M000015402

ANTHROPOLOGY WITH AN ATTITUDE

Cultural Memory

in

the

Present

Mieke Bal and Hent de Vries, Editors

ANTHROPOLOGY WITH AN ATTITUDE

Critical Essays

Johannes Fabian

STANFORD UNIVERSITY PRESS

STANFORD, CALIFORNIA 2001

Stanford University Press

Stanford, California

© 2001 by the Board of Trustees of the

Leland Stanford Junior University

Printed in the United States of America on acid-free, archival-quality paper.

Library of Congress Cataloging-in-Publication Data

Fabian, Johannes

    Anthropology with an attitude : critical essays / Johannes Fabian.

        p. cm.—(Cultural memory in the present)

    Includes bibliographical references and index.

    ISBN 0-8047-4142-5 (alk. paper)—ISBN 0-8047-4143-3 (pbk. : alk. paper)

    1. Anthropology—Philosophy. 2. Anthropology—Methodology.

3. Anthropology—Authorship.   I. Title. II. Series.

GN33 .F32 2001   2001032019

306'.1—dc21

Original printing 2001

Last figure below indicates year of this printing:

10 09 08 07 06 05 04 03 02 01

Typeset by Robert C. Ehle in 11/13.5 Adobe Garamond.

Contents

vi   *Contents*

Preface

It is a privilege to be allowed, for the second time, to publish a collection of essays (Fabian 1991a was the first); it is also a challenge to present such a collection as a coherent book. After some pondering of common themes and related arguments I came up with a division into two parts, "Critical Concerns" and "Critical Memories." In the first part the emphasis is on questions of knowledge production, while the second part further elaborates on themes derived from a project on colonial beginnings of ethnography that has occupied me for more than a decade (Fabian 2000). The collection is framed by a "Prelude" and "Coda," two short texts that, as befits the musical metaphors, set a mood rather than expound detailed arguments.

All but three of the essays (chapters 1 and 7, and the Coda) started as contributions to panels or plenary addresses at conferences; this accounts for traces of oral delivery (including some sermonizing), which I mostly decided to preserve. Half of the chapters have previously appeared in print and some of the others may be published in various places by the time this book goes to the printer. Though always tempted to reformulate, I have kept changes in previously published texts limited to a few cuts to avoid repetition, occasional changes of wording, some additional bibliographic references, and necessary standardization of headings, modes of citation, and so forth.

The term "critical" expresses no claim that a field of "Critical Anthropology" is here defined and systematically treated. It is descriptive of an approach, or an attitude (see chapter 5), toward the work of anthropology (a phrase I like because it encompasses all aspects of knowledge making in our discipline). This attitude was formed during the sixties and seventies—a fact that may give to the issues taken up, and perhaps to the language used, the flavor of what my cohort of anthropologists will recall as our fighting days. However, already in those days, I was opposed to thinking of critique as a specialty and trying to establish critical anthropology as a subdiscipline. "Critical," I still argue, should be a quality of whatever we do; and critique is not cumulative, it needs to be thought and formulated again and again.

Critical intent, as many have observed, makes us cast our writing in the form of essays—"attempts," or sometimes just exercises or experiments—which, in my experience, are the pillars that support our more ambitious book-length projects. Together, the essays assembled here do not describe a distinctive field of knowledge, let alone constitute a "textbook"; but they may well have their use as exemplary *études* in teaching and learning the craft of anthropology.

One does not expect a book like this to cover all major topics of current debate. If readers wonder why such hot issues as modernities (the plural is important), ethnicity, and globalization don't get much attention, I can only point out that almost all of the essays are occasional pieces; they reflect the expectations of my hosts who did not think of me as an expert in these matters. Rightly so. All three themes have occupied me at various times, especially when I struggled with the concept of popular culture. None of them imposed itself as a central, organizing perspective when I attempted to present results of field research conducted between the mid-sixties and the mid-eighties. That may change, however, if and when I finally get around to working on my field notes and recordings made during local manifestations in the Congo of the worldwide phenomenon of Catholic charismatic renewal.

I now briefly summarize the content of each piece, beginning with the Prelude, "With So Much Critique and Reflection Around, Who Needs Theory?" Here I argue, against a background of a- and anti-theoretical tendencies in postmodern thought, for debating the need for theory by considering not so much its "place" in marking positions and territories but its "time" in the production of knowledge.

Chapter 1, "Ethnographic Objectivity: From Rigor to Vigor," starts with reminiscences of the critical sixties. Rejecting positivist notions that prevailed at the time, I adopted a view of ethnographic objectivity that stressed its grounding in intersubjectivity and language. Then follows an attempt to understand the eclipse of the objectivity question in anthropology during the decades that followed. The chapter ends on a hopeful note: there is enough energy and imagination left in ethnography to justify our concern for objectivity. Our conceptions of what makes up the ethnographic knowledge process have broadened, and give new vigor to our questioning of the conditions that make ethnography possible.

Chapter 2, "Ethnographic Misunderstanding and the Perils of Context," begins with the observation that misunderstanding, though common enough in ethnographic practice, is seldom discussed. Also common enough has been a tendency to invoke context as a means of avoiding or repairing misunderstanding, especially in language-centered ethnography. Three exemplary cases of misunderstanding show that context is as likely to cause misunderstanding as it is to help avoid it. Following a dialectical approach to speaking and ethnography, further work should explore the conception of misunderstanding as not-understanding, and hence as part of a process.

Chapter 3, "Keep Listening: Ethnography and Reading," is an inquiry into reading as a subject and a mode of ethnography. Some reasons that this topic was seldom addressed until recently are explored in a sketch of historical and theoretical developments in anthropological studies of literacy. This is followed by a proposal to recast the problem of literacy and ethnography by paying attention to reading as part of any literary practice, including that of ethnography. This is then illustrated in a report on two projects concerned with the production and presentation of texts. Reading such texts calls for an ability on the part of the ethnographer to "listen" to them, that is, to (re-)enact oral performances that get documented in transcriptions of recordings as well in writings informed by "grassroots literacy."

In chapter 4, "Ethnology and History," I recall how a positivist heritage came to ethnology and African history from nineteenth-century historical methodology, especially through the work of E. Bernheim. His has been a long shadow, from which historically oriented anthropologists only began to emerge since the seventies. But relations between anthropology and history continue to be debated. As an attempt to understand the current situation, a triadic model is proposed. Not only two disciplines but three practices confront each other: academic anthropology, academic historiography, and popular historiology.

In Chapter 5, "Culture with an Attitude," the issue is negative thought as a prerequisite of both viable culture and viable concepts of culture. The argument is built on evidence of negation in popular narratology and of resistance and survival in popular culture generally, and on philosophical insights regarding negativity (such as Adorno's "negative dialectic").

Chapter 6, "Hindsight," is the earliest piece in this collection. It was chosen because it provides some humorous relief from epistemological seriousness and makes a transition to the topics of Part II.

Chapter 7, "Curios and Curiosity," recalls an episode in the exploration of Africa. A comparative reading of reports by Emil Torday and Leo Frobenius leads to interesting insights on links between objects, markets, and politics, and on the role that collecting played in the emergence of professional ethnography.

Chapter 8, "Time, Narration, and the Exploration of Central Africa," deals with temporality and narrativity. All-pervasive representations of time characterize a discourse that is condemned (or privileged) to tell stories; they have concerned and characterized anthropology even during its most "modern," that is, purportedly "synchronic" (or achronic) and systematic phases. This chapter brings together and further explores certain observations on the treatment of time in a number of travelogues reporting on exploration in Central Africa shortly before and during the famous "scramble" for the continent.

Chapter 9, "Remembering the Other: Knowledge and Recognition," addresses the question of memory and alterity. Based again on a reading of travelogues of African exploration, the argument takes its departure from, and develops, three connotations of the term "recognition" (*Erkennen*, cognition; *Anerkennen*, acknowledgment; *Wiedererkennen*, remembrance), concentrating on the role of remembrance in the production of knowledge about other cultures and societies. Must we, and if so, how can we, "remember" those who are strangers to us?

Chapter 10, "Africa's Belgium," returns Europe's "imperial gaze" on Africa with examples of Congolese views of colonization gleaned from popular historiology and ethnography that show how the Congolese intellectually appropriated their former colonizers. The focus is on the construction of critical memory.

The Coda is a reflection on the political and theoretical (though perhaps not practical) irrelevance of the millennium for the future of anthropology.

I dedicate this book to the memory of my friends Hermann Greive and Bob Scholte. Their untimely early deaths deprived me of more than intellectual companionship.

J.F.
Xanten, August 2000

Acknowledgments

I thank publishers and editors for making it possible to include the following previously published papers in this collection.

Chapter 1 appeared, under its present title, in *Annals of Scholarship* 8 (1991): 381–408. It was reprinted as "Ethnographic Objectivity Revisited: From Rigor to Vigor," in *Rethinking Objectivity*, ed. Allan Megill (Durham, N.C.: Duke University Press, 1994), pp. 81–108.

Chapter 2 was published as "On Ethnographic Misunderstanding and the Perils of Context," *American Anthropologist* 97 (1995): 1–10. It was reprinted in *The Problem of Context: Perspectives from Social Anthropology and Elsewhere*, ed. Roy Dilley (Oxford: Berghahn, 1999), pp. 85–104; and in *Pour une Anthropologie de l'Interlocution: Rhétoriques du Quotidien*, ed. Jean-Louis Siran and Bertrand Masquelier (Paris: L'Harmattan, 2000), pp. 81–106.

Chapter 3 appeared in *The Ethnography of Reading*, ed. Jonathan Boyarin (Berkeley: University of California Press, 1993), pp. 81–97.

Chapter 6 was published as "Hindsight: Thoughts on Anthropology upon Reading Francis Galton's *Narrative of an Explorer in Tropical South Africa* (1853)," *Critique of Anthropology* 7 (1987): 37–49. A German version appeared as "Hintergedanken zur Ethnologie" in Wissenschaftskolleg zu Berlin, *Jahrbuch* 1983/1984 (Berlin: Siedler, 1985), pp. 63–74.

Chapter 7 appeared as "Curios and Curiosity: Notes on Reading Torday and Frobenius," in *The Scramble for Art in Central Africa*, ed. Enid Schildkrout and Curtis Keim, (Cambridge: Cambridge University Press, 1998), pp. 79–108.

Chapter 8 appeared as "Time, Narration, and the Exploration of Central Africa" in *Narrative* 9, no. 1 (2001): 3–20.

Chapter 9 was published as "Remembering the Other: Knowledge and Recognition in the Exploration of Central Africa," *Critical Inquiry* 26 (1999): 49–69.

The Coda appeared as "Sur la (non-)pertinence du millénaire," *Anthropologie et Sociétés* 24 (2000): 15–19.

In addition, I most gratefully acknowledge the organizers of and audiences at the meetings at which the following pieces were originally presented, the colleagues who invited me to include essays in their volumes, and the institutions that extended their hospitality.

The Prelude was written as a keynote address to a workshop on "The Point of Theory" organized by Mieke Bal at the University of Amsterdam, January 12–13, 1993.

Chapter 1 is the result of a collective, interdisciplinary effort to rethink objectivity to which I was invited to contribute by Allan Megill.

Chapter 2 was first written as a discussion paper for a workshop on *Les rhétoriques du quotidien*, organized by Bertrand Masquelier and Jean-Louis Siran, Paris, May 22–23, 1992. Thanks to Dennis and Barbara Tedlock for inviting me to submit this paper during their tenure as editors of *American Anthropologist*, to Roy Dilley for including the piece in a collection on "The Problem of Context," and, again to Bertrand Masquelier and Jean-Louis Siran for reprinting it when their book, based on the Paris workshop, appeared.

Chapter 3 was first presented at the Annual Meeting of the American Anthropological Association, Washington, D.C., November 1989, in a panel on "The Ethnography of Reading," organized by Jonathan Boyarin and sponsored by the Society for Cultural Anthropology. I am grateful to Jonathan for inviting me to address a topic to which I had until then given little thought.

Chapter 4 is the somewhat expanded text of an address to the Biennial Conference of the Deutsche Gesellschaft für Völkerkunde, Heidelberg, October 3–7, 1999.

Chapter 5 is the text of an address at the annual meetings of the American Folklore Society, Columbus, Ohio, November 25–29, 2000.

Chapter 6 was originally a lecture delivered during my stay, most gratefully acknowledged, at the Wissenschaftskolleg Berlin in 1984.

The reading for chapters 7, 8, and 9 was made possible by a stay in 1990–91 at the Getty Center for the History of Art and the Humanities in Santa Monica, California. Its support is gratefully acknowledged. I also thank my tireless research assistant, Elisabeth Cameron; colleagues at the Center, especially Suzanne Preston Blier, for listening and responding to an earlier version; and Enid Schildkrout for including Chapter 7 in the volume edited by her and Curtis Keim.

Chapter 8 is the revised text of a plenary address at an international conference "Narrative 2000," April 6–9, 2000, in Atlanta, Georgia. Claude Calame and Mondher Kilani, as organizers of a colloquium on "Répresentations du temps: historiographie et anthropologie," University of Lausanne, June 7–8, 1999, allowed me to try out a shorter and somewhat differently oriented version.

A stay, gratefully acknowledged, as a visiting fellow at the Internationales Forschungszentrum für Kulturwissenchaften, Vienna, March–June 1998, allowed me to work on the topic of chapter 9. An earlier version was presented there as a contribution to the Forschungszentrum's research project on memory and identity.

Chapter 10 was written for a congress on "Belgium's Africa," devoted to an assessment of scholarly work on Belgium's former colonies. The meeting was organized by Jan Blommaert and Karel Arnaut at the University of Ghent, October 21–23, 1999.

The Coda responds to an invitation by Serge Genest to participate in a millennial appraisal of anthropology in the journal *Anthropologie et Sociétés*.

Not all occasions on which I was allowed to try out my work in lectures and seminars are included in these acknowledgments. I hope the colleagues and institutions that invited me and the audiences that attended will accept a collective expression of gratitude for their hospitality.

Finally I want to thank Mieke Bal and Hent de Vries for including this collection in the Stanford University Press series on Cultural Memory; Helen Tartar for supporting the project; Gavin Lewis for sniffing out interference from other languages in my English prose; and Anna Eberhard Friedlander for seeing this book through production. And it goes without saying, but should be said nevertheless, that I owe thanks to my department and to the Faculty of Cultural and Behavioral Science at the University of Amsterdam for their support.

ANTHROPOLOGY WITH AN ATTITUDE

With So Much Critique and Reflection Around, Who Needs Theory?

The way this question is formulated, only one response seems appropriate: "No one." I shall assume (rightly or wrongly) that such an answer has tempted many of us who worry about the point of theory, not because we are atheoretical empiricists but because we have seen through the false and often dangerous claims to hegemony and power that have been made in the name of theory.

What I shall have to say is intended to be polemical rather than just belligerent. I'll contend that our answer should be "We do." No matter how much critique and reflection we practice, we still need theory. I'll end up pleading for "critical theory," a position that unites what the terms of my question evoke as oppositions. I believe that, more than ever, critical theory needs arguing: not just the arguments that were formulated in what became solidified as "Critical Theory" (associated with the Frankfurt School) but arguments that have to be formulated again and again in response to actual situations and problems (an idea, incidentally, that is part of Critical Theory at its best).

We either need theory or we don't. If we do, which is what I want to propose—if only because it seems to be the more difficult and interesting position to take in this age of postmodern hyper-critical-reflexive thought—then the next question is: "What kind of theory?"

So as to avoid the stance that made us weary of theory in the first place—all those glib assertions that theory maketh knowledge and scientific disciplines—let me begin with a somewhat personal *mise en scène*. I received my training in anthropology under a disciplinary paradigm that combined culturalism and Parsonian grand theory. Put mildly, we were encouraged to be contemplative; put less innocuously, we were urged to take the view from above. The mark of the professional, we were told, was to be in control, to create theoretical order out of empirical chaos. But there was another requirement, something that anthropology adopted at first with reluctance and has since clung to with great stubbornness: the requirement to do "fieldwork," our Victorian euphemism for empirical research. I studied to be an anthropologist; fieldwork made me into an ethnographer. Today, I couldn't care less when I am variously stamped a cultural anthropologist, an Africanist, or even a philosopher—as long as it is understood that all of the work I do rests on ethnography.

Two things brought about a transformation from anthropologist to ethnographer. The first one was, as befits rituals of initiation, properly traumatic. The break occurred when I realized that my hypertheoretical training and the methodological orientation that went with it—geared as they were to seeing, observing, labeling, and classifying—simply found no object to work on, got no hold on the Afro-European religious movement that was my dissertation project. I met a founder who denied having founded a movement, members to whom the abstract category of membership in a movement was meaningless, and teachings whose status as doctrine, let alone as ideology, was vehemently disavowed. What saved me from despair was the realization that in these fleeting, ever evanescent situations there was something I could nevertheless get hold of, something that by sheer repetition became familiar and took on shape. It was not an object but a practice: talk.

Early on, while I was still "in the field," this brought about a break, radicalized because of the circumstances, with what I came to criticize much later as visual root metaphors of knowledge. It was not so much seeing and observing that brought me in touch with the object of my inquiries, but listening to people talking, and learning to talk like they did. Ethnography, I realized, is crucially, not incidentally, based on communication and language. Almost inevitably, this led to a choice of method—of gathering and interpreting data—that looked for guidance from linguistics. After an episode of toying with formal semantic analyses—then the supposedly most rigorous and advanced way of searching for cultural meaning—I fortunately found an approach that was more appropriate to my problems, the "ethnography of speaking" (also known as "interactive sociolinguistics"). Whatever else it entailed (for instance a critique of formalist structuralism in linguistics), it made it possible to conceive of talk, the one thing that gave some reality to my project, as *praxis*. And that is one way of describing a personal trajectory from theory to praxis.

But there was another aspect to my transformation into an ethnographer. Unlike the switch from subsuming to ingesting, or from seeing to listening, this one was neither sudden nor traumatic. In fact, it took almost twenty years before it became clear to me what it involved. That other aspect was *writing*. That writing was a problem I had noticed at the latest when, due to personal, mainly economic circumstances, I had to complete my dissertation in about seven months. But at that time I perceived the problem of writing, as I am sure did many others, mainly as one of execution, as a kind of nuisance that was only occasionally pleasurable and gratifying. Writing stood between gaining knowledge and expressing it. At first, I must admit, I took an escape route on which others had preceded me. Actually, it was an escape that ran on two tracks. On the one hand, I delved ever more deeply into texts—that is, recorded speech events which through transcription and translation I had transformed into written documents. On the other, I radicalized my critique of domineering theory and visualist bias (both conveniently exhibited by my favorite target, positivist scientism). I fell back on hermeneutics, to which I had been exposed prior to my Anglo-American training in anthropology, sometimes putting aside misgivings that came from the Marxian school (if it is one), which had first brought me to experience critical thinking as something I did rather than adopted and applied secondhand. I guess I partook of the "interpretive turn" in anthropology. When our field was hit by some high-powered literary theory which told us that *representation* was the problem with ethnographic writing and that, therefore, ethnography should be attacked with weapons taken from that theory's critical arsenal, I was tempted to go along for the ride.

What made me reluctant to jump the hermeneutic bandwagon is

not easily summarized. Through the years, I continued to put myself to a test as an ethnographer. Under circumstances and constraints that were quite different from those of dissertation research I went on to other projects of field research, albeit always in the same geographic and cultural area, with more or less the same people, and working through the same language. These projects included the study of experiences and conceptions of work, expressions of popular culture in painting and theater, and colonial history approached through the analysis of competing discourses of academic and popular historiology (a term meant to encompass both oral and written history).

Recently, I have turned to anthropology's beginnings by examining reason and madness in practices of research and representation in accounts of the exploration of Central Africa. The one insight that took shape during those years and that finally allowed me to tie together my ethnographic experiences and my critical reflections was quite simple. When we align writing with theory (thereby opposing it to research like representation to reality, or sign to thing) we may have a point. But the conclusion I have come to is that interpretation and representation are not our central problems. When we write we *act*. Writing (and of course, reading) is what I *do* during much of my working life. Writing is on my mind even in those periods in the field or in the classroom when I mainly listen and talk. Before ethnography can be a problem of meaning (hermeneutics) or signification (semiotics), let alone of explanation (positivist science), it is constituted as a *praxis*. When we study other cultures, our theory of their praxis is our praxis, I once said, and the foremost problem of ethnographic writing is not the extraction of meaning or the matching of signifier and signified but the meeting—I prefer confrontation—of kinds of praxis, ours and theirs.

Thus the insight that was forced on me by my work as ethnographer, that what we encounter is not an object but a praxis, and the gradual realization that writing-up is also a praxis, merged to define the point of theory in a radically different way. The question with which we began may refer to something like need (do we need theory?), or function (what is theory good for?), or even to rhetorical effect (how convincing is theory?). I would add one more item to this list. I think the question of the point of theory is almost always heard as a question of the *place* of theory.

What I mean is this. In hierarchical conceptions of knowledge, be they interpretive or explanatory, hermeneutic or classificatory, pleading for theory is a matter of claiming a place, usually above or upstream from that which becomes the object of knowledge. This positional quality of theorizing is too obvious to have escaped critique. Theory is then denounced as a token of power relations, of elitist, Western, male, and undoubtedly other forms of dominance. But if theory belongs to the things we do in the real world then we must take a further step: Theory has no place unless it has time. In the real world *theory happens*. And that is the reason why critique that targets only the place that is claimed for theory falls short of its aims.

This is not an occasion to rehearse the critique of theoretical domination as the denial of presence—something that was expressed, for instance, in Edward Said's statement that the Orient's theoretical presence has been predicated on its effective absence (1979: 208). I shall treat this insight as an assumption and proceed to think about its consequences for further critical thought about theory. A brief semantic exercise should clarify what I am searching for. Consider the following series of conceptual oppositions, all of which have already appeared in these reflections:

theory—method
contemplation—action
vision—confrontation

Presumably, such a list will be accepted as one, if not the only, plausible set of contrasts/oppositions between the terms. But what looks like an innocuous inventory is—like all lists—really a trick, a rhetorical imposition. It tricks us into accepting that the initial pair (theory and method) is indeed simply contrastive, a horizontal relationship, whereas in all scientific discourses I know of theory and method are in a vertical, indeed hierarchical relationship, something that also holds for a pair theory—praxis). Moving to the next pair, contemplation and action/movement are not in peaceful contrast either. They generate conflict because movement, which cannot be but movement toward something (certainly the kind of action/movement that is involved in empirical research), subverts contemplative rest and distance; we lose the safety of detached vision and get entangled in agonistic confrontation. Therefore, one should consider the point of theory in terms of antithetical relationships that describe not a state of affairs, nor just a progression from thought to action, but a process that involves transformation. To me this is a radical way of raising the question of theory.

Because I cannot shake my humanistic Greek-and-Latin upbringing (I always hear "roots" in radical) I dug out my old Langenscheidt Greek-German dictionary and looked up *theōria*. Here is a tentative translation of the German entry:

1. Gaze and watching (*An- od. Zuschauen*), contemplation (*Betrachtung*): a) *Schaulust* (not an entry in my German-English dictionary but roughly, "spectator's pleasure"). b) Festive spectacle (*Festschau*), participation in a festival (*Teilnahme an einem Feste*). c) Inquiry (*Untersuchung*), scientific knowledge (*wissenschaftliche Erkenntnis*), theory (*Theorie*).

2. A show (*Schauspiel*), spectacle (*Schaufest*), festival (*Fest*), festival delegation or procession (*Festgesandtschaft, -zug*).

Rather than getting weighed down by history—undoubtedly there are libraries of learned disquisitions on all these connotations of *theōria*—I savor this entry for its evocative, poetical qualities. The hardened little nut that "theory" has become in its present use is cracked open here. Inside the shell there is a world of interest and amazement, of desire and pleasure, of involvement and performance, of people who move in celebratory processions. It seems to me that recuperating these connotations could be a new beginning, food for fresh thought about theory. Certainly it could serve the aim I formulated earlier: to reconsider theory dialectically as praxis.

Not all of this can be done at once. So let me sketch the one line of further thought that I feel is most urgent, given the pervasive atheoretical mood regarding theory that seems to have spread from literary criticism into all kinds of cultural studies. I have no intention to proscribe (or even deprive myself of) the intellectual pleasure afforded by inventing theories and testing them on data. Nor do I think that projects of emancipation are well served by taking critical shortcuts and denouncing hierarchical conceptions of relationships between theory and reality as acts of domination and oppression. What can and must be done is to reflect, not so much on theory's place as on its time, that is, on moments in the production of knowledge leading from research to writing in which we must take positions: moments that determine how we get from one statement to another, from one story to another, indeed, from one sentence to another. Speaking for myself, doing ethnography needs theory that does more than subsume and classify, put order into the alleged chaos of perception. Critical theory, to return to a notion I used at the beginning, is the ability to show, as much as this will ever be possible, what drives and moves us when we produce and communicate knowledge. *Production* signals the involvement of theory in processes of confrontation and transformation, a conception that does not go together with contemplative distance. And when I invoke *communication*, I want to say that theory is what allows others to move along with us, or move elsewhere, when we theorize.

The view of theory I am pleading for—stressing time over place, movement over territory, confrontation over contemplation—ought to have consequences for the *teaching* of theory. To begin with we must question and preferably abandon presentations of theory that contribute to its reification as something outside, above, or behind our practices of gaining knowledge. Quite concretely, we can work on the symptoms of such reification that feed back to its cause: the separation, in our curricula, of theory and method courses from others. To make "methods and techniques" a separate subfield (as is prescribed, for instance, for certain disciplines by Dutch law) only looks like promoting scientific theory; it really canonizes and domesticates *theōria*. At best, it makes students hate or disregard theory; at worst, it gives them illusions of theory propelling them to higher levels of knowledge. Finally, if theory needs its time as well as its place, then two things follow from this. First, teaching theory means introducing theoretical reflection (including conceptual elaboration and refinement) at the right moments, moments that are created by the empirical matter at hand in any course that is not devoid of factual information. Second, our teaching should not aim at *theoria perennis*, timeless theory. Theory should be taught as that which makes it possible to reach a critical understanding of the history and politics of our disciplines. All this amounts to saying that the point of theory is praxis.

PART I

CRITICAL CONCERNS

Ethnographic Objectivity: From Rigor to Vigor

About thirty years ago I first felt the need to think publicly about criteria that make ethnographic research and writing objective (Fabian 1971b). Of course, many ethnographers had already concerned themselves with objectivity, but focused, sustained, general, and in that sense public discussions of objectivity in ethnographic work did not exist at that time.[1] I concede that entire schools such as structuralism, functionalism, and structuralism-functionalism aspired to provide the social sciences with theories, methods, and techniques that would produce scientific, and hence objective, knowledge. Characteristically, however, these approaches were concerned with theory and rules of method, rather than with foundations of knowledge. An outstanding example of meticulous critique that remained within the accepted frame of theory and method was J. A. Barnes's evaluation of the work on kinship by Murdock, Lévi-Strauss, and Fortes (Barnes 1971). For Barnes (who, incidentally, found most of that work wanting) scientific logic (as conceived, for instance, by the logical positivists) was the standard of evaluation. The question whether scientific logic in this sense was even applicable to anthropology remained, except for occasional reflexive asides, outside the discussion. Yet faith in science made him hope that his critical labors would help to discern and accumulate what was valuable in the analyses of the three earlier researchers (this although he cites Kuhn 1962 and even Scholte 1966, and qualifies anthropology as pre-paradigmatic). Divergence and discrepancies among and within the three approaches did not lead Barnes to doubt that scientific logic ought to be the sole standard of evaluation of scientific discourse.[2]

The implicit claim that objectivity was somehow built into the exercise of science and that remaining doubts and question were of a personal, private nature made me go public with my private worries about objectivity. Ever since, I have felt compelled to pair reflection on objectivity with assertions of subjectivity. Because I hold that knowledge that is worth working for must be mediated by experience (even if this is the case vicariously and indirectly when we "use" someone else's ethnography) I must conclude that all ethno-graphy is connected to (auto)bio-graphy. The autobiographical stance I assumed in the first sentence of this essay will be maintained in the reflections and arguments that follow. By the time I come to conclusions, it should be clear that autobiography need not be an escape from objectivity. On the contrary, critically understood, autobiography is a *condition* of ethnographic objectivity.

I

Things could, however, get hopelessly muddled (and may have gotten so already in some recent debates) if the subjective and the autobiographical are treated as synonyms. Subjectivity informs the production and representation of knowledge even in those cases of writing where autobiography is absent. The subject as speaker, as author, as authority is always present. Conversely, writing that is explicitly autobiographical (including even the so-called confessional variety) may be conventional and stylized and as such apt to hide the subject more effectively than "objective" scientific prose. Autobiography can, as I posited, be a condition of (rather than an impediment to) ethnographic objectivity in the sense that it allows the writing subject's actual history and involvement to be considered critically.

But back to the first crack I took at formulating a position on ethnographic objectivity. I had written my dissertation a year earlier, found a teaching job that was challenging, and was now given an opportunity to justify what I had so far presented as ethnography. That this would have to be a statement *defending* objectivity I did not doubt at the time; dismissing objectivity was not an imaginable option. But neither did I consider the obvious threat, subjectivity, as the problem. In the constellation of debates and controversies that entailed epistemological as well as political issues (and personally inspired by earlier contacts with hermeneutics and critical theory, especially through Habermas's first text on the logic of the social sciences),[3] I felt that objectivity was in danger of being perverted by two misplaced strategies for making it safe once and for all: There were those who *naturalized* objectivity and those who *socialized* it.

Naturalization I ascribed (although not in these words) to positivist tendencies equating legitimation of knowledge with its success, or epistemology with methodology.[4] Here was a conception of knowledge that presupposed a process containing safeguards that would make worries about ideological distortion, historical contingency, and the lure of special interests unnecessary. What made me reject the positivist option was not a desire to be worried, but the experience I had just had in my ethnographic work on a religious movement of the utter failure of positivism's recommended techniques and methods. Charismatic authority, prophetic thought, and membership through initiation could not be observed and studied *comme des choses*. Sources of assurance other than well-executed method and techniques were needed to make sure that the movement existed and that what I had to say about it was anchored in reality.

I found socialization, or perhaps it would be better to say sociologization, of the problem of objectivity (with echoes of Durkheimian social anthropology) in Thomas Kuhn's theory of scientific revolutions (1962), whose unparalleled impact outside its field of origin was just beginning. Among my undergraduate students it caught on like the manifesto of a liberation movement. In the perspective provided by Kuhn, it made sense to speak of objectivity only relative to a given, established paradigm and its attendant practices ("puzzle solving"). Commitment to science as a serious pursuit could be maintained without commitment to one indivisible truth. Again, it was not an aversion to Kuhn's relativism that made me doubt the usefulness of his "solution"; my qualms about relativism took shape only later. Rather, it was the fact that I could not detect in anthropology and ethnography the traits of a "normal science" that would have made Kuhn's epistemological position plausible. As if ethnographers did not have trouble enough defending knowledge that claims to transcend cultural boundaries, they also lacked the kind of security that comes from working in an established discipline.

At any rate, the adversary I decided to confront directly was positivism. I was aware that many who shared my distaste for its crude scientism thought that it could be overcome with the help of Max Weber, who promised *Verstehen* where positivists peddled explanations—this was, at any rate, the dominant view in anthropology. Similarly, Kuhn's ingenious yet somewhat bloodless social theory of scientific progress could be injected with strife and drama from a Marxist perspective. Weber and Marx can supply a great deal of ammunition to critiques that take naive faith in science, or in society, as their targets. But neither thinker offered help, or at least neither offered enough help, when I faced the epistemological problem of objectivity in actual ethnographic work. That they failed me in that crucial moment is probably the reason that I eventually abandoned the Weberian approach to the study of charisma that I had taken in my just-completed monograph, and also the reason that my commitment to Marxism has been firm, but never systematic.

Misguided and illusionary as positivist methods may have been, they had staked their claims in a territory that was not really contested by the dominant schools. (That, incidentally, is the reason that so much social science inspired by Marx and Weber on the level of grand theory has been carried out according to positivist canons on the ground.) Although it does make sense to raise the problem of objectivity as one of, say, class perspective or rationality, I did implicitly accept positivism's claim that objectivity must, first of all, be approached as a quality of knowledge production. Consequently, I began attacking positivist conceptions of objectivity by attacking what I felt were wrong ideas regarding the production of ethnographic knowledge. I tried to argue my case with the help of problems encountered in ethnography and then formulated two theses:

First Thesis: In anthropological investigations, objectivity lies neither in the logical consistency of a theory, nor in the givenness of data, but in the foundation (Begründung)[5] of human intersubjectivity (Fabian 1971b, 25).

Second Thesis: Objectivity in anthropological investigations is attained by entering a context of communicative interaction through the one medium which represents and constitutes such a context: language (Fabian 1971b, 27).[6]

At the end of the sixties, when these propositions were formulated, the challenge was to save objectivity from positivist objectivism. I thought this could be achieved by making subjectivity a condition of objectivity rather than its opposite. The consequence was a processual, historical notion of objectivity (as opposed to a static, logical notion according to which objectivity is a quality that either exists or doesn't); processual also because the notion involves the action of subjects who form and transform knowledge and who are doing this together. When I ponder this today I would like to add qualifications here and there (most of which will be discussed later in this chapter); but the two theses describe a notion of objectivity I am still prepared to defend.[7]

One thing is clearer to me now than it was at the time. The decisive difference between the positivist conception of objectivity and the alternative I was struggling to formulate involved a theory of *objectification*.[8] Claiming that social-scientific knowledge was based only on facts that could be studied like natural objects, positivism needed no theory of the constitution of objects. But a view of ethnographic knowledge based on what is intersubjectively and communicatively produced, and hence made, had to include a theory of objectification capable of specifying what in communicative interaction becomes an object and thereby the basis of objective knowledge. Like others, I opted for the one phenomenon that seemed to fill the bill, namely *language*.

The "linguistic turn" that characterized the first phase of discontent with positivist theories of ethnography, however, led anthropologists in quite different directions. Some saw it as saving "science" in anthropology; after all, in linguistics rigorous, quasi-mathematical methods had triumphed. Others thought that to make language and everything that was language-like the object of ethnographic investigation called for an interpretive and hermeneutic approach. From there it was a small step to postulating that *texts* were *the* objectifications with which ethnography should concern itself or, conversely, that whatever could be studied in a culture would have to be approached like a text.

To say that defending ethnographic objectivity requires a theory of objectification does of course not mean that a theory of objectification as such confers objectivity on ethnography. Take, for instance, the schools that see objectification as occurring in signs and symbols. Semiotic and symbolic analyses, even those that "work," are not absolved from giving epistemological accounts of how they produce knowledge. These accounts cannot be limited to reports on what is being done, especially not if they are again formulated in terms of symbolic or semiotic theory. To duplicate a procedure is not to justify it.[9]

II

If one wants to distinguish changing attitudes to the question of ethnographic objectivity it helps to discern first what theory of objectification, if any, a given theoretical approach favors. Turning now from retrospection to circumspection, I find the need to fill the epistemological gap in theoretical reflections on objectivity in ethnography and anthropology to be almost as pressing today as it was thirty years ago.

First an observation of fact, then some thoughts on reasons why this should be so. A search of major journals in anthropology since 1980 yielded disappointing results. Hardly any papers adressed objectivity as an epistemological problem.[10] The one paper that looked as if it might address the issue (Feleppa 1986) approached it in terms of the *emics* versus *etics* debate and was (as some of the commentators noted) unable to salvage a truly epistemological question from the confusion that has characterized that debate from its very beginning. Feleppa defined the problem of ethnographic objectivity, so far as he defined it at all, as one of overcoming ethnocentrism, or of gaining an insider's perspective on a culture. As I see it, even if either or both of these goals could be achieved, objectivity remains an epistemological problem. The very possibility of ethnographic knowledge production is problematic; bias or distortion are second-order qestions. This is not a plea for an ethnography that condones bias and distortion; it simply expresses an epistemological position according to which more is needed to make ethnographic knowledge valid than the absence of ethnocentric bias. That "more" is what we are trying to work out when we think about objectivity and objectification.

A picture similar to the one we found in the survey of periodicals emerged from the contributions by two anthropologists to a series of lectures on "Objectivity and Cultural Divergence" (Brown 1984). They seemed to feel that the question at hand really was cultural relativism—the position that stresses the specificity if not uniqueness of cultures—and the limitations it imposes on making general (and hence objective?) statements: J. M. H. Beatty (1984), focusing on knowledge and Paul Heelas (1984) on emotions, come to middle-of-the-road positions that fail to address objectivity as a quality-of-knowledge production. Reading Beatty and Heelas, and not only them, one gets at times the impression that relativism must be logically opposed to objectivity or, more exactly, to objectivism. That contradicts the history of anthropology where, under many different guises, the cultural relativist position appears as supporting the discipline's claims to being scientific, and hence objective. It also confuses cultural relativism with the moral rejection of ethnocentric bias. As if cultural relativism could *not* be the ultimate objectivist theory—*n* objectivities are more than one objectivity. Discrepancies among cultures regarding what counts as objective have been declared superficial and reduced to certain basic functions or averaged statistically; both procedures—functional reduction and cross-cultural statistical correlations—were at one time or another thought to give us objective measures of cultural diversity.[11]

In sum, there seems to be in current anthropology a lack of interest in objectivity as an epistemological issue.[12] Before I discuss more systematically some of the reasons for this, I want to make an observation that may shed some unexpected light on this issue. As someone who has preserved an interest in archeology and prehistory (ever since being forced to study these fields as part of a required program of graduate study) I am struck by a paradoxical situation. Whereas epistemology and the objectivity question seem to have all but disappeared from cultural anthropology, they found a most unlikely abode in archaeology. Thirty years ago, when attacks on misplaced scientism began to appear within cultural anthropology, the "new archaeologists" discovered Logical Positivism and saw themselves as a bastion of scientific objectivity within anthropology. Today, archaeologists read Habermas and Bernstein (see Wylie 1989, to cite but one example) and are concerned with epistemology. Perhaps this is just a matter of delayed reception of philosophical ideas. I think a more likely explanation may be found by going back to our observation regarding the common ground between positivism and critical theory: both consider objectivity to be problematic with regard to the production of knowledge. Archaeologists began to worry about how to justify their reconstructions of the past when they realized that their pronouncements about the past were part of a practice (intellectual, political, aesthetic, and so forth) that belonged to the present. Instead of being concerned only with the logical consistency of their "systemic" approaches they had to face epistemology, that is, a grounding of knowledge that cannot be given by recourse to method alone.

Precisely this view—that recourse to method is sufficient—was held by anthropological schools and approaches with a scientific bent prior to the advent of postmodernism. These schools were quite diverse and often antagonistic, yet they seem to have had one element in common. They considered objectivity as grounded in a "correct"[13] decision about what constitutes the real object of anthropological inquiry. Objectivity then becomes an ontological rather than an epistemological issue and a theory of objectification is not required. Most proponents of these approaches would of course have rejected the insinuation that taking the positions they took may have involved metaphysical choices.

Ontology is a difficult issue, and anthropologists, who often find ontologies in the cultures they study, are not usually inclined to discuss their own. My own position is roughly this: Tying the epistemological issue of objectivity to objectification does involve ontological assumptions; method alone may get along without ontology but it is therefore incapable of providing epistemological foundations. Method does not make the object. Approaches that profess to have no need for epistemology (and/or ontology) make ontological decisions nevertheless, and are in danger of ending up in the realm of metaphysics, that is, of ontology removed from critical discussion.

In current anthropology, concern with ethnographic objectivity as an epistemological problem has been conspicuously absent. We surmise that this is so because the object(s) of inquiry have been ontologized. Ontologizing, here understood as assigning to one or several kinds of objectification a comprehensive reality status (man is social, biological, symbolic, etc.) absorbs, as it were, the legitimation of knowledge into that reality. What remains is a legitimation that is limited to rules and techniques of knowledge procurement. It is concerned with operations, not with the grounding of ethnographic knowledge in some actual relations between knower and known.[14]

But that is not yet the full story of the disappearance of objectivity, if such can ever be told. We also need to ask why the critical language-centered position described above failed to have the impact it should have had. In retrospect, I come up with a fairly long list of shortcomings, but before I discuss some of these I want to offer a general observation: that in ethnography and anthropology the chance to develop a conception of objectivity that is not to be derived from natural science[15] hinges on a conception of intersubjectivity as something that is made, rather than given. Unfortunately, the term "intersubjectivity" alone was apparently reason enough to stamp concerns that were inspired by critical theory as "phenomenological."[16] In itself this would have been at least partly correct had it not been for the sad fate of "phenomenology" in the social sciences on this side of the Atlantic. Much of what went by that name had no title to it. Aside from Alfred Schütz, who was a secondary figure as a philosopher, few phenomenological theorists were accessible in English.[17] In the end, as some have remarked cynically, to be phenomenological in sociology, psychology, or anthropology meant, apart from taking an anti-establishment political and ethical attitude, little more than to reject quantification and statistics. And that obviously was not enough to support a serious counterposition to positivism.

Let us now consider some specific deficiencies of the critical language-centered approach that began to take shape in the mid-sixties. Because the turn to language initially took shape as a critique or further development of structural linguistics, its conception of language shared, almost inevitably, certain features of the Saussurean (or Bloomfieldian) view. There was notably a tendency to take language as a system of rules capable of being formulated in a sort of grammar, even though the emphasis was now on speaking. Less palpable, but nevertheless present, was a propensity to equate the role of language in communication with verbal communication. On the level of methodology, this often led to an exaggerated and misplaced trust in recorded verbal exchanges and their transcriptions/translations. In some varieties of the linguistic turn, culture was, as it were, substituted by language (an approach that had a long history in anthropology). Theories and methods developed in the study of language could, it was thought, simply be transferred to the study of culture. Strategies of that sort proved limiting because they were based on a truncated conception of language as a system of referential signs. True, to acknowledge what should have been obvious, namely that reference is but a small part of what language does, would have limited the methodological usefulness of the substitution.

Eventually, critique of this position gave rise to language-centered studies that stressed the importance of other than strictly referential language use. Tropes and figures of speech were now given attention. That in turn favored inquiry into rhetorical and pragmatic aspects of language which, because they opened up a tremendously rich source, soon were felt to need some kind of regulation. Grammarians came back in through the back door. An example of this has been the methodologization of the "ethnography of speaking." In fact, methodologization—turning epistemological insights regarding the role of language in establishing intersubjectivity into a "method" for producing ethnographic knowledge— has been the single most important failure of the critical turn to language, even if at times it may have looked like its greatest success. Methodologization occurred in several objectivist varieties of the linguistic turn, above all in ethnoscience and similar proposals for formal semantics. Such projects tended to assert that the study of culture through language was to be limited to inquiries into impositions of conceptual order onto perceptual chaos. This was said to be accomplished by reference ("labeling") and classification ("lumping"). As "cognition" became an object of inquiry, ethnoscientists and cognitive anthropologists thought of their study as basically of the same kind as its object; its procedures were thought to mirror the ones the human brain follows whenever it functions normally. So another situation developed in which objectivity could not become a fundamental question. Cognition either takes place or doesn't, it is either normal or impeded, either influenced by cultural factors or not, but it does not make sense to ask whether it is objective. In its extreme forms cognitive anthropology has no use for epistemology.

Arguably, methodologization also happened in certain formalized approaches to texts (often called structuralist) and may characterize some work that goes under the label of "hermeneutic," but cultivates a kind of textual fundamentalism.[18] Be that as it may, the language-inspired critical approach to ethnography which, during the sixties and seventies, kept a certain interest in the objectivity question alive was all but eclipsed in the eighties by yet another turn, this time to literature and literary deconstruction. This turn is said to have ushered in the postmodern era of anthropology.[19]

Given all the attention that has been directed in recent debates to what ethnographers actually do—having dialogues with their informants, producing ethnographic texts, writing ethnographies, experimenting with literary genres—what I now want to argue may come as a surprise. It is my impression that objectivity as an epistemological problem has once again disappeared, this time as a result not of methodologization, but of a displacement of focus from knowledge production to knowledge representation. Making representation the crucial issue has two consequences, one salutary, the other to be deplored. Postmodern awareness definitely does away with the lingering remnants of naive scientism. Ethnographic knowledge is no longer to be judged by the accuracy with which it mirrors the part or aspect of reality that it selects for study. As representation, ethnographic writing is considered more or less successful, depending on whether it meets criteria of rhetorical and perhaps aesthetic persuasiveness. Ethnography must make a case for what it states, but there is no longer any single canon according to which a case may be argued.

Not all proponents of the postmodern turn advocate abandoning traditional standards, such as conceptual rigor, parsimony, and logical consistency. Most think that ethnography as literary representation requires experimentation with new genres to which traditional standards of scientific prose may or may not apply.[20] As a result, self-monitoring reflection now tends to have recourse to literary criticism rather than to scientific method. Literary critics, however, do not seem to be greatly concerned by objectivity as a quality of knowledge production.

Emphasis on representation also favored a displacement of critical attention from scientific objectivity to literary authority. Attentiveness to an author's authority made the postmodern critique of ethnography much more sensitive to the play of power in human relations, including those that obtain between an anthropologist and the people he studies, or between an ethnographer and his readers. This may not always necessitate, but it certainly favors, a shift from objectivity as intellectual grounding to objectivity as political legitimation. Granted, the two need not be opposed to each other as long as politics is guided by rationality (I read Habermas's work as a stretched-out effort to understand that connection). Still, if author-centrism is coupled with the idea that ethnography is to be legitimized above all rhetorically or aesthetically, there is at least the danger that postmodernism, very much like the approaches it purports to overcome, preempts the objectivity question by ontologizing representation, writing, and literary form (all of which, by the way, may be connoted in talking about "ethnographic texts").

Incidentally—to give at least some indirect support to my observations on postmodernism—the index in *Writing Culture* (Clifford and Marcus 1986) directs us under "epistemology" only to Rabinow, in many respects the odd man out in the collection. Under "objectivity" I find, apart from a reference to Maquet's paper, only five entries, none of which leads us to a treatment of the issue in epistemological terms. Clifford sees objectivity and subjectivity as opposed to each other when he notes that they were thought to be kept in balance by participant observation (14), and he speaks of the "experience of objectivity" as (a subjective) mode of experiencing fieldwork (15). Crapanzano has a literary aside about Goethe's notion of objectivity (63) which relates to subjectivity as does outer to inner experience. Rosaldo has a brief section (93–95) on the "Rhetoric of Objectivity," and Rabinow adopts Hacking's (1982) proposal to save scientific objectivity (237) in a manner that has little bearing on the objectivity question as we are raising it here. Indexes are not exhaustive; but they can make pointed statements. In this case I take the statement to be that objectivity as an epistemological question is a nonissue in the "poetics and politics of ethnography."[21]

Although the objectivity question may only be raised by postmodernism to be dismissed—that is, a situation may be created in which it makes no sense to ask such a question—I am reluctant to regard the matter as settled. Thus, I prefer to speak of displacement. This allows me to keep looking for differences between postmodern objectifications such as writing, genre, or, indeed, "the Other," and the kinds of objectivist ontologizations I mentioned earlier. I think that, at least in some cases, it could be shown that these key concepts are being ontologized—not withstanding the postmodern claim that nothing is real—and that they are thereby given an objectivity that is not legitimized by critical reflection. I am not sure, however, which is more insidious—ontologizing basic needs, cybernetic systems, and genes, or ontologizing symbols, style, and authorship.

One answer to my quibbles might be that, given the failure of scientistic modernism, there is nothing wrong with the objectivity question disappearing from center stage. It no longer needs to be confronted, now that a better, more sophisticated approach to a critique of ethnography has been found. I cannot accept this conclusion. True, discussions of what is involved in ethnographic knowledge production have gotten much more sophisticated during the last decade. Yet no amount of subtlety, complexity, and ironic distance in critical accounts of ethnography absolves us from showing what justifies epistemologically the constitutive acts of ethnographic research (that is, the acts that we usually lump together as "fieldwork"). At the very least, keeping the epistemological question of objectivity alive means holding out against postmodern nihilism. The experience of ethnographic fieldwork, of its possibility, its reality, its changing and growing scope makes nihilism born from the quandaries of authorship unacceptable. Writing as representation simply cannot be the fundamental issue. Presence *is*, because before there is representation there must be presence; and in the end the question of ethnographic objectivity still comes down to the question of what makes it possible to have access to another culture, or to be in the presence of another culture—both of which seem to be required if ethnographic knowledge is to be more than projection or delusion.[22]

III

This brings us back full circle to the position I took in the retrospective section of this chapter. I think that the question regarding ethnographic objectivity was framed correctly in the seventies, at least in its essentials. In order to describe a position that can be defended now, I shall first briefly identify what I still consider to be basic in epistemological reflection on ethnography. Then I conclude with thoughts about changes, additions, and shifting emphases that impose themselves. I shall be drawing on my own experience as well as on insights produced in recent critical debates.

By now it should be clear that I am seeking to defend a notion of ethnographic objectivity that is equally critical of objectivism and of relativism; of objectivism because its faith in science makes raising the question of objectivity superfluous; and of relativism because it seems to assert that transcultural objectivity is impossible. The position I have been developing needs as its most general requirement a processual theory of knowledge. Knowing, such a theory posits, is acting. This means two things. Firstly, human acting is always acting in company; the social-communicative element is constitutive of thought, not just an additional determinant. Secondly, as I use the term here, acting is closer to Humboldtian productive activity (or "energy") than to sociological enactment; consequently knowing does not reflect reality but transforms what it knows.[23] Put differently, the *content of knowledge* must be transformed; how else could it be the product of a process? Defining knowledge as reflection may express a legitimate concern: That which can be known is not identical with that which is known. Reality remains unconsumed in the act of knowledge. Still, that concern is not met by adopting naive realism but rather by insisting on the limited, historically contingent nature of all knowledge.

I agree with such philosophers as Richard Rorty (1980) who reject the mirror metaphor of knowledge and postulate instead a social process in which "conversation" is basic in knowledge production. However, situating knowledge in social contexts (or "communities") does not take care of the legitimation of knowledge, nor does it make search for foundations unnecessary. It may be true, as Rorty argues, that Western philosophy's quest for foundations was conducted as an appeal to higher instances that govern knowledge without being themselves subject to change. The very metaphor of foundations poses problems, promoting, as it does, a spatial image suited to a view of knowledge as structure, system, edifice—a view I do not hold. Precisely if we want to assert the processual nature of knowledge we must maintain nonidentity (or negativity) in our conceptions of knowledge—nonidentity, that is, between its formulation and its legitimation. "Conversation" and "community" are too weak to assure this; something like critique and epistemology is still needed.

What goes for the theory of knowledge in general goes for the theory of ethnographic knowledge in particular. Ethnography that is emancipated from scientism cannot work, either explicitly or implicitly, with the assumption of a hierarchical relationship between knower and known, or more exactly, between knowing knowledge and known knowledge. Refusal to make such a hierarchical relationship an element of our theory of knowledge means that what the ethnographer is out to know does not as such exist as an object in nature to be "submitted" to inquiry. In other words, the ethnographic knowledge process is not initiated simply by turning our gaze on objects that are given. But neither is it sufficient to concede, as most anthropologists did even in more empirical times than ours, that our objects are scientifically constructed.[24]

In ethnography, to formulate another thesis, *the knowledge process must be initiated by confrontation that becomes productive through communication.* There is an agonistic connotation to "confrontation" that we need to maintain for at least two reasons: (a) to counteract the anodyne, apolitical, conciliatory aura that surrounds "communication" (and, for that matter, "dialogue"); and (b) to indicate that the "move toward ethnographic knowledge" can initiate a process only once it encounters resistance in the form of incomprehension, denial, rejection, or, why not, simply Otherness.

It is unfortunate that this requirement must be described in terms that sound psychological. What is really at issue is that we must locate the necessity for what I called the grounding of intersubjectivity, and that is an epistemological rather than a psychological problem. Recognition of the necessity to ground intersubjectivity is the moment where *objectivity* arises as an issue, as that which—apart from and beyond psychological attitudes, historical circumstances, ideological leanings, and power relations—provides us with the assurance (however temporary and open to discussion) that we actually make contact when we reach out with our ethnographies, and that the discourse we are producing gives form to experiences and contents which we could not have had without such a contact. But that is of course only the first, and minimal, meaning of ethnographic objectivity.

The next question must be: What makes it possible for us to sustain, develop, document, and reflect upon contact? The one medium which, as I used to say, both constitutes and articulates—makes possible and formulates—the ethnographic knowledge process is *language*. I still don't know of a better first step in gaining a position that offers an objective alternative to objectivism, as long as it is understood that language includes speaking, its lasting as well as its fleeting forms.

In practice, what makes ethnographic knowledge amenable to critical interpretation is its objectification in records which we conveniently call *texts*. Thinking backwards from texts as products along the lines of their production leads one to *genre* as a concept that gives concrete content to process and ultimately to the idea of the communicative event as the space-time-action fusion where epistemologically significant contact is made. Communication is therefore a precondition of objectivity, and not just an operational strategy or a methodological instrument.

Having learned from experience that "dialectical" is often disqualified as a token of jargon, I have avoided using the term so far. Now that I have spelled out in as much detail as it is feasible in this essay what I believe to be involved in the ethnographic knowledge process, I am ready to qualify my approach, as I did twenty years ago, as dialectical.[25]

So much for the basics of the position "revisited." If the conclusion should be that the basics did not change in the eventful years during which anthropology was shaken and transformed, this could mean that I am clinging to objectivity in a manner that has simply been bypassed by recent developments. While there is as such nothing wrong with being steadfast, I want to show now that what really encourages me to stick to my position is that it has shown the capacity to grow, matching the much greater sophistication we now bring to what I called the basics.

IV

Here, then, are some concluding reflections, not offered in any particular order, on where to go from here. First, a general observation. Changes in conceptions of ethnographic objectivity, we argued, are expressive of changes in what counts as objectification, a notion that is as indispensable as it is difficult. Objectification may cover anything from global metaphysical postulates regarding what counts as reality, to "language" as the objective medium of communication, to concrete action that runs into resistance (something one might call the founding acts of ethnography). Here I shall take up a few key words that have been used to designate aspects of objectification and see what has happened to them recently.

At the risk of repeating myself, the purpose of this list is to show that thinking about the conditions of producing ethnographic knowledge has considerably broadened in recent years. At one time the ideal might have been to assure objectivity by adhering to a set of rules small enough not to be in the way of data collecting and writing-up. Currently, I believe, there is more concern for the complexity of interaction that takes place in ethnographic research. It is easy to be objective if reported knowledge consists of a few algebraic transcriptions of, say, kinship terms or narrative structures; the number of conditions that need to be spelled out to justify such work is limited. Problems of a different magnitude are posed, for instance, when ethnography reports, in ordinary prose, on such extraordinary phenomena as ritual performances, the arts of story-telling, or even the transmission of ecological knowledge. There are those who think the quest for objectivity in ethnography must be abandoned because they claim that ethnography is not scientific and hence incapable of producing objective knowledge. Others declare that any search for objectivity is an illusion. I think that our concerns for objectivity should become more intense to the extent that the challenges multiply. In the title of this essay I suggested that recent changes in that direction involved moving from appreciation of rigor to a pursuit of vigor.

Text. There should be no need to point out how important the notion of text has become in recent theoretical debates. But as often happens in such cases, popularity has not promoted clarification. We may be told that the object of anthropology is a text, or like a text, and that text interpretation is a mode of knowledge. Others abandon such caution when they propose that texts *are* (ethnographic) knowledge because they are what ethnography produces by the only means it knows, writing. Textuality replaces reality. Earlier I acknowledged that valuable critical insights are gained when hermeneutics and literary criticism are applied to anthropology, but I also suggested that such diffuse infatuation with text may be a kind of ontologization that is detrimental to epistemological critique.

On the ground, where ethnographers not only invoke texts but work with them, the problems are of a different order. One insight that ought to be gaining acceptance is that we may have gone too far by granting the status of ethnographic texts only to records of verbal interaction (preferably records established—recorded, transcribed, translated—by the ethnographer). True, when we lost our confidence in other ethnographic sources, it was a relief to find in texts the cards that could be put on the table as tokens of ethnographic objectivity. The danger is a lapse into textual fundamentalism. Among the limitations of the textual approach is an overemphasis on orality or, rather, on the idea that the ethnographer's foremost task is to transpose ethnographic material from an oral into a literary mode of existence. I am not sure that there is a viable alternative to such a conception of ethnographic work, but that is not the point. What this conception promotes is disregard for the role of literacy on the "other side," that is, among the people we study. Especially if we want to go on assigning to texts a crucial role in the ethnographic knowledge process, we must stop giving the impression that "writings," and hence texts, are objectifications to be found only on the side of the knower. To the extent that texts become a common ground between knower and known, any vestiges of a positivistic conception of texts as "data" ought to disappear together with the false assurance of objectivity that textual approaches may have given us.[26] Once the one-way perspective on text and writing is abandoned, something else is bound to change. The role of literacy in ethnography can no longer be considered only as writing. Therefore, critical standards cannot be limited to those of writing. As part of a social praxis texts are *read*; not only does this open up a new field for ethnographic inquiry, but reading—what makes it possible and what it accomplishes—must now be examined as having a bearing on ethnographic objectivity. If anything, thinking about the ethnography of reading once again brings to the fore the communicative nature of ethnographic knowledge (see chapter 3 below).

Communication, Information, and *Performance.* A new appreciation of literacy helps us to recognize the limits of the standard semiotic model in accounting for the production of ethnographic knowledge. For instance, only parts of what happens in literacy as a social and cultural practice can be described by such notions as sign, message, and code (signification, information, encoding, and decoding). I had recognized this for some time. But only during later work did it become clear to me that recognizing limits in what can be covered by semiotic concepts also calls for rethinking the role of information in producing ethnographic knowledge. The point I am trying to make resembles observations that are critical of limiting the function of language to "reference." Only part of what members of a culture know is "informative" in the sense that it can be elicited and produced as discursive information. Much more is "performative:" it can be done, acted out, put on (Fabian 1990b). What is performative in ethnographic communication—and I am advocating a broad sense for the term, including aspects that are play-like—needs to be given more attention if we want to keep ethnography objective. Perhaps this, rather than the rubric of "genres" of writing, is the place where *poesis* should be seriously considered as being involved in knowledge production.

Time. As we begin to appreciate the performative aspects of ethnography we get a sharper focus on the most demanding criterion that must be met in initiating the ethnographic knowledge process, namely the *sharing of time.* Not just having been *there,* but having been *then* is what maketh the ethnographer. Sharing time has been recognized in phenomenology as a prerequisite for action that needs to be syn-chronized in more than a physical sense. Making music together (the example used by Schütz), working together, having a conversation, and certainly "getting an act together" in performing need shared time, not just as an enhancement but as a precondition for their occurring. If knowing resembles all of the above, shared time (not just in its almost abstract meaning which puts the emphasis on shared, but also in its concrete meaning that stresses *time passed together*) must be involved in the founding of ethnographic objectivity.[27] This is something most ethnographers will find compelling; it is a different matter, however, when we begin to think about time in ethnographic writing. Uses of tense and other grammatical categories linked to tense (persons, pronouns), other temporal markers, various temporalizing devices (most of them used to establish distance between anthropological discourse and its objects) need to be scrutinized because they have a bearing on the question of objectivity. To equip us technically for such critique is, in my view, the greatest service that a literary turn can perform for anthropology.

Observation and *Vision.* The belief that observation, albeit participant, is ethnography's most reliable source of knowledge is tenacious inside the field and, it seems, outside it as well. A cloud of connotations has gathered around this idea over the years and now obscures what should be questioned about it. Inasmuch as being an observer, and a participant one at that, demands presence, observation does seem to come close to what we said about ethnographic knowledge as action rather than contemplation. At the same time, observation clearly privileges vision as the most reliable source of knowledge. That this should have become one of the tenets of empiricism may or may not have something to do with the physiology of perception. It does express an ideological current that goes back to the beginnings of Western civilization and has now become the target of critique.[28] Whatever else such critique has achieved it is now no longer possible to limit oneself to concepts and images derived from vision when discussing questions of objectivity.

Materialism, Body, and *Embodiment.* Critique of the visual bias in a theory of knowledge is not just a matter of rehabilitating hearing (and hence sound) and the other senses. Its aim must be to undermine a conviction that visualism had been made to serve in our tradition. Vision requires distance from its objects; the eye maintains its "purity" as long as it is not in close contact with "foreign objects." Visualism, by instituting distance as that which enables us to know, and purity or immateriality as that which characterizes true knowledge, aimed to remove all the other senses and thereby the body from knowledge production (this, incidentally, is also a context in which the gender question needs to be raised). Visualism, nonetheless, needed some kind of materialization which it found in signs, symbols, and representation. If it is true, as we have said, that the question of ethnographic objectivity has been displaced by a shift of emphasis in critical thought from production to representation, then our response should be to explore again body and embodiment as involved in objectification and the grounding of objectivity.[29] It is in epistemology more than in, say, economics or even aesthetics, that we need to maintain, or rehabilitate, a materialist position. What is at stake here is whether we can give to intersubjectivity a more concrete, palpable meaning than that of an abstract "condition."[30]

Praxis, Ecstasis, and *Terror.* Not only does vision in its literal sense (as observation, visual recording) need to be put in its place; so also does contemplating and intuiting—concepts that betray a propensity to think about knowing as basically a process of reception and as a passage from an outside to an inside; as ingestion of experience that is then "processed" in the mind. All of this presupposes an individual knower who offers an inside to the outside world, and who gets active on passive objects. Such a stance, held even by some who reject visualism and crude empiricism, makes it difficult to conceive of intersubjectivity as an actual sharing of content that results in production and transformation of knowledge. How can we share what we believe to exist inside our minds? At this point the notion of praxis (as a concept of sharing that stresses the active as well as social aspects) appears more useful than the expected appeal to "culture" that would have been made traditionally when it came to "explain" how it is that ideas can be shared.

But we can go a step further. Ethnographers are more and more realizing that, to put this provocatively, some, perhaps much of our ethnographic research is carried out best while we are "out of our minds," that is, while we relax our inner controls, forget our purposes, let ourselves go. In short, there is an ecstatic side to fieldwork which, again, should not be written off as a quirk but counted among the conditions of knowledge production, and hence of objectivity. Many ethnographers have in fact undergone ecstatic rituals of initiation, taken hallucinogens or plenty of alcohol,[31] participated in exhausting dances, and gone sleepless during vigils and wakes. But as a rule, such experiences, if they were reported at all, only served as formal legitimation—as the strongest form of "having been there." What needs to be worked out now is the epistemic content that is produced in such a manner.[32] I expect that this call for more attention to ecstasis may be scandalizing. How, it could be asked, are we to distinguish legitimate ecstatic experiences from, say, those flights of imagination that made Carlos Castaneda's fame and fortune? The answer is: We cannot (unless we have some factual information on fraud in a given case). But that is no reason to discard vital sources of ethnographic knowledge.[33]

Incidentally, these recommendations for ecstasis make empathy, once a strong term in the critique of positivism, rather pale. They also help to clarify a distinction that is often difficult to make—the one between epistemology and method. While the sources of ethnographic knowledge that I called ecstatic need to be considered critically (and while they thus have a bearing on the question of objectivity) they can obviously not be recommended as "methods."[34]

One last observation regarding the passivity often ascribed to knowledge when visual, receptive, contemplative aspects are stressed. To the reasons already mentioned for rejecting such a view we should now add the following: Accepting passivity as an appropriate stance leads us to overlook the role of "passion"—understood as drive but also as suffering—as a condition of knowledge, and hence of objectivity. Recommending passion, I realize, is playing against odds that are even higher than those that make pleading for ecstasis so risky. In our tradition, passion has always been denounced as an impediment to reason. Yet, how else than by giving room in our theories of knowledge to passion—indeed, to terror and torture (see Taussig 1987)—can we hope to deal objectively with the peoples and cultures whom Western imperialism made the subjects of brutal domination as well as of ethnographic inquiry?

2

Ethnographic Misunderstanding
and the Perils of Context

Alles Verstehen ist daher immer zugleich ein Nicht-Verstehen, alle Über-
einstimmung in Gedanken und Gefühlen zugleich ein Auseinandergehen.

(Thus all understanding is always at the same time a not-understanding,
all concurrence in thought and feeling at the same time divergence.)

—Wilhelm von Humboldt, *Über die Verschiedenheit des menschlichen
Sprachbaues und ihren Einfluss auf die geistige Entwicklung
des Menschengeschlechts.*

Ethnographers report what they understand: sounds are transcribed
into texts; utterances are presented as stories or conversations; events and
processes are interpreted or explained. If what is reported is not to be dismissed as mere recording or description, it must be recognized as understanding. Understanding must be relevant to what the discipline wants to
understand and it must be shown to have been arrived at by methods and
procedures that are accepted as valid. After all, our efforts are expected to
result in some kind of enlightenment, even if analysts and hermeneuts,
explainers and interpreters, disagree, sometimes vehemently, about what
constitutes enlightenment.

Where there is light, and where there are objects, there are shadows.
On the dark side of understanding there is not-understanding and misunderstanding.[1] The conventions of scientific discourse make provision
for this, but always in such a way that light prevails in the end. Misunderstanding, by the very logic of the concept, can be envisaged neither as

the goal nor as the result of scientific work. Even those who maintain that falsification, not verification, is what science can accomplish, and those who state that all interpretation is partial, strive for some kind of positive gain in knowledge. In presentations of anthropological knowledge, misunderstandings may be focused on and reported, though not very often, and discussions of misunderstandings usually serve as methodological or rhetorical strategies destined to enhance the discipline's (or the writer's) authority.[2]

I will begin by discussing a few examples of ethnographic misunderstanding from my own work, which has been language-centered in two respects. First, almost all my empirical inquiries were conducted through speaking and listening to (and recording) speech. Second, language and communication have been central to me in conceiving a theoretical approach within anthropology.[3] Needless to say, I never made an inventory, much less a systematic study of misunderstandings in my work. Therefore, my examples will be necessarily anecdotal. Nevertheless, I tried to strengthen my case by considering misunderstandings on not just one but several levels that are conventionally distinguished in the study of language. It did not take much searching to find instances that involved phonology, grammar, semantics, and pragmatics.

One hesitates to point out the obvious: By the time they have been made to serve as examples, misunderstandings have been understood. Or have they? We begin to suspect that what happens when we (mis)understand cannot be envisaged adequately as a flow through a chart of binary branches marked either + or −. Should the question be rephrased? Do misunderstanding and understanding relate to each other like error and truth? Perhaps a case could be made for misunderstanding as committing an error; but not for understanding as attaining truth. Scientific, discursive understanding is both less and more than truth. It is about less than truth, because understanding is related to a "discipline" and expressed in the language of that discipline. Always doubly limited, it is thus removed from any absolute notion of truth. There does not seem to be any other notion worth positing; "relative truth" is a compromise, not a solution. Scientific understanding is about more than truth because, when we speak of understanding, we do not only signal an abstract quality; we offer specific content, statements about the world as experienced, direct or reported.

Because a myriad of possible questions can arise on every level of (mis)understanding, I shall try to give my comments on the examples some focus by concentrating on one issue: different ways to repair ethnographic misunderstanding which have in common that they summon *context* as a corrective. In anthropology, context usually is invoked to point out shortcomings or misconceptions that arise when analysis falsely reifies items or entities, confuses logic with explanation, or sells generalizations as cultural universals.[4] Examples of false reifications can be easily found, for instance, in semantic approaches to kinship studies, but similar critique can be leveled against formalist linguistics in general. As a field, sociolinguistics, or the ethnography of communication, has resounded with appeals to context. When, in what follows, I speak of the perils of context, I partly draw on self-observation. Precisely because I sympathize with the "contextualizers" in linguistics and language-centered anthropology, I feel that critical reflection is called for.

I will conclude this chapter with a more ambitious argument. The significance of misunderstanding can be appreciated when we begin to struggle with the notion of not-understanding. Only then will it be possible to proceed from questions of method and rhetoric to epistemology.

Ethnographic Misunderstanding and Not-Understanding

Transcription: Sounds

In ethnographic work based on the documentation of speech, understanding begins, as every practitioner of that approach has painfully experienced, with work that has often been considered problematic only in a technical sense: transcribing recorded sounds.[5] This is not the place to face the multitude of problems that arise, ranging from distinguishing speech sound from noise to deciding what must go into a reasonably accurate graphic representation of recorded speech.[6] Instead, I propose to look at an instance of misunderstanding which is of particular interest regarding the role of context in misunderstanding. The task was to transcribe a brief passage of dialogue, followed by a song from *Le pouvoir se mange entier*, a play created by a group of popular actors in Lubumbashi, Zaire.[7] The language in this, as in all the other examples to be discussed, is a local variety of Swahili. The general theme is power, a story of its exercise, corruption, and restoration. Here is the fragment as it appears in translation:

> *Notable*: Stop it, stop it . . . but what is this noise here?
> *Villagers*: [vociferous protest; impossible to transcribe]
> *Notable*: What is all this rejoicing about? This is what ought be done, what ought to be done [. . . .] everyone cultivates his fields. When the fields are worked you can take a rest and a little glass, isn't that [. . . ? . . .] pass the ladle.
> *Woman*: Let them first give you a small one.
> *Man*: He should first sit down in the furrow over there.
> *Others*: In the furrow. That's how we see it [. . .]
> *Woman*: Singing! Singing! Get into the dance!

Both the scene and the speaking are thoroughly performative rather than discursive, which makes the recording quite difficult to transcribe. In our translation, gaps and incomprehensible passages are marked by dots within brackets. The text that can be recuperated is elliptical but sufficient to get the gist of the exchange: An elder (*notable*) is sent by the chief to remind the villagers of their duty to work in the fields. He finds them feasting and decides to join the drinking and dancing. The scene ends with a song expressing resolve to defy the chief. The songs that were interspersed in the play posed special problems. In addition to the fact that it is always difficult to lift, as it were, the lyrics from a musical performance, most songs were in languages other than Swahili. I therefore settled for transcribing just a few lines of each and then indicating the content as best I could. In the case we are considering here, I initially noted, at the end of the scene: "A sort of fighting-song is intoned, consisting mainly of repetitions of *tutabawina*, 'we shall beat them' (in local Swahili; derived, possibly via Bemba, from English 'to win')." Later I checked my transcriptions with the help of that provider of context par excellence—a native speaker of Shaba/Katanga Swahili. He confirmed my reading of *tutabawina*. Not only that, he volunteered additional information: This was the type of song that would be intoned by supporters of a soccer team.

But we had both misunderstood what we heard. Because I continued to have difficulties with other songs I wrote to the theater group in Lubumbashi to ask for help. They responded with a letter giving the opening lines of five of the songs together with a French translation. As it turned out, the song in question was not in Swahili but in Kizela (a language spoken east of Lake Moero). And it was not a fighting song but a marching song. According to the letter, it went:

> Tuta Mawila, Lumundu
> Kwa Mwenge I Kula
> March on, Lumundu
> It is still far to Mwenge's.

I am unable to check whether the transcription and translation provided by the group are correct. But that they call for a correction of what we had heard cannot be doubted. As misunderstandings go, failing to identify the language (Kizela rather than Swahili) as well as the genre (a marching rather than a fighting song), certainly constitutes one. The point of giving this case our attention is to show that failure to understand can be due precisely to the kinds of sources on which we base claims to understanding: language competence and knowledge of context. This is how it worked in our case: Because Shaba/Katanga Swahili was the language of the play it was to be expected that its sounds were heard in this song. That a string of sounds was identified as *tutabawina* was, if not demanded, at least encouraged by context. *Context* here means the semantic environment of the song in a text that expresses defiance. Context also evokes a cultural environment that has fighting songs in its repertoire, constructed around the expression *kuwina.*

It could be argued that correction was in this case provided by a double break with context. One break was the decision to suspend trust in the "natural" workings of context (through linguistic and cultural competence), a trust that would normally seem to be required to make the task of transcription possible. The other break consisted in leaving the context of orality and of ethnographic routines we develop in working with oral "data." Rectification was demanded by a written document that was not a transcript; the recorded play was improvised, without a script to quote from.

Translation: Grammar and Semantics

On April 25, 1973, I recorded a conversation with the painter Kanyemba Yav at Kolwezi in Shaba/Katanga. In the course of discussing his life history we came to a passage where he recounted his involvement with the Bapostolo, a religious movement that originated in Zimbabwe and had reached the Kolwezi area by 1953. At one point I told him that I had often seen Bapostolo walking around in their colorful biblical attire and had observed some of their open-air meetings from a distance. I said that I found it difficult to make contacts with them. This led to the following exchange:

> *Kanyemba*: It is not difficult because right now we have a white [person] from America who is a member of our group.
>
> *JF*: Of the Bapostolo?
>
> *Kanyemba*: Of the Bapostolo movement, yes.
>
> *JF*: Here in Kolwezi?
>
> *Kanyemba*: Not here in Kolwezi, I think [the person] made the contact first during a trip to the Kasai region. From the Kasai region they took [the person] to Lusaka in Zambia because the Bapostolo religion is a religion that came there from Southern Rhodesia. That's what I think, yes. That is where this religion came from.
>
> *JF*: Was it not Yoanne . . .
>
> *Kanyemba*: . . . Malungu, yes John Malangu [John Maranke, the founder]. And thus it arrived in Lusaka. Now, some of the local leaders [from Zaire] went there to Lusaka to fetch [the person] and then they arrived here. That is where they met this [person who was like a] white [person]. This is now the first white [person] here among us. [The person] had to get there to Lusaka because that is where the leaders are.
>
> *JF*: I see.
>
> *Kanyemba*: They arrived there and baptized [the person]; now we are with that [person] in our community.

The translation, which is as literal as possible, poses several problems of understanding. The most obvious one is caused by the fact that in Swahili neither nouns nor pronouns (or pronominal infixes) are marked for gender. Grammar (in this case morphology) is no help in deciding whether the person that is reported to have joined the movement is male or female. I signal this uncertainty by enclosing references to that person in brackets. A few other passages require paraphrases or explanations (some are provided) but they are marginal to the point illustrated by this example.

I transcribed this text from a recording sometime in 1975 without translating it (other, that is, than the kind of translation that is involved when one transcribes from a language he or she understands). However, I distinctly remember storing the information as "A white man joined the Bapostolo movement." At about the same time, Bennetta Jules-Rosette published *African Apostles* (1975), her dissertation on the Church of John Maranke, which must have come to my attention during the same year or early in 1976, when I was asked to review it (Fabian 1977). In this book, Jules-Rosette describes her conversion to that church. I do not remember exactly when I made the connection, but eventually it became clear to me that she must have been the person I had taken to be a white man. That revealed a first misunderstanding: the person was a woman, not a man. But there is another twist to this story: Bennetta Jules-Rosette is an African American and that signals problems with translating the Swahili term *muzungu*. It distinguishes one class of non-Africans (there are others) on the basis of origin, socioeconomic status, and political position, but not color.[8] Black Americans are *bazungu* (plural of *muzungu*); Italians, Greeks, and other Mediterranean groups, as well as Jews, may be excluded from the class of *bazungu*.

What brought about the misunderstanding I had stored in my memory? When I recorded the conversation with Kanyemba I knew that pronouns and pronominal infixes are not marked for gender and that *muzungu* does not correspond exactly to "white." Yet, when decisions had to be made in order to translate the phrase into English—where pronouns have gender and "European" means "white"—I let myself be guided by context—not, of course, the specific context of this particular utterance, but the context of "normal" expectations derived from experience and prejudice.

The point I want to make with this case of misunderstanding is not that we should mistrust our expectations and improve our competence as translators. We should, of course; but we must, as I have said, make decisions and settle for a version we can live with, otherwise we will end up with unreadable texts like the one quoted, full of gaps and cautionary paraphrases. So the useful lesson to be learned from this case must be elsewhere. I would argue that the example demonstrates that, even on the level of interpreting grammatical and lexical meaning, translating requires *historical* background knowledge. In this case, such knowledge was obtained after the fact, though it could have been gotten during the original exchange, had I been bothered by ambiguities of gender and the meaning of *muzungu*. History, despite expressions such as "historical context" that come easily to most of us, provides connections that are contingent, unpredictable, and unsystematic, and are therefore not really "con-text" in either the linguistic or the literary sense of the term.

Interpretation: Speech Event

As we have seen so far, misunderstanding may be due to a failure to decode sounds or to reduce grammatical and semantic ambiguity. I have tried to show how such misunderstandings, far from being merely failures, can become ethnographically relevant. By being made the object of reflection, they reveal what should have happened to make us understand what we in fact misunderstood. Misunderstandings can reveal conditions of understanding.

Misunderstandings, whether or not productive, are usually identified after the fact. That they have occurred is reconstructed from a record available to us in the present: the recorded text. This means, strictly speaking, that recourse to a corrective context is dependent on the availability of a text. In this perspective, a hermeneutic stance is not all that different from a positivist view stipulating that a theory needs to be tested against data; if theory is the text, data become the corrective context.[9] Doubts about such an approach caused us to reflect on misunderstanding. These doubts concern the notion that ethnographic understanding happens always after the fact and that it is possible to distinguish the collection of information from interpretation or analysis. Opposed to this is the idea that collecting does not (or not adequately) express what happens when anthropologists do field research. The founding acts of ethnography are communicative events. Hence, to confront misunderstanding must be a task that poses itself already in those moments in which the knowledge process gets under way—that is, in those verbal exchanges of which a selection eventually becomes documented as ethnographic texts. When we participate in speech events, our questions regarding (mis)understandings are not addressed to information deposited in texts but to potential breakdown in an ongoing process of communication. Perhaps the difference can be marked terminologically if we distinguish misunderstandings of texts from mistakes in communication. On the other hand, every textual misunderstanding was once (part of) an event. As we shall see, communicative mistakes occur when some sort of text invades the event. We should add that mistakes can in turn be communicated only when they have been turned into texts.

Elsewhere I took a mistake in communication—a wrong choice of what Dell Hymes would call the "code" component of a speech event—as the point of departure for a critique of reified sociolinguistics (Fabian 1979a, reprinted in 1991a, chap. 5). Here I want to confront a similar "key" experience which has taught me that in ethnography things sometimes go right when they go wrong. I must admit, however, that my comprehension of what happened remains incomplete and that my interpretation of the text I am about to quote is tentative.

In 1986, I undertook, as a sideline to other projects, some rather incidental research on Catholic charismatics (the neo-Pentecostal *renouveau charismatique*), in the same language (Swahili) and in the same area (Lubumbashi) from which I took my other examples. I had been introduced to several persons involved in the charismatic movement and made a number of recordings, something that had become a routine in my way of doing ethnography. Matters were everything but routine when I met Mama Régine, leader of one of the "prayer groups," as the charismatics are known locally. We hit it off, as the saying goes. There may have been other reasons, but in the end it was a case of kinship of mind that, I felt, allowed us to transcend gender, culture, politics—and religion. Whenever we talked at her place, one or several other persons were present and, as the recordings show, they occasionally intervened. Nevertheless, I carried in my memory the impression of conversations between only the two of us.

Not that the beginning of our exchanges was especially auspicious. Mama Régine, then a statuesque lady in her forties, received me because I came with a friend who was among her followers.[10] She took control, as it were, by reciting a brief prayer before we sat down around a coffee table. I began by making conversation, telling of my past work with the Jamaa, another religious movement in Katanga of Catholic background. Eventually, her husband came and joined us; drinks and cake were offered. This could have been the end of our meeting. But then our conversation came to a critical point and took a new turn. Régine must have had some information on me before we met because she now confronted me with my past (more about that later). Whatever she knew about me did not stop her from asking me a question that I immediately felt was loaded with significance beyond the meaning of the words that were spoken: "Do you pray?" This sort of head-on challenge made me uncomfortable. I did say "no," but basically I stalled. I suppose ethnographers of religious enthusiasm acquire the ability to hang on in moments when they sense that an important conversation may otherwise be cut off. To bridge what I feared was becoming a gap, I countered with a question: "You want to know who sent me?" She did indeed, and that gave me an occasion to direct our attention from her work, prayer, to mine, research sponsored by my university (not, as she had obviously feared, by the church).[11] "Empty research (*recherches ya bule*)," she muttered. Then she insisted on telling me her life history. When she had finished we took our leave, but not before agreeing that I would come back soon for more questions.

Before I continue my account of conversations with Régine, I want to stop for a moment for an ethnographic aside. It should illustrate why I find the notoriously difficult study of religious enthusiasm theoretically rewarding. As we left Régine's house, my friend, an eminent folklorist, expressed his surprise at not seeing me taking notes. This had been his first occasion to watch me at work, and I had the feeling that his question implied a gentle professional chiding. Two reasons accounted for my unscientific behavior. One was habit. I have always found the posture of the scribe extremely embarrassing. Except when the subject matter was very specific and technical (eliciting, say, a terminology), I never took notes while I conversed with people during field research. My notes were assembled as soon as possible after the event, sometimes assisted by tiny scribblings that I make to aid my memory, but not necessarily at the time or the place to which the notes refer. I have been able to cultivate that habit because, in the end, I always taped what I considered truly important—after learning what was important. That this may leave bits of information unnoted is a small price to pay for the richness of well-prepared recordings.

But there is another reason to abstain from note taking, which is epistemological. If what I were after in a conversation such as the one with Mama Régine were primarily knowledge in the sense of something *known* (such as a folktale, a genealogy, a historical recollection), then what I learned could and should be noted immediately. But if I were primarily after knowledge as process, after *how* charismatics know what they know and how I can know what they know, then we are involved in a social undertaking, and it would be crucial not to disturb the dialogue situation (for epistemological rather than ethical reasons). In practice, this means that one must refrain from turning process into product too early. The risk of missing information is small compared to the risk of being excluded from a practice of knowing.

The preceding, by the way, is an elaboration of thoughts I noted in my diary right after the event. That entry was followed by reflections which I now want to quote (slightly edited):

One of the questions M. Régine asked me was whether I "pray." Being put on the spot I had no choice but to say no. She responded with a smile and a gesture saying "I thought so." Why, damn it, should I be put on the spot? And am I reacting the way I do only because I fear losing contact and rapport? I only have to imagine someone in my everyday surroundings asking such a question [meaning: I would express resentment and brush off questions of that kind]. Nor is this sort of challenge—because Régine's question is *not* a question of information but a challenge—simply a matter of religion. Would it be put up by a practitioner of "traditional" religion? He/she might ask me to *do* things. M. Régine's question was not about whether or not I *do* something but whether I do it as an expression of faith; with the implication that we will never have a common understanding except on the level of faith. Therefore, her invitation to participate in the next meeting [of her group] is aimed at *conversion* not *conversation*. But what if all that is just a projection? Yes, there might be a challenge to convert—but perhaps not to a faith but to *doing*. (Lubumbashi, June 15, 1986)

Three days later I made a partial recording of a séance of Mama Régine's group—two and a half hours of song, prayer, preaching, and testimony. Afterward, we sat together for a while and talked about this and that. Before I left, another meeting was scheduled. "We part on good terms," I noted in my diary, without being able to say why. At first, not much came of that meeting. I arrived at the appointed time but I caught

Mama Régine just as she was leaving. I gave her a lift to the market, where she had to see after her business, and we agreed to meet again in the afternoon. We did, and this time I asked permission to use my cassette recorder (spending some time to explain the purpose). Régine did not hesitate for a moment. Once again she began with her life history, dwelling especially on early experiences that made her certain that she had the gift of prayer, as well as other gifts. This took up about one-third of the 130 minutes of the recording. A second part was devoted mainly to events since 1973, when she began to gather a group together. A third part, in which her husband joined us, was spent, as Mama Régine put it, discussing the "conclusions" from her life story. It was in this reflexive metaperspective that she resumed the line of questioning that had provoked in me the angry reaction I noted above. As it turned out, the rather timid suspicion I formulated then—that I might be projecting rather than understanding—was proven correct.[12]

> *Régine*: Alright. Now I have a question for you . . . You told me, excuse me, you see things from a distance—aren't you a Catholic?
> *JF*: Hm.
> *Régine*: [making several starts] Even though you have . . . I am asking
> 5   you. You are . . .
> *JF*: We were talking about that with your son, the one who studies statistics.
> *Régine*: Yes.
> *JF*: He asked me the same question.
> 10   *Régine*: So, did you give him an answer?
> *JF*: Tsk [I click my tongue]. We looked at each other . . . He asked me: Are you a Catholic?
> *Régine*: Ah.
> *JF*: So I said: Hm, tsk. And he, too, said: Hm. [I laugh] He understood.
> 15   We are searching, mama.
> *Régine*: Are you searching for God? [chuckles] Is that what you understood there [when you questioned each other]?
> *JF*: Yes.
> *Régine*: Voilà, and I, when you questioned me, did I not give you
> 20   answers?
> *JF*: Ask, go ahead, ask. So, your first question was: Am I a Catholic?
> *Régine*: [repeats] Am I catholic. Now, earlier you used to be a [Catholic].

JF: I was, I was . . .

Régine: You were a Catholic.

25 *JF*: I worked very hard . . .

Régine: Amen! [passage omitted] . . . In the end you did everything. Now [pauses]—you see farther. The matters of God go on outside. You used to be a Catholic; [now] you are in the world.

JF: Mm.

30 *Régine*: You see further.

JF: Mm.

Régine: [somewhat obscurely] We haven't died yet, we are still alive.

JF: Mm.

Régine: You see further. As far as that is concerned, I also speak the way

35 you spoke. As when you made your "Mm." That is what I said, too. I told you about that. When they [the official supervisors of the charismatics] call me to a meeting, then I don't tell myself first that this not a Catholic meeting.

JF: True.

40 *Régine*: Mm.

JF: That's how it is.

Régine: [sighs]

JF: But these are difficult matters, mama.

Régine: [chuckles]

45 *JF*: Go on, ask. Ask.

Régine: [laughs out loud, turns to her husband] Nestor, what else do you want to ask?

Nestor: No, you ask [him]: When you finished everything . . .

Régine: When you finished everything, sorry, you finished everything . . .

50 *Nestor*: . . . did you enter?

Régine: He entered. He entered . . .

Nestor: Alright, after you had entered, did you leave, did you return to what was before?

JF: I left.

55 *Nestor*: Why?

JF: That's the question [laughs].

Régine: That's what I am trying to ask.

JF: [sigh] To begin with, I did not think a lot about it.

Régine: Right.

60 *Nestor*: Yes.

JF: It was like growing up. I was thinking, now I left this behind me. I

have my work, my work as a professor. I am going to put a lot of
effort into this work. It's going to be alright.

Régine: Right . . . [passage omitted] I know. This is why I asked you:
65   Those people whom you saw [when you were a Catholic], they say
they are Catholics. Right?

JF: Mm.

Régine: [chuckles] But—I just use my eyes.

JF: Yes, indeed.

70   *Régine*: That's what I kept telling you the other day. You were sitting here
[when I said]: They should stop getting on my nerves. They should
stop getting on my nerves. Here I am, to pray to God, and that's it.

In this episode Régine confronts me for the second time with a
question I experience as embarrassing. No longer being a Catholic, I fear
that my answer may be embarrassing to her. Hence the clever dodges
(lines 7–15) that help me avoid giving a direct and clear answer. Régine is
not fooled by this and insists: The questions you asked me were of the
same kind as those I am asking you—did I not give you answers (lines
19f.)? But this is still allusion. Only in lines 34ff. does she put into words
what had begun to dawn on me a few moments earlier. In my reaction to
her question and in my anticipation of her reaction to my response I had
been mistaken. She had no intention whatsoever of criticizing me for my
past, or of bringing me back into the fold; she was quite simply interested
in how one gets away from Catholicism and how one acquires the ability
"to see farther" (a notion expressed right at the beginning of this exchange
in line 2). Once I had realized that, we had a new basis for our conversation and we therefore started it again with another version of the first
question (lines 21ff.). Accordingly, my answer is more detailed. Régine
can identify with my recollections (see lines 26ff.). At the very end of the
exchange quoted here, she announces, as it were, that she intends to put
her cards on the table (lines 71f.). The rest of our conversation (recorded
until the tape ran out) consisted of one example after the other of ways,
direct or indirect, subtle or rude, in which the Catholic Church, as represented by the local hierarchy, had become an intolerable burden for this
devoutly religious woman.

Before I get further embroiled in this episode let me stop and consider what this can contribute to our inquiry into ethnographic misun-

derstanding. In this instance, there were no problems with phonetic decoding or with semantic interpretation. The misunderstanding that I felt had occurred regarded the interpretation of intentions. Conventionally speaking, something went wrong on a metalinguistic level: A mistake was made that was perhaps akin to a failure to recognize irony or parody. On the other hand, the "ethnography of speaking" holds that the "linguistic" includes, above the levels of phonemes, morphemes, lexemes, and sentences, that of speech events and genres of communication. And this is where we might locate the mistake: Although I should have known better from previous experience, I simply misunderstood the nature of the event. I approached this conversation as an "interview," certainly not preset and hardly directed but, nevertheless, as an exchange whose purpose was to elicit and record information about charismatics. Hence my concern, expressed textually in what I called "dodges," with not endangering the flow of information. While I was pursuing an interview, Mama Régine was engaged, and was trying to engage me, in a different genre: testimony.[13] Had this been clear to me, my communicative competence should have included knowledge of the fact that the "rules of speaking" for defining testimony among charismatics require that those who give testimony and those who receive it assume positions of absolute, perhaps utopian, equality. The Jamaa movement, whose teaching is quite explicit about these matters, often expressed the required attitude as one of self-humiliation (*kujishusha*). That gave the event a moral tinge and eventually resulted in a ritualization of testimony exchanges as "encounter" (*mapatano*), a necessary step in the process of initiation. With the charismatics, the definition of this genre is somewhat different. It, too, is ritualized in form and often also in content, and is part of the typical meeting of a prayer group. Incidentally, our text contains a discursive marker to confirm this. Just when I begin to respond to her question about my Catholic background with an account, Mama Régine responds with a typically charismatic expression of assent and encouragement: "Amen!" (line 26).

Ritualized or not, speech we classify as testimony has intellectual functions we should briefly consider. Testimony/witness is given where there is something to prove or verify. Proof/verification is needed when there is an argument, when something is contested. The more precarious faith becomes (because it is more and more isolated in an individual, or because it goes more and more against common sense), the stronger the need for testimony. Through the years, I have become convinced that there is a fine line where testimonies can be exchanged between ethnographers and the people who are being researched. The result need not be agreement or conversion, it seldom is; but it can be the promise of nontrivial understanding that is produced by researcher and researched together (see Fabian 1979b).

This means (returning to our reflections on the significance of ethnographic misunderstandings) that this kind of mistake can be repaired by invoking as context certain culturally defined rules of communication. But it is also clear that context here is not "given."[14] What is not given cannot be called upon or applied; it must first be created. Furthermore, there is nothing inherent in context that makes it a corrective for misunderstanding. A text "reduced to writing" may give us the illusion of an inside and an outside, of a part and a whole, or of lower and higher levels of understanding. In reality, in acts of producing ethnographic knowledge, creations of text and creations of context are of the same kind. This confronts ethnography with an insight that is now accepted widely in literary and cultural studies. Jonathan Culler wrote some years ago:

[The] notion of context frequently oversimplifies rather than enriches discussion, since the opposition between an act and its context seems to presume that the context is given and determines the meaning of the act. We know, of course, that things are not so simple: context is not given but produced. . . . contexts are just as much in need of elucidation as events; and the meaning of a context is determined by events. (1988, xiv)[15]

The particular route by which we came to a similar conclusion—the problem was misunderstanding rather than a matter of interpreting meanings—can, I believe, be traveled further. From examining misunderstandings and their repair with the help of context, we can, having overcome the positivity of context, go on to direct our attention to the significance of not-understanding in the production of (ethnographic) knowledge.

The Significance of Not-Understanding

At this point I should address a likely objection. In my examples, misunderstanding was identified reflexively—the same person was involved in misunderstanding and in understanding that something was misunderstood. What about situations where one person "corrects" the misunderstandings of another? Can understanding be collective? Is reflexivity collective? In order to get a grip on these questions we should briefly stop to consider reflexivity. I would argue that at least three aspects of reflexive understanding need to be attended to: critical intent, memory, yes, but above all a personally situated process of knowing. By "critical intent" I mean an intellectual habit directing attention not just to the possibility of misunderstanding but to actual cases. "Memory" I take to be the capacity to connect present with past understanding (every misunderstanding was once an understanding). Finally, "process of knowing" signals a notion of understanding as a praxis of constant transformation, rather than as the accumulation of understandings and the elimination of misunderstandings. The latter view would presuppose a position of distance or transcendence, outside the process of understanding—one that does not seem attainable if that process is, as I said, personally situated. Contrary to the endearing ethnoscientist fiction of an "omniscient ethnographer," our work is necessarily historical and contingent because it is autobiographical.

It seems to be a different matter when another person catches or diagnoses misunderstanding. But critical intent, although individually mobilized, is a socially shared habit connecting both analytical and reflexive practices. How is memory involved? I must remember that someone reported something as understanding in order to confront this with evidence that is available to me but not, or not yet, to the author of the reported understanding. But whose is the misunderstanding in that case? Whatever the answer may be, it will necessarily point to a communicative view of the pursuit of understanding. After all, even in cases where I am the author of both the misunderstanding and the understanding, I act with communicative intent as soon as I report my (mis)understanding.

I realize that choosing to address the problem of ethnographic misunderstanding has led me onto dangerous ground. As a matter of elementary logic, it is impossible to determine the significance of a negative proposition with any degree of exactitude. Establishing that something was misunderstood tells us, as such, nothing about how it should be understood. But my examples should have shown that, in practice, the diagnosis of ethnographic misunderstanding is not a matter of logic alone. The reason is, of course, that it is impossible to specify axiomatic truth conditions for anthropology. Unless we are able to deal with statements such as "a white person is black" in ways other than rejecting them as contradictory, there is no point in doing anthropology. What I want to argue is that misunderstanding needs to considered epistemologically and that it is but one kind of not-understanding.

Misunderstanding, with its conceptual aura of mistake, error, failure, and falsity, serves conceptions of knowledge that measure validity with a standard, if not of absolute truth, then of the degree of match between representations (ethnography, in this case) and realities. If this is applied rigorously, validity becomes a matter of either/or (true or false). The very rigor of that position requires that the idea of approximation be introduced if knowledge is to expand beyond first assumptions. Approximation, however, reaffirms what it qualifies: proximate to what? To the truth. Although such an approach to knowledge can subjectively be experienced as continual search, as the never-ending work of eliminating misunderstanding, it does not really conceive of knowledge as process. How one gets from one state of grace to another is not part of what is known, but belongs to the realm of rules, of method or theory, all of which are posited as being outside of the "context" of intentions, communicative purposes, and historical conditions, at least while knowledge of (a) reality is being established.

In a processual, dialectical theory, knowing is not envisaged as a succession (and accumulation) of states of agreement between representation and reality, but rather as the production of knowledge through practices of interacting with, or confronting, reality. It is essential for such a process, and not a regrettable weakness, that negativity be involved in every conceivable step: not-knowing, as I think of it here, is not a logical but a dialectical negation. It is that which makes of knowing a process and of knowledge a product. Hegel could be invoked here, but we may as well stay with Humboldt who provided the epigraph for this chapter.[16]

He makes his intriguing statement about all understanding being not-understanding in a discussion of the dialectical relationship between language and speaking. We may speak of the individuality of a language when we distinguish one language from an other; but "true individuality"—that is, true actualization, realization—is achieved only by the individual speaker (1963 [1830–35], 439). On that level,

Nobody means by a word precisely and exactly what his neighbor does, and the difference, be it ever so small, vibrates, like a ripple in water, throughout the entire language. Thus all understanding is always at the same time a not-understanding. . . . (1988, 63)[17]

Let me now bring these reflections down to earth, and consider our problems with misunderstanding in language-based ethnography. I suggested that we might get a better understanding of the epistemological significance of ethnographic misunderstanding if we were to concentrate on a claim that presumably is accepted by those who are theoretically inspired by the ethnography of speaking, namely that full understanding, and consequently overcoming failures to understand, requires recourse to context. What I have been struggling to make clear, at least to myself, is that the potential of the ethnography of speaking to go beyond semiotic (and certainly beyond purely methodological) uses of language in ethnography—the potential, that is, to move ethnography from knowledge as representation to knowledge as praxis—may be endangered precisely by unreflected appeals to that which distinguishes it from other "linguistic" approaches: context.[18] Context, I argue, works dialectically, not logically-methodologically. Context cannot, except trivially, be "cited" (as context). Context does not coexist with text "synchronically"—a qualifier that, rather than affirming temporal coexistence, really asserts the irrelevance of time. A "synchronous" or paradigmatic notion of context may be involved, for instance, when Dell Hymes appears to use "context" and "setting" synonymously in his discussion of the components of a speech event (1974a, 13).[19] If there is a conclusion to be drawn from our reflections on examples of ethnographic misunderstanding, then it is something like the following. Context must be constituted in a practice that is individually and therefore historically situated and determined. Ethnography is biography is historiography—a position that can escape tautology if it rests on a dialectical conception of knowledge. The point of insisting on "dialectics" is to overcome facticity through overcoming positivity. The positivist definition of facts as *choses* needs negating, not just breaking down or refining. Dialectics opens up a view of history as uniting the general and the specific in a process. Positive social science ends up with something like "pluralism." In that case, historiography/ethnography is envisaged, at best, as a matter of negotiation and, at worst, as a game of classification. Of course, if a dialectical theory of knowledge is descriptive, not just programmatic, then positivists produce knowledge dialectically like everyone else. But the problem is not one of ontology; not what knowledge *is*, but how it can be presented and communicated. This is what can be discussed by people holding different theoretical positions. I should hope the cases I discussed show that we stand to lose much if we deal with (mis)understanding by sweeping our failures under the rug of invariably positive accounts of success.

3

Keep Listening: Ethnography and Reading

The Study of Literacy and the Neglect of Reading

Nothing human is supposed to escape anthropology's attention. Yet reading, an activity on which many humans spend more time than on eating, having sex, or participating in rituals, has not been among the rubrics of standard ethnographic research and writing. Why this should have been so is a question to be asked, now that reading seems to become a topic of ethnography. In the first part of this chapter I want to show that answers may be found if we begin to think about the ways in which literacy has been approached in anthropology.[1]

There is a story which goes like this. In the beginning, anthropologists (and their predecessors) studied the invention/origin and diffusion/evolution of systems of writing. This was taking literacy literally. Later it was realized that literacy might be looked at more broadly, not just as a "technology" but as a social practice that involves more than using a script. And finally the idea appeared that literacy may be a political-ideological complex which is involved in the exercise of power, in the maintenance of inequality, and in imperial designs. This opened up a global perspective. Literacy, it was realized, had a real presence in much of the world—not as popular mass literacy but as something that belonged to the aura of religious and secular power—when those who began to propagate mass literacy in the service of the Scriptures, at home and in the newly conquered parts of Africa and America, invented "orality." It has been said that the Reformation was the one event that offered, by combining the power of the Scriptures in the vernacular with that of the printing press, the incentives for the spread of generalized literacy (Harbsmeier 1989). Then, at the latest in the eighteenth century (Gusdorf 1973), orality took its revenge; it became a weapon of "critique" (Bible criticism, literary criticism). Orality (and aurality) became epistemological issues in the nineteenth century; Herder and Humboldt built their theories of language and, indeed, culture on speech and sound (rather than writing and sight). Orality went into the foundations of modern anthropology—where it remained buried. Above the ground, the seeing eye became the root metaphor of knowledge. The observing gaze delivered the material; visible order created by classification provided its meaning.

When anthropology became established academically toward the end of the nineteenth century and began systematically to study "peoples without writing," orality was usually regarded as little more than that which remains when literacy is subtracted from a culture: a sign of a lower stage of evolution. Oral peoples were depicted as intellectually rather dim; their thoughts were said to be short-lived due to the absence of means to preserve them; their capacity to organize major work projects or to govern large populations and keep records on them was deemed limited. In short, they were the kind of people who "cried out" (orally) for the blessings of literacy.

While orality was thus used as a means to establish distance from one's own place, with distance implying inferiority given the prevailing equation of evolution with progress, there was some lingering envy, inherited from the Romantics. Orality makes peoples verbose and lively, great entertainers and performers, free from the constraints of script and scripture. Still, except for serving anthropology by demarcating its territory, orality as nonliterateness continued to lead a shadow life; it remained the dark side of what was brought to light about human history.

Then came Walter Ong and others. They cast doubts on the blessings of literacy within our own culture by showing how the promotion of the graphic and the visual had depersonalized language and speaking. Worse, they found that most of what had for centuries been regarded as sound pedagogical method had in fact been invented in order to make knowledge a matter of internalizing signs, graphs, and diagrams (which fitted the printed page), rather than disputing about matters that matter in live dialogue—an interesting discovery (of Ramus and his works by Ong), and a productive critical position (and a very popular one in the form it was propagated by Marshall McLuhan). Still, it took decades before it was appreciated widely by anthropologists.

Then came Jan Vansina (see chapter 4) with a book on oral tradition—at a time when the idea that there was history only where there was writing was becoming less and less accepted. Initially at least, he convinced as many people as he did because he offered a "method" whereby oral tradition "there" could be processed such that it would meet more or less (mostly more) the same standards as those held in esteem by historians "here." (Vansina came again, a generation later, but it was a different book.)

Then Jack Goody and others showed two things. (1) "Traditional" (by which he meant oral) societies were much more involved with, touched by, literacy than had previously been assumed: therefore processes of transition deserve above all our attention. (2) Literacy in the narrow sense of writing, has been but part of a graphic technology whose development had its own "logic" and ran its own course with a necessity that seems to be characteristic of major technological advances. One can see an element of contradiction between these two assertions. The first one seeks to dismantle received ideas about absolute barriers between literate and illiterate societies; and that is good because it undermines claims to superiority on the part of the former. The other asserts an inner, necessary connection between literacy and "domestication"; and that is bad, because it somehow excuses the domination of illiterate by literate societies when it makes the effects of literacy an inevitable outcome of technological evolution. But, if there is contradiction, it is only in ethical terms; logically and, ultimately, historically, the two theses envisage two sides of the same coin, the coin being the victorious march of technological progress.[2]

Then Brian Street, Goody's most thorough critic, argued that

Goody failed to realize that literacy was only in part a matter of technology; whatever technology was available could become effective (or not) depending on whether literacy emerged as an ideology. As ideologies varied greatly so did practices of literacy, and attempts to understand links between literacy and imperial projects are not well served by ignoring these differences.

Through this somewhat fictionalized sketch of anthropological concerns with literacy there runs a line: from the invention of writing as a material, visible, lasting token of speech and as something achieved for humanity as a whole, through literacy as a mark on the scale of technological evolution, to literacy as social and political ideology serving special interests. Undeniably, this trajectory has resulted in increased sophistication about the ways humans have with writing; the questions asked and the answers given became more and more general in their application, to a point where literacy research now takes its place on the same theoretical level as, say, the study of religion, law, or modes of production. The price of such theoretical progress, however, seems to have been a dematerialization of the object of research—much along the same lines which led to the dematerialization of language in linguistics. There are probably many ways to show how dematerialization worked. One is to consider how the fascination with signs and symbols, in short, with representations (going back to the medieval idea of nature as a "book") favored mirror theories of knowledge.[3] Elsewhere (Fabian 1983) I have tried to show how this in turn encouraged a visualist bias both in the choice of the sources of empirical knowledge and in its presentation.

Studies of the social history of reading in the West show that it came to be conceived as something almost exclusively ocular not too long ago. As a result of changes that affected especially the role of the body, reading underwent, as one author puts it, a "loss of sensuousness." I am referring to a study by Schön (1987) which is limited to literacy in German but is probably applicable to most Western societies. Following, rather selectively, Norbert Elias and Michel Foucault, he situates the crucial changes—the immobilization of the body, the end of reading aloud, solitary reading, reading as consumption, and others—in the eighteenth century. This richly documented and methodologically sophisticated treatment (and others like it, see Schön's bibliography) should be required reading for those who embark on ethnographies of reading. One may surmise that the dis-embodiment of reading described by Schön is all the more pervasive because it precedes encounter with other cultures. It shapes attitudes and habits in Western bourgeois ethnographers that limit their imagination and capacity to ask concrete and interesting questions about reading as a social practice.[4]

All this has a long and complicated history; the point of at least evoking it was to suggest that the absence of concern with reading as an activity (not just as the logical complement to writing) may be indicative of what I called "dematerialization," and that, conversely, attention to reading may provide a much needed corrective for our views of literacy.[5]

Literacy and the Work of Anthropology

Wherever one stands in current anthropological debates, there is no escaping the realization that investigating literacy is part of the phenomenon it tries to comprehend. Critical anthropologists—anthropologists who reflect on the practice of writing as part of the process whereby knowledge is produced—could not fail to realize that they might themselves be handmaidens of imperialist literacy, and some began to agonize about a dilemma which seemed to be: either not to serve literacy, that is, to stop writing and stop being anthropologists, or to go on writing and contribute to the oppression of those they wrote about. Most settled for going on with writing, critically. The best argument I can think of for not giving up goes roughly like this. That one can take sides for or against literacy is an illusion; literacy is, for better or worse, a global phenomenon and, at least on that global level, there is no boundary to cross, no inside to be left for an outside. Sides can be taken only in concrete antagonistic situations of conflict or of domination/submission and, given the conditions that prevail, taking sides will have to be done (if it is not to remain a purely personal moral gesture) publicly, that is by acts which, sooner or later, involve the use of literacy. This, I realize, does not dispose of the dilemma; it may help us, though, to recognize its true nature.

It would be wrong to assume that anthropologists who think of themselves as social scientists—and most of them probably do—are habitually plagued by the dilemma just described. Still, it is fair to say that critical self-awareness was propelled to a new level by a literary turn in anthropology, a turn affecting even those who did not take it. Reams were written about the ethnographer as writer and about ethnographies as texts. Yet it has largely gone unnoticed that this new awareness did little to change one of the oldest convictions informing a scientific approach—namely that speaking and listening, important as they are in conducting research, are, as it were, left behind when the ethnographer's work proceeds from research to writing. To be sure, there is talk of locution and rhetoric in ethnographic writing, of devices to capture an audience, but all this is discussed in a rather abstract, derivative sense; hardly anyone literally means speaking when discussing rhetoric, nor is a literary audience really envisaged as a group of listeners. Writers can be dumb and readers deaf as long as literacy is imagined to exist on a plane of signs, above, outside of, or apart from the agitations of voice.

Be that as it may, a generation of anthropologists emerged which could no longer maintain the illusion of clear distinctions between literate and illiterate societies even if they wanted to. Almost all ethno-graphers (even those who work in the "interior" of Africa, Melanesia, or South America) now face people-writers: natives who use literacy for their own projects of survival. The fact that the label ethnographers attach to themselves is a Greek one may be expressive of their intent to hold on to old privileges (claimed in times when they wrote and the others talked); it does not absolve them from coming to grips with a situation in which literacy is routinely, not exceptionally, shared by anthropology and its objects.

Interestingly, a similar breaking down of barriers seems to go on in the one guild from which the high priests of literacy are usually recruited. Literary critics and experts on linguistic texts have begun to argue that orality has never been exorcised even from the most literary texts. Much of what texts have to tell us, they now say, can be understood only by listening to them while reading them.[6]

Those who have had experience with literacy outside of domains that are more or less rigidly controlled by specialized institutions (schools, churches, administrations) are beginning to realize that imperial designs have been served, inadvertently or not, by thinking of literacy mainly as the capacity to *write* while neglecting that any literacy can of course only have the insidious effect we ascribe to it when what is written is also *read*. When literacy ceases to be understood as the one-way activity of in-scribing, this must have consequences for the global assessment of literacy as an instrument of domination; such a change of perspective should therefore also be considered with regard to the writing work done by ethnographers. The ethnographer's critical dilemma should then appear in a different light. I now want to explore how ethnographic work with written texts may, paradoxically, help us to subvert the dictates of literacy to the extent that we concentrate on reading.

Writing and Reading: A Report from Ethnographic Research

Parts of this section may tax the patience of readers who have no linguistic expertise. To begin with, there is the clumsy label Shaba/ Katanga Swahili for the language of my documents. The double tag reflects the vagaries of recent Congolese history, in the course of which the region where this variety of Swahili is spoken was known as Katanga, then as Shaba (at a time roughly coinciding with the Mobutu regime), and then again as Katanga after Mobutu's demise. Furthermore, to make the point of this exercise in the ethnography of reading, certain basic linguistic terms must be used. When I speak of morphemic and syntactic segmentation, this means, roughly, the way syllables that make up words and phrases that make up sentences are kept together or not in transcribing recorded texts or in trying to read written texts.

Being committed to a language-centered approach, I have in my own ethnographic work in the Congo sought my "data" mainly in the form of recordings in the common language of Shaba/Katanga, a variety of Swahili. Like many others I assumed that analyzing and interpreting field material required, above all, transposing it into *writing*. At least this is what is foremost on our minds when we "write up" our research. We are of course aware that, while we write, we also read—to check, correct, edit (all in the service of writing). Why even ethnographic work conducted in terms of a language- or speech-centered approach should be fixated on writing is a question which deserves some thought. It may be due to a lingering epistemology that stipulated that seeing and observation were the most important or at any rate most reliable sources of ethnographic knowledge. "Saving the oral" then requires making it visible. Although it has been said that anthropologists ought to approach the cultures they study as "ensembles of texts" (Geertz), when we consider *reading* as part of the ethnographer's work we usually do not think of the people or phenomena we intend to de-scribe. After all, ethnography is supposed to make us different from historians who do their research in archives and other depositories of writing. We read our colleagues' writings because we want to learn from them or argue with them; perhaps we study some written documents which come in handy for dealing with historical context, demography, economics, and all those wider aspects that cannot be known from face-to-face interaction. The people we study are usually not read, at least not before the ethnographer has transformed their utterances into written texts.

Paradoxically, it was struggling with a text written and published in Shaba/Katanga Swahili[7] which made me realize more clearly than before that producing an ethnographic text, here taken in the narrow sense of a spoken text, is not limited to, and does not come to an end (even provisionally) with, a successful trans-scription of recorded speech. The reason is elementary, once we think about it, yet it may have complex consequences regarding our conceptions of the ethnographer's task. Writing ("scription") is inseparable from reading. The kind of writing that occurs in transcribing recorded speech from tapes is never just a straightforward transposition from acoustic signals to graphic signs. It is an activity that is geared to, guided and constrained by, the aim of making the transcript *readable* according to criteria which are always relative to culturally and historically specific situations (of both the source and the "target" text).

In this regard, there is little difference between the efforts and competences required to transcribe a recorded text and those one needs to read a text written in the kind of literacy that speakers of Shaba/Katanga Swahili—a language which during its colonial history was denied access to official literacy (Fabian 1991c)—employ when they write their language. Both kinds of activity, even though one may be seen as graphic encoding, the other as decoding, require an ability to recreate the oral performance of speech. A special kind of ethnographic work, namely discussing and conversing about what is written or read, is therefore required no matter whether the task is transcribing and thereby producing a text, or understanding/translating a text. I will now report on and discuss two instances of such work.[8]

When I began work on an ethnography of conceptions of power in Shaba popular culture (Fabian 1990b), my starting point was an intriguing proverb-like saying ("Power is eaten whole"), but most of the material consisted of recordings of a play constructed around that saying and performed by a group of actors.

When I worked on the final version of the texts presented in that study (in the original Shaba/Katanga Swahili and an English translation) I had the privilege (and luxury) of having my friend Kalundi Mango, a native of Lubumbashi, literally at my side. His contribution was not only to help me fill gaps and correct errors; this affected perhaps less than 5 percent of the work previously done by myself. More importantly, the conversations and occasional heated disputes we had about correct transcriptions and translations made me realize that both acts, establishing the text and translating it, are to the core dialogical.[9] Such an insight may be obscured by the fact that this phase of ethno-graphy is usually carried out in the absence of informants with whom we can negotiate signs and meanings. To be carried out successfully, making and translating ethnographic texts in the absence of interlocutors still calls for (the substitute of) an inner dialog in which the anthropologist who writes ethnography must *listen* and match recorded sounds and graphic symbols with communicative competences, memories, and imagination. (And, of course, with that body of knowledge that gets deposited in ethnographies and lexica. Good dictionaries are always both.) In this sense all ethno-graphy is ethno-logy—recuperation of the spoken word (*logos*) through reading as "re-collecting" (legein).

The situation I am reporting here is perhaps not typical; much work based on recordings is done with the help of native speakers who assist the ethnographer by transcribing and often also translating the spoken texts. There is much professional lore about the problems of working with interpreters and "native assistants," but only recently have these problems been recognized for what they are: integral parts of the production of ethnographic knowledge—hence epistemological problems and not just a practical nuisance or a minor issue in methodology.[10] And that is what I am trying to argue about the role of reading.

Kalundi Mango also played a crucial part in the project I briefly mentioned above: The *Vocabulary of the Town of Elisabethville*, a written text, typed and mimeographed. It is presented in a kind of uncontrolled literacy that makes reading the document, let alone translating it, a forbidding task. Because the author did not have at his disposal a system of standardized rules for writing Shaba/Katanga Swahili his text is characterized by erratic segmentation on both morphemic and syntactic levels: very often word and sentence boundaries are not marked or not clear, at least not immediately. More than the inconsistent orthography and the confusing punctuation, this makes the original text very difficult for a foreign reader and, I should add, may pose problems when working with a native reader. Lack of consistency in writing is matched with inconsistency or, put positively, much freedom in reading. In the kind of literacy we meet here the written text is approached as but one *aide mémoire* between one oral realization and another, without ever commanding the sort of reverence our kind of literacy pays to texts. This, rather than indifference or incompetence, is yet another reason why native speakers are notoriously "unreliable" as transcribers of language recordings. More than "a little training" is required to do what really involves a profound reorientation toward the kind of disembodied literacy that is the product of our culturally postulated distinctions between writing and speaking.

Yet before some kind of agreement on segmentation is reached, translation of substantial parts of the document remains impossible. With untiring help from Kalundi Mango a relatively simple and elegant solution was eventually found although not without many compromises, as we shall see presently: Kalundi Mango was asked to read the *Vocabulary* aloud and this was recorded (in Lubumbashi in 1986). The intonation patterns and other prosodic features in that recording made it possible to mark syntactic segments in the written text. Many passages remained doubtful and had to be corrected later with the help of semantics. Morpheme and sentence boundaries became further clarified when we proceeded to translating the text.

The next step was to ask Kalundi Mango (who, like many speakers of local Swahili, is used to writing this language mainly for the purpose of private correspondence) to rewrite the original in what he felt was the manner he and other Shaba/Katanga Swahili speakers like him would currently choose (in Amsterdam in 1987). The results of that experiment were rather more problematic than expected. As could have been foreseen, Kalundi Mango showed too much respect for the written text of the *Vocabulary* and achieved only a partial transposition of the original into current Swahili.[11] Nevertheless, his transcript became the starting point for establishing a Shaba/Katanga Swahili version of the *Vocabulary* (in Amsterdam in 1988). The latter is the result of rereading aloud Kalundi's typed text together with him, word by word and sentence by sentence, and of negotiating a mode of transcription which is at least moderately uniform. Thus this version, or "reading," is really a *reoralization of the written original.*

To give an idea of what this accomplished, here are the first few sentences of the *Vocabulary* in their three versions:

Original:

abali ya wazungu kwakutufikia mu inchi ya Afirika na mu Congo (Mukongo) yetu na pia bakatufikia na sisi wa toto wa Katanga ya mashariki ni:waka gani?

Shaba/Kantanga Swahili Version:

Habari ya wazungu: kwa kutufikia mu inchi ya Afrika: na mu Congo: mu Congo yetu: na pia bakatufikia na sisi watoto wa Katanga ya mashariki/ ni mwaka gani?

Translation:

Concerning the news of the Whites arriving in the country of Africa, in the Congo, in our Congo, and especially when they arrived among us, children of East Katanga. Which year was it?

Comments:

—abali is a possible but not a frequent variant of East Coast Swahili habari (with h before a deleted and alternation between r and l).

—The Shaba/Katanga Swahili version has after Katanga ya mashariki a tone pattern indicating a full clause (marked by a slash). This suggests that the phrase beginning with habari ya wazungu and ending with yetu is proleptic and best translated as "Concerning, etc.," making it a sort of heading.

—Connective kwa should be separated from kutufikia; the prefix wa should be joined to toto.

—The expression mu Congo (locative particle + name of the country) is followed by (Mukongo) (prefix mu-, indicating person, singular, + generalized ethnic term). The parentheses make it look like a repair due to insecurity about writing. This "complication," however, can be disregarded when the text is read because both forms have the same phonic realization.

—The end of the first phrase after mashariki is not marked in the original while the colon between ni and mwaka is not motivated.

Notice that this is not one of the difficult passages. Still, as the comments show, a direct translation from the written text would have had to be justified with numerous notes and explanations, most of them based on the editor's/translator's ability to recognize Shaba/Katanga Swahili speech in the graphic signs of the original.

The experience gained in this preparatory phase eventually determined the presentation of our edition of the *Vocabulary*. The original was produced in facsimile. The oralized Shaba/Katanga Swahili version appears, on facing pages, with the English translation. For reasons that pertain to this discussion of ethnography and reading, I eventually decided to present the oralized Swahili and the English texts under the common heading "translations." This began as a defensive move when a historian friend reacted with what I felt was excessive discomfort to the oralized version. To him it was a threat to the original and authentic text, a false limb not needed by readers who are speakers of Shaba/Katanga Swahili and never to be used by most readers of this edition of the *Vocabulary*. His reaction (or, at any rate, my perception of it) reflects an approach to written texts that builds the authority of its interpretations on *keeping the act of reading invisible*, or rather inaudible. As I have argued and tried to exemplify, oralization, that is, recourse to audible speech, actual or imagined, is an essential part of our ability to read texts. Yet our ideology of literacy seems to put a taboo on revealing what we actually do when we read, for fear that oralization might subvert the authority of the written text.[12]

Such an attitude may be described as a kind of textual fundamentalism (shared by many text-oriented anthropologists and true believers in the Scriptures). Any fundamentalist notion of a text's authority, I submit, is false for at least two reasons. It obscures the nature of authorship (that is, of the process of writing) as well as the nature of reception (that is, of the process of interpretation and translation which occurs whenever we read a text). It is a falseness that becomes particularly insidious in the case of ethnographic texts, which are most often produced/transcribed as well as translated/interpreted by the same person. Fundamentalism should also be avoided whenever texts are approached ethnographically even if they were not transcribed by the ethnographer but already collected in written form. Thus, if we return to the example of work on the *Vocabulary*, the oralized Shaba/Katanga Swahili version needs to be included in the presentation of texts inasmuch as it is a record of a phase in the process of *reading* the original text. It is a phase which consists of negotiating signs and signification either with native speakers or with the ethnographer's own competence—most often with both. It seems especially ironic to keep this part of our work under our hats if we remember that anthropologists turned to texts in the first place because they realized that there is no such thing as naked data in cultural research. Why commit the same error, once removed, by pretending that there could be such a thing as the naked authenticity of texts?

Lessons from Grassroots Literacy

Apart from its extraordinary content, it was its literary, or more specifically, its graphic form which made the *Vocabulary* such a challenge. I referred to it as an instance of grassroots literacy, that is, of the appropriation of a technique of writing by speakers of Shaba/Katanga Swahili which was relatively free from the ideological and technical constraints that characterized literacy taught to the same speakers in other languages (French, some regional languages, and a variety of Swahili spoken by no one but considered fit for literacy). From the results—in this case the written text—we can infer that it is a literacy which works despite an amazingly high degree of indeterminacy and freedom (visible in an erratic orthography, a great disdain for word and sentence boundaries, and many other instances of seemingly unmotivated variation). These negative characterizations should not obscure what really determined the peculiar shape of this document. It was the attempt to read the *Vocabulary* that made us discover the immediacy and indeed primacy, not of orality in some vague general sense, but of *oral performance*. As we learned from the ethnography of speaking (see chapter 2), such performances come in specific forms reflecting cultural definitions of speech events. Texts that document performances/events carry their semantic meaning not only in linguistic units up to the level of the sentence; participants, setting, topic, genre, channels, etc., and relations between these components, all have significations a competent reader must be able to understand.[13]

The *Vocabulary* is a text whose representation in writing cannot be conceived as mere encoding in graphic signs, certainly not in signs that exist—other than physically—as a system apart from the utterances they represent. Consequently, reading such a text is not achieved by the mere ability to decode graphic signs. It demands a capacity to reenact or re-create the oral performance which is the source of the text. To return to the notoriously unreliable native assistant as transcriber and translator of ethnographic texts: What is negatively deplored as lack of exactitude should be seen positively as expressive of a great degree of freedom which the native speaker enjoys both as a writer and a reader.

Interpretations of ethnographic texts that pretend to require nothing but a decoding of sign systems must eliminate or, rather, hide constitutive acts of understanding that are communicative and dialogical. These acts demand attention to how a text sounds and not just to what it looks like. A rehabilitation of reading in the sense I have tried to give to the term should make such ethnographic hiding games unnecessary.

There is much to be learned about the ethnography of reading from the struggles of philologists with early writing systems such as Sumerian (Larsen 1987) and Greek (Svenbro 1987, 1988). The early Greek practice of *scriptio continua*—writing without what I have been calling segmentation—necessitated recourse to orality in reading, and about the cuneiform system Larsen makes a statement that is echoed by my observations on the *Vocabulary*:

From the beginning, the cuneiform system as used for the writing of Sumerian texts was basically a logographic system in which signs stood for words; syllabic values for signs were used to indicate only the absolutely essential grammatical elements, which has the effect that Sumerian writing was really a mnemotechnic device, and that the texts were not meant to represent fully any spoken message. A text gave cues, so that for instance a literary text must be understood *as an aid to an oral performance*. (Larsen 1987, 219; my emphasis)

What I had to say about the necessity of oralizing texts such as the *Vocabulary* may be compared to the following observation by Svenbro:

> . . . reading aloud is part of the text, it is inscribed in the text. At first this may seem a paradoxical proposition. How can an audible [*sonore*] act be part of a silent fact? How can one be comprised by the other? . . . the Greeks . . . wrote in *scriptio continua*, that is, without intervals between words, which, as experience shows, makes reading aloud practically necessary. It is in this way that audible reading is part of the text which is incomplete, unfinished by itself. Therefore the text is more than the sum of the alphabetic signs of which it is made up: these signs are to guide the voice through which the text will take on a body—an audible body. (Svenbro 1988, 54; my translation)

This brief excursion into philology should not create the impression that I see recourse to orality in the ethnography of reading also as returning to an older, or earlier practice. Such an evolutionary perspective is irrelevant to the practices I try to understand (and certainly to those who are involved in them).[14] A much more fruitful approach has been adopted and exemplified in a recent paper by Kenneth George. With acknowledgments to Brian Street he advocates a position which holds "that oral and textual practices exist as mutually shaping *contemporaries* embedded in social, ideological, and historical contexts" (1990, 19; my emphasis).

Conclusions

> Should someone, in the future, read this fairy tale in print and doubt that it could have had such an effect, he should take into account that man's true vocation is only to act effectively [*wirken*] in the present. Writing is a misuse of language; to read silently for oneself is a sad surrogate of speech.
>
> —J. W. von Goethe, *Dichtung und Wahrheit*[15]

If this essay makes a contribution to an emerging ethnography of reading it does so by articulating questions and tentative insights that result when seemingly narrow, specific problems of routine ethnographic work with texts are placed in broad historical and theoretical contexts. The narrative of anthropological study of literacy I offered in the first section can now be continued and concluded. The discovery of reading as both a subject and a mode of ethnography has been linked to the discovery of orality. We can now add some precision to that insight.

A first discovery of orality was made due to the *absence of written texts* (that is, of ethnographic and historical sources or documents). A key notion that developed from that discovery was the "oral tradition" which, we begin to realize, has really been a program of methodologizing the oral by imposing on it forms and criteria that assured (in Foucault's terms) its "passage" into literate discourse (see also Chap. 4).

A second discovery of orality is now taking place due to the *presence of written texts*. This discovery is based on the realization that a reading of ethnographic texts demands attention to speech and oral performance. Linguists and literary critics have prepared a field of inquiry that should now be entered by ethnographers. In discussing problems with reading I faced in two projects based on texts I have only given some general and rather disconnected indications of issues that need to be addressed in detail and as systematically as it has been done, for instance, by Dennis Tedlock in his proposals for dealing with the spoken word (1983).

Whatever shape or direction this work takes it will have to be carried out with an awareness of the historical and, indeed, political nature of anthropological inquiry into literacy. The point is this. Two discoveries of orality have been made, one forced on us by the absence, the other by the presence of written texts. However, we must keep in mind that "written texts" may be an equivocal and confusing notion. The texts of Western ethnographic discourse and the texts produced by autochthonous, grassroots literacy, although both are written, cannot be read unproblematically as members of one and the same class. Apart from relations of power and submission that determine all reading, we also need to consider the specific relations that exist between elitist and popular literacy (which are not identical, but may overlap, with relations between literacy in Western and non-Western languages).

Perhaps it is useful to recall in conclusion that, although we raised some very general questions, this chapter has concentrated on an issue that is primarily reflexive. What, we asked, is the role of reading in the production of ethnography? Not for a moment do I pretend that this exhausts the agenda of an ethnography of reading. Other practices of reading need to be confronted and while we confront these, however crit-ically, we cannot be expected to address reflexive issues at the same time. We must go on with the work of recording, describing, and interpreting. Still, their practices of reading and ours exist at, or better in, the same time, and that is why the reflections on the current place of reading in anthropological studies of literacy should be neither elevated nor dis-missed as "meta"-problems. Deep-seated attitudes and habits inform our practice of studying other practices of reading. It would be sad if future ethnographies of reading did little more than catalogue conformities and deviations from our own dematerialized conceptions of literacy. Our chances to do more than that will increase to the extent that we keep lis-tening to writing, while writing.

4

Ethnology and History

When I was asked by the German Ethnological Society to address the topic of this chapter I named two reasons that made me hesitant to accept the invitation. First, I told them, I have neither the competence nor the courage to attempt a general synthesis or synopsis of a topic as broad and deep as that of relations between history and ethnology. True, much of my own work as an anthropologist has been concerned with history, theoretically and ethnographically. However, I have not really participated in debates about the ethnologization of history writing or those concerning the historization of anthropology.[1] Second, I asked myself, is it not presumptuous to speak to German ethnologists about ethnology and history or, worse, about the need for ethnology to become historical (that is, to take historical approaches to the object of its study)? Anyone who is even slightly familiar with the history of ethnology in German-speaking countries knows how much thought has been given to relations with history ever since ethnology emerged as an academic discipline.

Ethnology and History: Bernheim's Long Shadow

First a note on the title of this chapter, "Ethnology and History." For the sake of convenience I will continue to use this formula even though it is conceptually fuzzy. "Ethnology" can, in other discursive contexts, be synonymous with "Völkerkunde" and "anthropology." Attempts to give "ethnology" precision, for instance, by distinguishing it from "ethnography" go back a long time (see below), but have never succeeded in eradicating synonymous use of the two terms. Similar confusion affects "history." Strictly speaking, we should acknowledge that we mean historiography or something like *Geschichtswissenschaft* when we use the term. On the other hand, it would, in my opinion, be shortsighted to write this confusion off to mere convention or conceptual laziness. This is not the place to develop such an argument, but there can be no doubt that failure to distinguish between making history and writing history has its historical and political reasons. Who would maintain that the recent German *Historikerstreit* is about historiography, not history?

Culture is what ethnology studies, but in Germany there has long been a sort of obligatory connection between culture and history (*Kulturgeschichte*), comparable to the predictable "pattern" or "system" that American anthropologists felt obliged to pair with culture. The history of German ethnology, one could argue, is a history of relations between history and ethnology. Yet, on second thought, if that story were told, I fear it would be a sad one. As I see it, ethnology paid for its recognition as a scientific, academic discipline by sacrificing a poetic (hermeneutic, processual) conception of history inherited from Romantic thought for a prosaic, basically positivist and taxonomic enterprise. To put this concisely, if a bit elliptically, Herder and Humboldt had to make room for Comte and Bernheim.

With his *Methode der Ethnologie* (1911), Fritz Graebner, who was originally trained in medieval history, played a decisive part in this fateful development (encouraged by W. Foy and followed by W. Schmidt). There he stated that "our discipline can and must count, in substance as well as form, as a branch of the science of history (*Geschichtswissenschaft*)" (1911, 3). In the following sentence Graebner tells us what ethnology got out of its submission to history: "History belongs to the sciences with the most thoroughly worked-out methods; I often had occasion to lean on Bernheim's excellent book on historical method" (3). The consequences were momentous and not only academic. Methodologism took the place of epistemology; *Quellenkritik* (critique of sources) preempted political critique. This made ethnology, if not forget, then at least bracket its colo-

nial underpinnings; even more fatefully, it was of little help in immuniz-
ing the discipline against racist and fascist ideologies. Of course, the theoretical and methodological recommendations made in Graebner's book
were not the sole cause of developments in German ethnology.

But why invoke Bernheim? Is he not thoroughly forgotten, and was
he not largely ignored even at times when his work was an obligatory reference?[2] Maybe so, but there are routes through the tangled history of
relations between history and ethnology that take us back to him. One of
these I would like to explore by making, as it were, a second start with my
reflections. This time I shall address the topic from an angle provided by
African studies. Unlike in many European countries where linguistics (or
philology) served as the core of *Afrikanistik* or *africanistique*, African
studies developed in the United States as a multidisciplinary undertaking;
anthropologists and political scientists, not linguists, were in the lead, followed by economists, a few psychologists, and sociologists. Only in the
seventies did the humanities, above all literary studies, appear on the
scene, but before that happened we saw a new discipline emerge whose
designation was at one time perceived as a contradiction in terms: African
history. Jan Vansina, who can claim to have been one of its founders, has
given us an interesting account of this development (1994).

Two reasons make Vansina's work a good starting point for reflections on interdisciplinary relations between ethnology (here taken as synonymous with anthropology)[3] and history. First, he pioneered ethnographic fieldwork in the study of African history; the practice has
remained part of the training of historians of Africa, many of whom conduct research in a manner that would also qualify them as anthropologists. In other words, within the context I indicated, relations between
history and anthropology have not been merely theoretical or programmatic; they have been an established practice. Further probing of the
question of relationships between anthropology and history could be
done by critically studying that practice with an eye, say, to how it
affected disciplinary boundaries and academic careers: double appoint-
ments and changes of affiliation from anthropology to history and vice
versa are not uncommon. Second, through the work that was probably
the most important first step toward establishing African history as a special field—his *Oral Tradition* (original published in 1961, translation in

1965)—Vansina's influence reached far beyond African studies. In *Living With Africa*, Vansina recalls his days of studying medieval history at Louvain under Albert De Meyer and Jozef Desmet, in a seminar whose founder had been Ernest Cauchie, pupil of "the great methodologist Ernst Bernheim at the end of the nineteenth century" (1994, 6). Though he remembers with obvious glee how he and his fellow students "satirized these masters of method," he admits: "We became, without ever being aware of it, thorough historical positivists" (6). No satire is detectable—but this is perhaps excusable in a dissertation—when, in *Oral Tradition*, Vansina leans on Bernheim to introduce his historical methodology (1973, 3–4). I wonder how many of those who adopted *Oral Tradition* as an authoritative text realized that Vansina had opened a back door to the spirit of Graebner and the much maligned or ridiculed *Kulturgeschichte.*

Vansina felt attracted to Bernheim because of the latter's arguments for admitting *oral* traditions as sources of history. That, in Bernheim's scheme, oral traditions became grist for the methodological mill only in "published form," that is, once they were written down, Vansina acknowledges only in passing (1973, 205 n. 7). In *Oral Tradition*, Vansina was prepared to have oral accounts validated essentially by the same procedures that Bernheim recommended for literate, archival sources. Graebner, as if sensing what would cause Vansina eventually to undertake a radical revision of *Oral Tradition* (more about that later), takes a certain distance from Bernheim when he states: "There is a large gap in his work, which accounts for the one point where the methods [of ethnology and history] appear to diverge significantly: Bernheim directs his attention too exclusively to the part of history that is based on written sources" (1911, 3).

Bernheim himself acknowledged the existence of relations between history and ethnology.[4] When he addressed the question explicitly (1908, 99–101) he came up with statements that are perhaps predictable but still worth pondering. He begins with terminology. "Anthropologie" is the label encompassing "die Ethnographie oder Ethnologie oder Völkerkunde" (ethnography or ethnology or *Völkerkunde*) (99); following Bastian, he distinguishes ethnology (a general, theoretical discipline) from ethnography (the description of specific peoples belonging to the "lowest stages of culture"). The latter is of greatest use to the historian. Ethnography actually "takes over part of the work of the science of history" (100) while the services which the other two disciplines perform for history are "indirect" (100). What Bernheim says about the uses of ethnography may at first look much like the statements that reflect anthropology's current popularity among historians; a careful reading of this and a few other passages shows that he pleads for making ethnographic knowledge part of history because ethnography reports "situations and accomplishments [Zustände und Leistungen] . . . [that] must by no means [be] excluded from the historian's horizon" (100). In other words, what ethnography brings to history is substantial; it affects (enlarges and changes) the historian's scope or horizon. One gets the impression that Bernheim considered this substantial contribution more important than the methodological services that may be performed by ethnology, which can be an "auxiliary science [Hülfswissenschaft]" insofar as it informs history of other peoples indirectly, "by means of analogy" (46).[5] In the first case (the one I called a substantial contribution), ethnography affects history because what ethnography studies is part of history; in the second case (its methodological contribution) ethnology/ethnography caters to history by revealing analogies that, presumably, confirm historical inferences and explanations.

Incidentally, when Bernheim speaks of ethnography's substantial contribution he designates its "times and peoples" as "prehistorical [prähistorisch]" (46). But note that he does this in a move contrary to allochronic tendencies in later anthropology; the "pre" *includes* these peoples within the "horizon" of history. The statement is important enough to be quoted in full:

We can accept the designation of times and peoples as prehistorical in the sense that the historian leaves it to the ethnographer to explore them, but not if this means that they should remain outside the horizon of the science of history. We must unconditionally reject the limiting view that wants to exclude certain times and peoples as *ahistorical* from scientific contemplation. (46)

A View of the Current State of the Question

Current talk about rehistorized anthropology has disparate backgrounds/motivations. One among them is the idea that anthropology simply needs to become historical again after a period of theorizing that ignored history. To some extent this makes sense, but history can rule even a theory that professes disinterest in history. In that sense functionalism and structuralism—prime examples of ethnology without history—were anything but ahistorical. It is at least possible to read these approaches as theoretical defenses against the violent realities of colonization and incipient decolonization. Was celebration of a "synchronic" ethnographic present not directed against the colonial present through which history loomed large and ugly and threatened to mess up neat scientific models of structure and function?

Be that as it may, aside from actual collaboration between historians and anthropologists (see note 1 above) and the spillover from historical work conducted in a frame of area studies (Vansina was our example from African studies), it was the need to come to grips with the history of Western expansion and the emergence of global connections and processes that must be counted among the more obvious reasons for the recent "historization" of anthropology. In this respect, the work of Terence Ranger and his students and collaborators has been more important than Vansina's in linking history and anthropology, especially since it helped to introduce anthropologists to the "social history" approach championed by E. P. Thompson and the History Workshop that also made us include work by Peter Burke and Carlo Ginzburg in our reading lists.[6]

Today journals such as *History and Anthropology* and *Culture and History* offer a forum for critical work on anthropology and colonial history. Anthropologists see the need to back up their ethnographic work with historical studies and there is the impressive development in the historiography of our discipline, initiated in the sixties by G. W. Stocking. I will not pursue this line—things will turn out to be complicated enough—and I can only hint at yet another connection between history and anthropology, little suspected and less explored: the one between history and autobiography. If ethnographies have tended to become more autobiographical, this may be symptomatic of anything but navel gazing; where and how else are we connected to the historical realities we study but through our personal experiences?[7] And what else could make the need to become "historical" more urgent the loss of faith in transsubjective objectivity?

Responding to work by Marshall Sahlins, discussions of history and anthropology briefly took center stage in theoretical debates.[8] With the decline of structuralism a theoretical void had to be filled, and another one was soon to appear when at least the more rigid forms of Marxism lost their footing a decade ago. As I read him, Sahlins's was an ingenious attempt to save most of both structuralism and Marxism by combining them. But the two intellectual movements had grown up, at least in anthropology, in opposition to each other. To lift their theoretical constructs from their discursive contexts and then combine them may be logically possible; but that does not yet assure a practical synthesis of history and anthropology.

The End of a Twosome: Toward a Triadic Model

I duly note these developments because they touch on relationships between ethnology and history, but here I would like to offer for discussion a view of the current state of the question that, though it owes much to all of the above, takes a different stand. I want to advance the thesis that to think of relations between ethnology and history as dyadic—and certainly any picture of a cozy twosome—is outdated. In retrospect, I find that I formulated a first inkling of a triadic model in an essay titled "Language, History and Anthropology."[9] This paper was a reflection on the doctoral dissertation I had written a few years earlier; as I mentioned in chapter 1, it was theoretically inspired by Dell Hymes's ethnography of speaking and Jürgen Habermas's critique of positivism in his *Zur Logik der Sozialwissenschaften* (1967). "Language, History and Anthropology" marked a turning point in my thought and I have, through the years, returned to it several times, either to revise and expand some of its points or to explore implications I had not caught earlier—such as the relation between anthropology and history, a question that was somewhat overshadowed by the attention I gave to language (which appears first in the title but was conceptually a middle term I introduced to expand the other two).

Here I should like to return to an insight that, I believe, has a bearing on our question. The subject of my doctoral ethnographic research had been a religious movement in the southeastern Congo, the Jamaa. For reasons that need not be spelled out again, this movement did not present itself as an entity of the kind that methods of social-cultural anthropology were equipped to study (such as clans, lineages, tribes, age groups, or even certain ritual associations). As I have put it elsewhere, I found myself with a founder who denied having founded a movement; with a movement whose members denied belonging to a movement or any kind of organization; and with teachings that were said not to differ from Catholic doctrine. In other words I found myself in a situation where the very entity to be studied could not be presumed to be given. Its shape and boundaries first had to be historically identified (that was the term I used). Given the then recent origin of the Jamaa, this particular case did not seem to demand much elaborate historical work, but that did not weaken the theoretical insight I derived from the situation. In cases such as the one I faced, ethnography demanded recourse to history, and that necessarily, not just as a matter of deepening or shoring up whatever findings I could report. Turning to history did not come as a result of adopting an interdisciplinary approach, certainly not in the sense of borrowing historical methodology; it was the result of a critique of positivism in anthropology. This led me to emphasize the communicative and eventually the text-centered nature of ethnography. In other words, what needs to be considered is not, as it were, direct recourse to history as another discipline but a mediated necessity to "turn historical"—mediated by the realization that we have access to the realities we study above all through interaction and communication with others who cannot simply be subjected as given objects to the procedures of either anthropology or history. This, I believe, forces us to introduce into our thought about relations between the two disciplines a triadic model, composed of the following elements: academic ethnology; academic history; and others, in which "others" serves as a convenient term for those whom we study, our "objects of research" which are accessible to us through subjects who are agents in the same arena. They are engaged in relations with us that can no longer be conceived as merely transitive (as matters of description, analysis, or explanation). Others are not consumed, as it were, by either ethnology or history; they remain present and confront us.

There are perhaps other ways to arrive at such a position and other ways to envisage it; that this view is now widely shared seems beyond doubt. Vansina, who has little use for the critical postmodern vocabulary to which the "other" belongs and who does not like to spell out political implications of scientific positions, was nevertheless moved to a radical revision of his approach to "oral tradition" by insights derived from the ethnography of speaking and studies of verbal performance (1985). That he also began to consider what I called "confrontation in the same arena" is expressed in his proposal to recognize in oral traditions levels of reflection, arts of memory, and forms of presentation that qualify as *historiology* (contrasted to historiography; see Vansina 1986, 109). This term, even though it has to my knowledge not been widely adopted, aptly signals the end of an era during which writing was considered to mark the difference between peoples with and without history (or whenever history was equated with historiography).[10] This allows us to reformulate the triadic model as follows:

> academic ethnology   academic historiography
>
> popular historiology

The contrast "academic-popular" may be objected to. Should we not be more precise and speak of Western academic ethnology and history and recognize the challenge that comes from ethnologists and historians who are academics but do not identify with whatever characterizes "academic" as Western? There is more than one way to respond. One could be cynical and observe that many, if not most, non-Western academics receive their training, and then work, in Western institutions and even if they don't, still have to submit to Western standards if they seek international recognition. Those whose positivist faith in the unity of science is undaunted will consider this "natural." This is emphatically not my view. The only position from which I can think and write is that of a practicing Western academic who is willing to confront challenges wherever they come from. One of them I find in popular historiology, and I think I made it clear that what it challenges includes our ideas regarding the nature or status of academic ethnology and history (Fabian 1996, chap. 5; 1998a, chaps. 3 and 4).

I prefer the adjective "popular" to "traditional" for several reasons. It emphasizes the contrast to "academic" and it asserts the contemporary nature of other historiologies, and that has again two far-reaching implications. To assert the radical co-temporaneity of the three elements in our diagram leads us, first, to think of them as three practices that, however distinct, can no longer be evaluated or ranked in terms of a status we may call "disciplinarity." Second, given this changed view of the constellation, we must identify common denominators or rather common tasks faced by the three practices.

Consequences: The Challenge to Disciplinarity

The changes in constellation expressed in the triadic model were not brought about by simply trying out a different logic of relationships; they are the result of historical and ultimately political developments forcing us to rethink our relations with those whom we study and with those to whom what we study matters. A consequence of such revisions, perhaps unsuspected but inescapable, is that relations between ethnology and history can no longer (only) be assessed in terms of "disciplinarity." If being disciplines were the major quality that makes the two practices relate to each other (or: if the two could and should relate primarily as disciplines) that relation would exclude popular historiology, a practice that can hardly be qualified as a discipline.

For the same reason, disciplinarity is a problem for which interdisciplinarity is emphatically not a solution. If belonging to a discipline means "to be among our own kind," must interdisciplinarity not be something like "to be among our own kind with those who are among their own kind"? Even before we ponder the compounding of insecurity as disciplinary boundaries become permeable we should ask who is excluded when we are "among our own kind." Everything I said so far suggests that the obvious answer—other disciplines, or other interdisciplinary arrangements—is no longer sufficient.

Matters appear in a new light as soon as we consider the possibility that the emergence of academic disciplines may not just be a kind of differentiation—a sort of natural process of evolution—inherent in the history of science. Perhaps more than others, relations between ethnology and history point to connections between discipline and empire, between academic and colonial divisions, divisions that separate practices of research along the lines that separate colonizers from colonized, literacy from orality, and so forth. To the degree that the world in which we operate becomes postcolonial, we should expect that our practices become not inter- but postdisciplinary. What this entails may as yet be too difficult to recognize or predict, but there is no doubt in my mind that such processes are under way, not only on the level of discourse where border crossing and hybridity by now seem to be the rule, but also on the ground, in the institutions and organizations where we make our living. Crossovers between anthropology and history of which we spoke earlier affect the employment histories of the persons involved, and so do changes that no one mistakes anymore for mere squabbles about names. This is the case, to cite one example, when an entire discipline, folklore, calls itself "European ethnology" (in Europe) or seriously envisages merging with anthropology (in the United States). Grouping together history and anthropology (with sociology, certain kinds of psychology and geography, and economics) under the umbrella of "social sciences," a long-standing practice in the United States, may take on a new meaning and have unpredictable consequences if, and to the extent that, it responds to postcolonial conditions of research, teaching, and publishing. The threat of anthropology dividing itself into several disciplines recently became reality when at Stanford University the department split into two, one sociocultural, the other biological. This case is often cited in recent debates as expressive of a struggle for power between "humanistic" and "scientific" conceptions[11] (an ideological issue that may also enter debates about relations between anthropology and history) but it may have those deeper causes that I have identified as the postcolonial crisis of disciplinarity.

To sum this up: The changed constellation in relationships between ethnology and history that I signaled by a triadic model expresses a convergence of historical-political developments and of epistemological revisions regarding the conditions of knowledge production. As a result, any discussion of relationships between the two disciplines must include questioning disciplinarity itself. It is likely that older conceptions—the feudal model: *Wissenschaft–Hilfswissenschaften* (science–auxiliary sciences), or the democratic/communitarian model: *Wissenschaft–Nachbarwissenschaften* (sciences–neighboring sciences)—will be adhered to by those who have no taste for radical questioning. In fact, there are even signs of interdiscplinarity itself being submitted to discipline when it comes to claiming academic status for regional specializations ("African

Studies") or, even more dramatically and apparently successfully, for "Cultural Studies." It is precisely the latter that, with more historical hindsight than we have now, may reveal the price of disciplining inter-disciplinarity. One of the acknowledged founders of cultural studies was Raymond Williams. How much of his original intent—a Marxist critique of literary theory and criticism—will survive the current fashion-ableness of this new "discipline" and its academic entrenchment?[12]

Tasks: The Challenge of Memory

The triadic model was proposed as a way of addressing the topic of this chapter on the current level of anthropological critique of positivism. This, as I just tried to show, opens the very notion of disciplinarity to serious questioning. It also becomes impossible to hold on to a view according to which the two disciplines may simply share a common object. Once we recognize (or at least have reasons to argue) that the three practices—academic ethnology, academic historiography, and popular historiology—confront each other in a common arena, arrangements and "deals" between ethnology and history that exclude the third party may still be worked out; but they don't work any longer under post-colonial conditions. Instead, we should now seek to identify terrains of contestation and tasks shared by the three players in our triadic model. Among them there are the many unresolved issues that have been the subject of postcolonial debates: national and ethnic identity, democrati-zation and human rights, economic justice, access to media and informa-tion, and so forth. Here I would like to focus on one theme that in recent years has received much academic as well as political attention and clearly has a bearing on these reflections about ethnology and history: memory.

Once again, I should like to introduce the topic by reporting briefly on how I came to confront memory in my own work.[13] I already sketched one "route to history" that imposed itself epistemologically when I con-ducted research on a religious movement in the sixties. Language became a crucial issue but I did not fully realize its implications until they began to dawn on me in the course of another research project I conducted dur-ing the seventies. It was titled "Language and Labor Among Swahili-Speaking Workers" and was planned as a language-centered ethnography.

A great amount of documentation was accumulated but somehow it would not take shape as a monograph (and it still hasn't). Two things became clear to me; that my ethnographic (mainly sociolinguistic and ethno-semantic) approach needed, first, more historical depth than was usually probed by ethnograpy and, second, a wider scope than the one provided by anthropology's guiding concept, culture.

To begin with historical depth, it was impossible to understand, or even adequately describe, current linguistic practices without having a grasp of the social and, indeed, colonial history of the language under investigation. This made me embark on a historical study, *Language and Colonial Power: The Appropriation of Swahili in the Former Belgian Congo: 1880–1935* (1986, 1991c). In essence, it argued that local Swahili, as a medium and practice of communication, had emerged in a space of freedom that colonial language and educational policies had inadvertently left unoccupied. At the same time I began to understand that the process by which the language had developed was intimately connected with, and deeply involved in, the rise of a vital urban culture at the core of which there was the shared experience of life under a colonial regime. This helped to widen the scope of my inquiries, and I now began to see my earliest work on religion and the later sociolinguistic inquiries as but partial forays into the many expressions of *popular culture* that soon included popular painting, theater, and historiology. From then on, time, history, and memory as constitutive of cultural practices became a major concern.

The beginning was the discovery of a regime of remembering—a bounded and internally structured architecture of memory—that found its expression in Shaba genre painting (Szombati-Fabian and Fabian 1976). A shared and, at that time, still mainly colonial experience was here made visible and displayed in private and public spaces in a huge number of genre pictures produced by local (usually untrained) artists for exclusively local consumption. Far from being merely decorative objects (though they would not have been produced if there had not been walls in living rooms that needed "decoration"), these pictures were conversation or, better, narration pieces. They made it possible to tell stories of the past whose narration, because it articulated an underlying regime of memory, always rose above the level of personal anecdote yet could not be confused with, or reduced to, the kind of material that served historians as "oral traditions."

It was only when I turned to a written document with the intriguing title *Vocabulary of the Town of Elizabethville* (discussed in the preceding chapter) that I began to realize how far the people of Shaba/Katanga had gone in giving shape to shared memories of a traumatic past through a historiology that no longer could be treated as mere grist for the mills of ethnology or history. It was the insights this document forced on me when I eventually edited, translated, and interpreted it in *History from Below* (1990a) that confirmed views I had begun to envisage in the triadic model that is before you. Finally, I was able to combine earlier epistemological critique of ethnography and more recent findings regarding popular historiology when I faced the challenge of writing an anthropological account of a truly astounding accomplishment, a history of Zaire by the Shaba painter Tshibumba Kanda Matulu. The ethnographic "material" of this project consisted of 101 paintings, the artist's narrative of his country's history, and our conversations about each of the pictures, about his life story, his views of art and politics, and indeed, his metahistorical reflections or historiology. In the resulting work, *Remembering the Present: Painting and Popular History in Zaire* (1996), I devote much space to what may be the most disturbing assertion I make with my model, namely the need to move from interpretation (as far as popular historiology is concerned) to confrontation. What I mean by this is evoked, though of course not adequately summarized or argued, in the concluding sentences of the book:

Tshibumba, being aware of contesting discourses [of ethnology and history], made it clear from the very beginning that his ambition was to paint and tell history, *tout court*. I have tried to develop the argument that a relativist escape is not necessary when we grant to Tshibumba's History the same status we must grant to academic historiography: that of a dialectical process, itself historical and hence contingent. Such a process necessarily (with epistemological necessity) runs into pièces de résistance, islands of untransformed material. Truth is a matter of emancipation from imposed ideology, unreflected opinion, and seductive images, not just the result of matching facts with transhistorical standards of verification. (1996, 316)

At the very least, we may conclude, the triadic *Denkmodell* (model for thought) forces us to take cultural memory seriously. I say "seriously" because I want to draw a line against fad and fashion; it would be sad if the current boom of memory studies on the academic market were our only reason finally to pay attention to popular historiology. "Seriously" also signals that I think we should be wary of attempts to, as it were, domesticate memories, for instance, by declaring them cultural and thus integrating them into existing theories of culture and identity. In my view, this preempts the potential of memory of leading us away from the trodden paths of culture theory (discussed in chapter 9 below).

I cannot resist ending this section on memory with an aside. It lies in the logic of the triadic model that what we discover about memory in popular historiology—especially also about traumatic political and personal experiences—should also be an essential element in the practices of academic ethnology and history. I have been told by knowledgeable colleagues that in current German ethnology, "ethnology and history" is also a kind of code for projects of *Vergangenheitsbewältigung* (coming to grips with the Nazi past) in this discipline. Without trying to preempt serious discussion I want to register doubts about the chances of attempts to achieve this by (selectively) denouncing complicity or, for that matter, of endeavors to recuperate respectable ancestors for German ethnology. The target of critique must be the theoretical and methodological foundations of German ethnology which permitted its complicity with racist and fascist ideology, and my guess would be that historical positivism—Bernheim's long shadow—which facilitated that unholy alliance, remains such a target.

Conclusion: Hegel, After All?

I stated my thesis and indicated some of its implications. In concluding I should like to return to more familiar ground (familiar but nonetheless treacherous, as those who have been treading it know all too well). I began with some observations on collaboration between ethnology and history. I showed how the case for African history—not so very long ago an oxymoron—was finally made. In *Living with Africa* (1994),

Jan Vansina reports how this new discipline emerged and became established. There is today even an establishment of sorts of African historians of Africa. But the fact remains that most of the published historiography of Africa is written by, and read by, non-Africans. Absenteeist historiography seems to match the absenteeist colonialism that goes with the postcolonial period. As things appear to be going—toward a widening of the gap between African and non-African academe in terms of access to information, sources, publishing outlets, and so forth—any notion that the disparity would be temporary (an idea that seems to have driven Vansina and especially the leftist British sponsors of history departments in the universities that were founded in the former colonies) becomes increasingly difficult to entertain.

Nor can we, while we regret the situation, enjoy the comforts of cultural relativism when we assert something like "Africans are not people without history; they are people who have their own kind of history." We know that Hegel was wrong when he denied history to Africa. But perhaps he had a point, after all. If we could for a moment suspend our outrage at his scandalous pronouncements and consider that Hegel was talking about history and about Africa only incidentally, we may consider that what he said about Africa tells us more about what he thought about history than what he knew about Africa. In that case we can ask again the question that was probably on his mind, or rather turn it around: What kind of history is it that we are after if we must, if not preclude Africa from having it, then for all practical purposes insist that it be produced outside, and imported to, Africa?

This question was brought to the fore in the subtitle of a collection of critical essays on African history (Jewsiewicki and Newbury 1986): *What History for Which Africa?* Having rehearsed explanations in terms of ideological links between (post)colonialism and academic ethnology/historiography, we are still left with a puzzling problem: Even if it were possible to imagine academic historiography free of ideological twists, self-serving interests, and political entanglements, how could we justify African historiography as a praxis largely carried out on "behalf of" its own subject?

The answer can only be something like this: Africa is not a "separate but equal" subject of ethnology/historiography. The current field and praxis of African studies where ethnology and history seem destined to collaborate is justified only if we assume that there is only one subject on which history can be predicated—humanity. But that means that having history "like we do"—as producers and exporters—is not really history. It is just another story. In other words, as long as we persist in the relativist frame we don't have history either. We need, I am arguing as many have done in the past, a universal history—a task that, as Hegel's example but also that of our predecessors in ethnology and history shows, always remains a project.

What we can still learn from Hegel and Marx is that the establishment of universal history is itself a historical and political process (not to be confused, incidentally, with "globalization," which can be conceived without a [Hegelian] subject). When we do African history we are not simply making contributions to an already existing world history; we are involved in practices establishing universal history. That leads us to a new kind of "relativism"—not to gratuitous pronouncements on the diversity of value systems but to recognizing the interrelatedness of practices of history-making in an process that encompasses all of them. That is the idea behind the triadic model, and that is where popular or vernacular historiology (history by the people for the people, history from below) comes in: its discourses and images are not merely sources (oral tradition) for academic historiography. Nor should popular historiology be appreciated primarily as a reaction to colonial and postcolonial oppression (that is, as discourses of identity and resistance). As I try to see it, and as I know many of its authors see it, popular historiology is part of universal (and universalizing) practices that cannot be reduced to mere enactments of power relations.

Culture with an Attitude

We agree with them more readily when they are witty and cynical than when they are wholly serious. Their negations rather than their affirmations enable us to treat them as kindred spirits.

—Carl L. Becker, *The Heavenly City of the Eighteenth Century Philosophers*

Title and tone of this chapter need an explanation. The text, somewhat expanded and reformulated, goes back to notes for a plenary talk delivered at the 2000 meetings of the American Folklore Society. The general topic was "Contesting Concepts of Culture." When I thought about a title I remembered how, a few years earlier, a folklorist whom I respect and like introduced me to his students as someone who "has an attitude."

A great compliment, I thought, and something to live up to on the occasion of addressing a discipline other than my own. I was encouraged to show attitude by the term "contesting" in the stated theme of the meetings and even more so by the plural, "concepts." On the part of the organizers, the plural was a wise choice, leaving open whether we should discuss conflict between concepts of culture (and presumably between those who make them) or simply contest concepts that are deployed in current debates. The sense I got from the programmatic statement was that the task was set for mediation, perhaps reconciliation, between contesting concepts. Improvement by consensus is an ideal I also subscribe to morally, but—and here attitude begins to show—it bothers me intellectually, as did "dialogue" when that idea was in vogue in discussions of the nature of field research. Consensus and dialogue can become suffo-catingly positive. I assume many share that feeling. I am less certain that many are ready to accept the thesis that the concept of culture and, even more so the plural, concepts of culture, have this aura of positivity, and that positivity is a fundamental problem we ought to address. There are compelling philosophical reasons for such a critique (and I will bring up some of them)[1] but my—hopefully not misguided—ambition is to for-mulate arguments against positivity that I derived from my empirical work as ethnographer and anthropologist.

Culture and Non-Culture: On Capturing Negativity

A critical attitude toward the concept of culture in the form in which it was dominant at the height of structuralist and structuralist-functionalist theorizing can serve as a point of departure. Culture (and its predecessors such as custom and tradition) had the undeniable merit of getting us out of a morass of racist theorizing. Still, the concept deserves being castigated for its emphasis on integration, conformity, and equilib-rium; for privileging identity over change; for advocating purity and authenticity over hybridity and syncretism; for being fixed on symbols and meaning rather than on performances and praxis. All this is assumed in my argument but it is not quite the point of pleading for negativity. When I began my work as an ethnographer with a study of a religious movement, initially guided by Max Weber's theory of charisma, it was carried out within the theoretical frame critical of the dominant paradigm of "culturalism." It was in the course of this work that thoughts about negativity came to me first as an empirical discovery.

The occasion was a task that should sound familiar to folklorists: to make sense of a story I had been told by a member of the Jamaa move-ment in Shaba/Katanga. The text, duly transcribed and translated from a recording in local Swahili, was a fable, the story of a contest of wits, a popular genre well known from studies of "Bantu tales" in this area. Had it simply been "collected" in the course of routine research it could have been filed away under its category for further study. However, the ethno-graphic circumstances of the exchange that produced the story were anything but those of purposeful collecting. The conversation took place on a day during an acute political crisis. The threat of imminent violence united my interlocutor and myself in a moment of critical doubts—about the innovative, positive potential of charisma, on my side, and about the movement's claims and promises, on his side. The usual social-scientific procedure would have been to write off the political crisis as an incidental element of "context," to book my critical qualms as progress in my theoretical understanding, and all but dismiss my interlocutor's self-doubts as untypical behavior, deviating from the cultural and social norms of the movement. And that would have been, perhaps not the happy, but certainly the expected ending of this episode of research. Instead, when I later returned to the text I felt compelled to formulate an alternative interpretation, arguing the need, or at least possibility, to consider negativity—negation of the concepts we work with, or of the beliefs we hold—as a condition of forming concepts or holding beliefs, as the case may be. Without meeting that condition, I became convinced, social conduct would be reduced to a quasi-pathological automatism controlled by culture, and scientific inquiry would amount to mindless exercises prescribed by posited theories and conventional methods. The negative view I then formulated of both social conduct and its study[2] is in philosophical terms "dialectical," and this describes the epistemological position from which I have reasoned and carried out my research ever since. However, I try to avoid the term as much as possible because I do not want to be burdened, every time it comes up, with the task of disavowing meanings of dialectics I consider trivial, mechanistic, or mystifying.

Once I had crossed the threshold of anxiety that conventional social theorizing seems to have set up against negative reasoning, I followed this approach in addressing such varied questions as the critique of the anthropological concept of culture, views of the nature of ethnographic inquiry and of ethnographic writing, and the generally affirmed importance of "context" in ethnographic understanding.[3] But rather than embarking on a possibly tedious summary of previous findings I should like to discuss here two exercises in negativity that have occupied me recently. The first consists of some as yet tentative thoughts on narration; the second, of a brief report on my views of popular culture as applied in the study of contemporary African cultural production. Both are offered as examples of how one may live up to Adorno's demand (1966, 159) that, in order to avoid a stultifying "mathematics" that has dialectics compute the negation of a negation as positivity, we must shun generalities and keep negations specific, determinate.

Popular Narratology: Narration and Negativity

Here is a premise I start with: The positive aura of culture that has until recently irradiated the so-called behavioral sciences shines more or less undiminished on a field of inquiry shared by anthropologists and folklorists—the study of folk narratives.

True, current consensus has, if not abandoned evolutionist, taxonomic, and semiotic structuralist approaches—enacting classical positivist ideals of scientific method—then put them in their place, as it were, as useful but inadequate.[4] However, in its most widely accepted form, the impetus for critique of positivist ways with narratives came from arguments for restoring cultural context; and that notion was based on positive concepts such as tradition, identity, and authenticity. The background of this trend has recently been demonstrated in a brilliant study by Regina Bendix (1997) exploring the historical depth and tenacity of authenticity as a guiding concept of folklore studies.[5]

True, too, much progress has been made in removing another classic positivist principle—the injunction to treat texts as objects, *comme des choses*, to recall a rule of social research formulated by Durkheim. We owe that critical move above all to Dell Hymes (1974a). For those of us in folklore studies and anthropology who were inspired by his ethnography of speaking (and the notion of communicative competence) his ideas offered prospects for inquiry into the pragmatic, historical, and political dimensions of storytelling practices. By now we are young Turks with grey hair but, speaking for myself, the program formulated in the sixties still inspires my work even though the emphasis may have shifted from communication to performance.[6]

However, while most students of folk narratives may have abandoned positivism, I do not know of theoretical reflections concerned with what I called capturing negativity. Borrowing such reflections from philosophy will not get us very far as long as there is too little empirical work apt to convince us that we need negativity. Yet there are such challenges and here I want to take up two examples.

In a study of urban storytelling in Lubumbashi, Marjolein Gysels found a proverbial expression, frequently quoted as an opening formula: "*Kulitoka hadisi: kulitoka bongo.*"[7] Gysels's Dutch translation—"*daar waar het verhaal van start gaat . . . daar blijken de leugens,*" "where the story begins, there appear the lies"—is an elegant rendering of the original, but for reasons that will become clear a little later, I should like to suggest an alternative reading: "Story appears, lie appears." This brings out two aspects of the original. One is the absence of any marking of number in either the nouns or the verbs[8] (hence the possibility, but no compelling reason, to put "story" in the singular and "lies" in the plural); the other is the stark parallelism of the two phrases that makes it possible to read them in sequence (and thus suggest implication or even causation) but should in my view be seen and dealt with as juxtaposition.

Gysels's interpretation of the saying is supported by her translation. According to her, this opening formula announces a story by asserting the fictive character of the narrative that is about to start. As she points out, a similar function can be attributed to the local idiomatic expression for "to tell a story," *kutega hadisi,* modeled on *kutega mtego,* "to set a trap": Storytelling is entrapment. Such conscious, reflexive framing of a cultural practice, applied routinely, not just in exceptional moments, certainly testifies to a capacity to negate literal interpretation and thereby to a concern for affirming a real, a nonstory world outside the story. At the very least, it demonstrates that not only we, the students of a culture, but also those who live it can take a critical distance through negation (remember the exchange with the follower of a movement I reported earlier).

Such findings cast serious doubt on the positivity of "folkloric" notions of storytelling, but the challenge they pose becomes deeper and more radical when we face the juxtaposition of *hadisi* and *bongo* and consider a stronger reading of *hadisi* as "telling the [or a] truth" and of *bongo* as "lie" rather than "fiction." In that case, we no longer have before us a distinction and separation of two worlds or two kinds of discourse about the world, but a contradiction between truth and lie. That this is not just speculative was—coming to my second example—demonstrated to me in work with Tshibumba Kanda Matulu, an extraordinary popular painter and narrator of the history of the Congo who grew up in the storytelling tradition described by Gysels.

To appreciate Tshibumba's project and his relation to the tradition he came from, it is important to recall that he consciously and explicitly qualified his work as that of a historian, an ambition that called for resisting (and negating) habits he shared with other producers of popular culture in Shaba/Katanga. As a painter, he worked "negatively" against the constraints of genre painting and, as a narrator, against both mere storytelling and academic historiography.[9] This general stance, though not expected from the average popular painter and storyteller, seems not to pose much of a problem because it fits, at least superficially, our own modernist ideas of an artist or scientist (I say "seems" because that impression does not stand up to closer scrutiny). Matters are different when we consider some of the specific ways in which Tshibumba practices negation, among them juxtapositions of truth and lies. Let me briefly take up several statements I documented and commented on in *Remembering the Present*.[10]

We were looking at a particular painting depicting Lumumba's flight to the Brussels Round Table talks after his release from jail (Fabian 1996, 87) when Tshibumba made one of his reflexive remarks on painting as a matter of thought and composition:

So now [Lumumba] takes to the air and goes away. These are thoughts I had [*njo mawazo niliwaza*]. That is the kind of thought you had in mind when you talked about thoughts [referring to an earlier discussion about the role of thoughts in painting]. . . . As far as I am concerned, [with a chuckle] they are my thoughts which I work out [lit. "make"]. Lie and truth [*bongo na kweli*][11] I put in it, so as to compose [the painting]. (Fabian 1996, 87, 314)

Later, when I suggested that he might conclude the series of paintings telling the history of his country with a few that would represent his thoughts about the future, he had this to say:

As regards the future of the country, I can think [it, about it]. I will say things that are true or that are a lie [*mambo ya kweli ou bien ya bongo*]. But if I am lucky, you will see and you are going to say . . . ? . . . [voice trailing off]. I'll just try. That's what I think. (Fabian 1996, 313)

The point I want to insist on is that these juxtapositions may express deliberate efforts to describe how "thought"—Tshibumba's own term for painting and narration—works; they are not symptoms of a confused mind. Elsewhere in our conversations, Tshibumba called what he considered a lie a lie, and truth what he claimed to be true. There is also one statement—the context is that of taking a potentially dangerous position on an issue—where the juxtaposition can be interpreted as a rhetorical move, a kind of *reservatio mentalis*:

When I thought about it, [I told myself]: It is true [*c'est vrai*]. So the things Mobutu began to think—he began to think [things] that were true—or else [they were] a lie [*ya kweli ou bien bongo*]. But that is something I keep to myself [*inabakia mu roho yangu*, lit. "it remains in my soul"]. (Fabian 1996, 313)

To sum up, we know *kulitoka hadisi, kulitoka bongo* to be a widely shared axiom. Tshibumba's use of such juxtapositions (with further support from statements I did not quote), I think, entitles us to qualify his approach to thought and artistic creation as dialectical, expressive of what, following Adorno, we could call a negative dialectic. The term stands for a critical mode of reflection that, certainly not methodically—dialectics is never a method to be applied or operated—but at crucial, "critical," moments negates what a culture affirms, be it truth in a story, accuracy in a painting, indeed the very notion of historical truth, and, as we shall see presently, the idea of culture itself.

It is tempting, now that the empirical point is made, to bring up some heavy philosophical artillery, perhaps—since we treated lying not as a moral failure to speak the truth, but as its negation—some Hegel. We might even argue that there is more than a hint in the Swahili saying of what we find in Nietzsche's famous essay "On Truth and Lying in Its Extramoral Sense."[12] But closer to home is an essay by Werner Hamacher, titled "One 2 Many Multiculturalisms" (1997). Statements such as the following explain why I think this brilliant tirade against positivity should be mentioned here. Hamacher asks what makes it possible to maintain a (concept of) culture:

The rescue of culture lies in the affirmation of cultural self-suspicion, in the explicit split of culture into itself and its suspicion of itself, that is, in the regulated distribution of its forces into a dyad of science and non-science, culture and nonculture. (285)

What is called a cultural ideal is not a peaceable, unified entity, but a battleground. (291)

But every culture is a culture only because it is history: the history of dissent [I would say negation, but that is a concept Hamacher seems to avoid] and of separations from previously attained stages of culturization [= becoming culture]. (324)

And finally, summing up his position on the theme that takes up most of his essay: "A multiculturalism for which the unity of a given culture counts as an established fact is still a disguised monoculturalism" (324).

These few quotations, I think, speak for themselves as well as for the lesson I have tried to draw from a brief excursion into an ethnography of narration. One may object that I am taking too quick a leap from one cultural practice to the concept of culture as such. But I assume that concepts of culture do not interest us "as such"; they must help us understand, account for, or at least give reasonable accounts of, specific practices. If we come up with findings of the kind I presented here we not only can but must draw conclusions on the level of encompassing concepts.

Popular Culture: Negation and Survival

Those who don't have a taste for dialectics may find my examples of negative thinking interesting and still remain unconvinced. What I have shown, they may say, are nothing but intradiscursive practices in popular narratology and critical philosophy; they are, at least in the case of popular narratology, aspects of material we study. But is this reason enough to fashion our interpretive discourse likewise? And what, in the material we study, compels us to accept the arguments of critical philosophy?

In a general manner, one could respond that knowledge production in our fields rests on interactive, communicative research and that the discursive and performative practices studied are not, or should not be, thought of as different in kind from the discourses we pronounce about them.

A more specific answer can be given when we turn to an example of negative thought about culture that should illustrate the need for attitude. We can seek that answer, not so much in the realm of philosophy, which is not our professional avocation, but in the arena of theoretical debates that all of us who deal with culture empirically must enter. The issue I have in mind is one that neither folklorists nor anthropologists can stay aloof from: the uses and perhaps abuses of the concept of popular culture. At first glance, this may not look promising, given the lack of agreement on definitions, the vast growth of literature on the subject, and the conflict between the vested interests of subdisciplinary specializations. Still, I have found in my own work on expressions of contemporary African culture that popular culture can be deployed as a critical, illuminating, and productive concept—under certain conditions that I would like to spell out as briefly as possible.[13]

First, we need to realize that talk about "culture," as Zygmunt Bauman stipulated long ago (1973),[14] is itself a cultural practice, a rhetorical strategy, and that this is also the case with (talk about) popular culture. Therefore, conceptualizing popular culture is not about establishing an entity different from, say, high culture, or primitive ("traditional") culture. It is a means to understand, in fact to perceive, certain expressions and creations in their own right, without assigning to them some lower rank in a hierarchy or dismissing them as derivative or epiphenomenal. Such was the fate of much of contemporary African culture in sociological and anthropological writing until well into the seventies.

Second, the rhetorical strategy of opposing popular culture to culture *tout court* is not just a theoretical game. The concept allows us to recognize negation of culture in the form of resistance. For the producers of popular culture, negation is not just a matter of logic, nor is it a style of expression that may be chosen or not; it is matter of survival under historical conditions that are not exhausted by, but would not exist without, oppression and deprivation. Creative resistance is a political act that, I became convinced, cannot be accommodated by the concepts of culture we inherited from our disciplines. The reason is that they have all been predicated on thoroughly positive notions such as orientation, integration, and identity.[15]

Third, though resistance to oppression is probably a necessary condition for popular culture to emerge, making resistance against colonial or postcolonial oppression a distinctive feature of popular culture would defeat the purpose of using the concept of popular culture. That purpose, as I stated in the first premise, is to challenge the concept of culture itself. What makes a culture, any kind of culture, viable, that is, imaginable as a way of living and surviving, is the capacity not only to negate and resist that which attacks you but also to contest that which embraces you or makes you embrace it.

That such a view of negativity is not just playing with words can be shown empirically—for instance, in the ways genre and generic differentiation work in expressions of popular culture such as religious discourse, painting, theater, and, bringing us back to the domain we started with, narratology. The need to negate, to resist the power of stories but also of rules and habits, is as manifest within popular culture as in its relations to posited high or traditional culture.

This last statement should meet objections that I romanticize popular culture as resistance (although I have no qualms admitting that recognition of negativity owes much to Romantic thought and that both anthropology and folklore would profit from cultivating that heritage instead of disavowing it). But if I don't romanticize, do I intellectualize popular culture's capacity of negation? There are two answers to this question.

First, there is no need to be bashful about using all the evidence we can muster to show that popular narrators, theologians, painters, actors, and poet-singers are thinkers, a title to which many of those I met actually laid claim (see Fabian 1998a, chap. 4). Among the stereotypes applied to creators of popular culture there has been one that depicts them perhaps as aesthetically impressive but also as "naive," that is, not self-conscious and in that sense rather mindless. This image proves untenable as soon as ethnographic research goes beyond the mere collection of products of popular culture and folklore. All the same, this fact has not led to the image's demise, and there will be, for some time to come, no harm done if we foreground critical and reflexive thought wherever we find it among those who make and live popular culture.

Second, though I came to it later than others with whom I share inspiration from the ethnography of speaking, the concept of perfor-

mance has been a useful and much-needed corrective to the communica-
tion- and text-centered ethnography I had developed through the years
(Fabian 1990b). I believe that attention to performance can keep us from
overintellectualizing popular culture, not because I take thought (or discourse, or semiosis) to be separate from, or opposed to, performance, but
rather because I have come to see that in the societies we study, the reflexive, critical (and negative) potential of culture is realized and has its pragmatic, indeed political, impact through performance.[16] This may be most
literally the case with popular theater and song; performance is, as I have
tried to show, also an essential aspect of popular painting and historiography, including popular literacy. In fact, one of the most interesting
insights I took away from these studies has been that the work of negation
may be inhibited on the level of discursive statements and can still be carried out on the level of performance. Irony and parody work that way.

A lateral thought: All-pervasive positivity and the concomitant
taboos on negative reasoning may also account for the conspicuous
neglect of humor in the work of social scientists (and of the glaring
absence of humor in theoretical debates such as the one about multiculturalism to which I will presently turn). The only general anthropological
(and linguistic) study of humor I am aware of is no laughing matter,
either (Apte 1985).[17] "Incongruity" is said to be at the root of humor but
I have the impression that, on the whole, Apte (and most of the authors
he cites) see humor and jokes (and narratives such as trickster tales) as
socially functional, and hence as positive ways to deal with incongruity
rather than as moves of negation that enable us to counter false claims
and expectations of congruity. The latter view is that of Ron Jenkins in
his *Subversive Laughter* (1994), an engaging book on clowning and comedy, based on participative fieldwork in none less than seven different
contexts. He has a quote from Charlie Chaplin, who said about the
comic: "Ridicule is an attitude of defiance" (3).

Showing attitude through irony and parody is not among the
rhetorical strategies habitually practiced by anthropologists and folklorists, nor is irony conspicuous in debates about multiculturalism, presumably the context where a theme such as "Contesting Concepts of
Culture" belongs.[18] Between two possibilities of approaching that
theme—as a contest of definitions, of theories, and research paradigms

out to recruit the largest crowds of followers, and a view that sees nothing but ideological battles obfuscating real struggle between nations and classes, classes within nations, and so-called ethnic minorities within classes and nations—we must find an intellectual space where we can breathe freely. We could and should learn how to find and create such a space from those who practice "the arts of resistance,"[19] from the popular narrators who tell stories tongue in cheek, from actors who cast critique as comedy, from singers and musicians who dance on volcanoes. And with the attitude thus gained we should return to challenging, in our theorizing about culture, those ideas that make us so terribly positive and serious.

Conclusion

"Contesting concepts of culture" should be taken as an invitation to do just that: contest concepts. Neither anthropology nor folklore are in a shape to suggest an alternative, which would be to assume some position above an arena where concepts are in contest and then offer arbitration based on long expertise and proven staying power. To argue culture theory—something that necessarily raises the question of identity—from embattled positions, or perhaps "on the fly" while trying to find a new identity and academic abode, is in my view a better qualification for entering the contest than the complacency to which anthropology seems to return after each of its crises, each time finding peace in a slightly changed version of the culture concept it has held for more than a century.[20]

Among proposals for alternative views of culture made by anthropologists there is one I should briefly mention. Jean-Loup Amselle (1998, [1990]), like other critics, begins by looking for a way to overcome the perpetual impasse between culturalism and evolutionism in his critique of culturalist anthropology. To the essentialist and ultimately racist model of a unified culture determining human conduct he opposes one where we call culture what people come up with when they succeed in meeting the demands of multiple, different practices. Negotiation is then the alternative to submission (or enculturation, or internalization, etc.). Hybridity rather than purity is the normal outcome of such negotiations, hence the provocative designation "mestizo logics" whose workings Amselle then demonstrates with detailed examples, mainly from his research in Africa.

If critique of culturalism is the aim, privileging hybridity is a commendable step in the right direction. But as far as I can see, it, too, raises conceptual problems that cannot be resolved without recourse to negativity. Negotiate (rather than obey) may be what people do when they make culture, but the concept leaves a fundamental question unanswered. Why would one negotiate in the first place if there were no differences or contradictions, in other words, if one party did not contest, negate, reject, resist, what the other affirms? Furthermore, negotiating connotes interaction that leaves the participants unchanged, and that makes it difficult to account for creative processes (more about this in chapter 9 where I discuss a related question, knowledge and identity).

Where negativity is not at the root of thinking and experiencing culture, where reflexivity, self-mockery, and other ways of subverting positivity have withered away, there looms collective madness (remember Burke's "metaphor without madness"). Such madness manifests itself in ethnic cleansing and massacres, as well as in legally unassailable ways of keeping class and national borders closed in the name of cultural identity, and, indeed, in certain views of multiculturalism (see also chapter 9). "Multiculturalism must not be a culturalism," says Hamacher and goes on to spell out why:

[Multiculturalism] must be concerned neither with the mere conservation of the purported integrity of cultures, nor with their mere perpetuation. A culture [and, I would add, a discipline studying culture] that does only this, that is not active—even if inexplicitly and in a mediated fashion—as protest against social and political injustice and which does not stand for social and political practice of justice is nothing but an amusement park, a technique of entertainment, "garbage," as Adorno writes. (1997, 325)

I fully agree with the substance of the statement but I have reservations about something that Hamacher does not take into consideration when he mentions amusement and entertainment (and something that Adorno, the same Adorno whose negative dialectic has much to teach us, was unable to see with his notorious disdain for popular culture). Anthropologists and folklorists should know that being unserious about culture, being amusing and entertaining about it, showing attitude when the culture cops stop to interrogate us, can be for us a way to join forces with those whose creations are the object of our study.

Lack of seriousness has been among the charges leveled against postmodernists. Where this has been an accurate observation (and not just a vague expression of positivist discomfort) critics may have failed to see that this alleged weakness is in fact among the strengths of the movement. Writing at the risk of not being taken seriously has often been the mark of innovative work contributing to the survival of the serious disciplines we practice.

Negativity, to come to a conclusion that is anything but a closure, is not a method; neither is it a mood or disposition (one does not have to be a "negative person" to think negatively). If anything it is a dis-position, a habit of distrust in positing and in positivity that goes with taking positions. That is why I recommend negativity as an attitude. It will keep us going until we get to a point where there is nothing in persons, actions, and things we study that challenges our understanding and theorizing. And that is not likely to happen soon.

Those who still want to be careful should consider one of the conclusions in Brumann's paper, a work above any suspicion of attitude:

Therefore, I propose that we retain "culture" the noun in its singular and plural form and clarify for those non-anthropologists who are willing to listen what the phenomenon so designated really is—which, as I have tried to emphasize, requires very clear and definite formulations about all the things it is *not*. (1999, suppl. 13; his emphasis)

PART II

CRITICAL MEMORIES

6

Hindsight

Anthropology has been in a permanent state of crisis during the roughly one hundred years of its existence as an academically recognized discipline. A crisis which is coextensive with the subject it affects is, of course, a questionable diagnostic notion. In the end, it only tells us one thing: that anthropology began precariously, that it never managed to assume an existence of unquestioned routine, and that it calls for critical examination now. Put optimistically, this means that anthropology is alive, pessimistically, that is is not quite dead yet.

It is all the more curious, therefore, that our discipline should enjoy so much popularity in the most varied intellectual fields ranging from literary criticism to the history of science. We seem to have made it *per aspera ad astra*, from bad times to the stars, or at least to stardom. In such a situation, I feel, our self-questioning must be intensified. We may be pleased with our popularity, but we are also saddled with the responsibility for many doubtful pronouncements on "primitive" or "traditional" societies that are based on anthropological literature being mined by Western intellectuals for their own purposes.

Foremost among critical queries has been a global question: To what extent has our discipline, the pursuit of scientific knowledge about other societies and cultures, been implicated in imperialist expansion, in military, technological or economic domination over the very same societies we study? The problem is not only one of moral implication; what we need to understand is the extent to which the intellectual substance of anthropology, its methods and techniques, its concepts and theories, have been affected, or corrupted, by the fact that our encounter with other cultures has always been determined by relations of power.

Macht verdummt, power makes you stupid, says Nietzsche; is ours a stupid science? Perhaps. But if one seeks clarification rather than indictment, other, more limited questions must be asked. How far was anthropology involved in formulating concepts, providing theories, and creating a rationale for colonization? Or: Was not the very idea of domination for the sake of civilization a product of that new science of man that eventually became anthropology? Is there in anthropological language and writing a *fond*, a substance we can consider valid because untouched by political conditions? This is one, the fundamental line of questioning that we could follow. There is another one, less radical but more practical at the moment. Where exactly do we find points of articulation or convergence between anthropology and colonial ideology? Where, methodologically speaking, should one look for original implications before these become overgrown by scientific and political jargon?

In the course of working on a project not directly connected with the topic of this paper I had to examine numerous travelogues, administrative texts, political pamphlets, practical manuals, and so forth, relating to early phases of colonization in Africa (see Fabian 1985, 1991c). It occurred to me that some of the answers to the questions I just formulated could be found in these documents. One of them caught my particular interest. It is one of the lesser-known works of the famous Francis Galton (1822–1911), inventor or innovator in the fields of statistics, meteorology, geography, heredity and eugenics, criminology, and a few others, among them, of course, anthropology. The book's full title was *The Narrative of an Explorer in Tropical South Africa: Being an Account of a Visit to Damaraland in 1851*, first published in 1853 and then widely circulated in the Minerva Library edition of 1891 which I am using.[1] It is the narrative of an expedition up the Swakop River, with side trips south, east, and north, in what is today Namibia. The book earned Galton immediate public acclaim. Later it seems to have been eclipsed by his famous handbook, *The Art of Travel; or, Shifts and Contrivances available in Wild*

Countries, which came out in 1855, ran to eight editions by 1893, and is now once more available in a reprint of 1972.[2]

The Narrative (as I shall call the 1851 account) is no longer representative of the Enlightenment genre of "philosophical" travel but is, on the other hand, not yet constrained by the conventions of the professional monograph. It has been said (see Middleton 1972, ix) that *The Narrative* was to Galton's later development what the journal of the *Beagle's* voyage was to his cousin Charles Darwin's later writing—presumably the starting point for projects of great innovative power. Galton himself seems to have felt that way.[3] In an appendix published with the Minerva edition and written more than thirty years after the original account he states: "I recur with keen and sustained pleasure to the memory of the journey. It filled my thoughts at the time with enlarged ideas and new interests, and it has left an enduring mark on all my after life" (Galton 1891, 193).

I shall now consider first what made Galton venture on his expedition and how it was conducted. Then I will present what he had to report on problems of language and communication; not that this was his foremost preoccupation—he spent more time hunting than talking, it seems—but because early colonial views on this matter are of special interest if one seeks to understand how colonial rule got established. Then I will trace some of the steps by which the Africans Galton encountered were transformed from the bunch of strange creatures he first beheld on the shore of Walvis Bay into political subjects and scientific objects. A concluding remark will raise a question much discussed in anthropology these days: In what sense can it be said that anthropology is a matter of imagination?

Travel and Sports

In 1846–47 Francis Galton had traveled to Egypt and southward to the "Sudan" (at that time the term simply designated "the country of the blacks"). In *The Narrative* he chose to say very little about that trip, except to express his conviction that only one reason could inspire the "African tourist" (his words) to venture into the unexplored regions of the continent: "fascination," described as an affliction that acts like a poison and makes one "cling with pertinacity to a country which, after all, seems to afford little else but hazard and hardships, ivory and fever."

Fascination provided the pull; the push came from "love of adventure" and an extreme fondness "of shooting." Only in the third place does Galton mention the motive that in later times was declared to guide the African traveler, namely the "probability of much being discovered there, which, besides being new, would also be useful and interesting" (industrially useful and commercially interesting, that is). Thus, for Galton, African travel was above all sport, in the peculiar upper-class British meaning of the word not to be confused with the mass activities and mass entertainment that now go by that name. Hunting, the aristocratic privilege, became an obsession with a rising bourgeoisie whose status claims rested on money rather than land and title.[4] Francis Galton, son of a banker, belonged, in the words of Dorothy Middleton, to the "many well-to-do inheritors of the Industrial Revolution" in whose opinion "the traveler must enjoy his journey rather than strive anxiously for a goal; travel is an experience rather than a quest" (Middleton 1972, 7, 8).

It was always vaguely recognized and occasionally stated that modern anthropology began with people of Galton's type, as a gentleman's pastime in which travel served only as a sort of private trigger for public scholarly careers made from an armchair. To contemporary anthropologists, very few of whom belong to the class of well-to-do gentlemen, Galton's frank admissions regarding the motives of his travels should be a reminder: Anthropology, perhaps more obviously than other fields, was the product of conditions marked by surplus wealth and leisure. Its current institutional shape can, therefore, be understood as the outcome of two concurrent transformations. Sport and leisure had to turn into method and work—hence the notion of field work, the distinctive manner in which anthropologists acquire their experiences; the place of private and individual wealth had to be taken by public funds and large anonymous foundations. In his later life, as we shall see, Galton contributed to both transformations.

In short, if one wants to understand what modern anthropology does and how it is done, funding policies and ideas regarding fieldwork need to be looked at in some historical depth. Leaving aside the former— i.e., capital in search of "useful and interesting" ways of being spent—it is striking how persistent Victorian notions of travel have been in the lore of anthropological research. Fascination, adventure (intellectual and physical), disdain for narrowly defined goals and purposes must, according to that opinion, at least accompany our methodical labors. "Experience rather than quest" (to repeat Middleton's formula) is still, and in recent years with increasing emphasis, considered a mark of good field research. If we are honest we must admit that those whose work would follow the canons of positive science to the letter would have little chance to be counted among the elite in our discipline.

Emphasis on experience takes nothing away from the fact that, from the beginning, scientific travel was firmly anchored in practical interests and backed up by established institutions. Galton's trip to Southwest Africa was prepared with the help, and had the blessing, of the Royal Geographical Society; he even sought and received a sort of political mission from the colonial secretary (see Galton 1974, 122, 123; also Pearson 1914, 214–15); and his expedition was to link up with other projects such as the recent discovery of Lake Ngami by Oswell, Murray, and Livingstone. After his return he was awarded the society's Gold Medal (in 1854) and given a position as its honorary secretary (1857). In his memoirs, published more than fifty years later, he stated "The Geographical Medal gave me an established position in the scientific world" (1974, 151), and, we may add, was the beginning of a career as an official of learned societies that culminated, as far as we are concerned, with the presidency of the Royal Anthropological Institute in 1885. Galton, the sporting man of means and leisure, had a keen eye on the commercially and industrially interesting, and more than once he describes the role of the traveler as that of a "spy,"[5] that is, the advance man of political penetration and rule.

Strange Sounds and Language

Galton traveled together with a Swedish "naturalist" by name of Andersson[6] and a party of European and African servants. Except for two forays into Ovamboland to the north and Bushman country to the east he had mission stations and trading posts to fall back on for guides, interpreters, and supplies. Like many other explorers, he never really left the sphere of already established commercial and political links and routes. It was on a mission station (at Schepmansdorf) that, during a church service, he first came into close contact with the language of the Damara, the group he was to spend most of his time with: "The natives crowd the church and sing hymns, which, being about three-quarters articulate and one-quarter clicks, produce a very funny effect" (1891, 18). Not exactly a promising start for a scientifically minded traveler. The observation bears the Galton trademark with its statistical, or in this case pseudostatistical, form. But why should a linguistic datum, the use of clicks—implosive and explosive sounds that are not part of our phonetic system (with some exceptions, to be accurate, in the area of ideophones or interjections)—produce a "funny" effect? Galton is free to note his reaction in such a manner because he is not yet bound to the kind of pedantic seriousness, all-embracing and understanding, but often hiding contempt, which modern-day cultural relativism imposes on ethnographers. He reacted naively, humanly, in fact much like the people he observed. Later in his narrative he reports: "Several Bushmen came to us here, of the tribe that lived at Tounobis; the Namaquas can hardly understand them, they laughed excessively at the odd double way in which they pronounce their clicks" (164). A reaction which might have been dismissed as ethnocentric in the first instance, now becomes anthropologically significant. Amusement or embarrassment, probably a mixture of both, can be examined as a widespread human reaction to that which is strange.

Amusement and embarrassment about foreign appearance and habits need not be a problem as long as the ethnographer only describes what he observes but when he needs to learn a foreign language he must eventually overcome these attitudes. Language is not as easily kept at a distance as are other elements of an exotic culture. If I use a language at all, I must to some extent identify with it.

Galton experienced this special authority of language and he foresaw some of the classical problems of communication between Europeans and Africans at the time when colonial rule was about to be established. At one point he notes:

I now lived at Mr. Rath's [the missionary's] house, copying his dictionary of Damara words, and hearing the results of his observations on the people. Timboo [Galton's servant] continued learning the language. . . . The time passed pleasantly enough. I put my map of the country, so far as I had gone, into order, practised a good deal with my sextant, but made very little progress indeed in the language; I could find no pleasure in associating and trying to chat with these Damaras, they were so filthy and disgusting in every way, and made themselves very troublesome. (50)

For the European, to transform strange sounds into a language usually meant to "reduce" (a commonly used contemporary expression) speaking to writing. Missionaries, as in the case just quoted, played a leading role in this form of appropriation; explorers, military men, administrators, and anthropologists have profited from their labors. It has been said that missionaries thus provided the tools for colonization. However, learning to speak a language is unlike learning the use of a tool (although many anthropologists who should have known better convinced themselves of the contrary). Practicing with a sextant is pleasant enough, Galton tells us (see also 161); conversing with Damaras requires closeness, interaction and a willingness to set aside claims to authority over "troublesome" natives. That was more than could be asked of a British gentleman.[7]

As Galton notes in the passage quoted, his servant Timboo made progress in learning the Damara language; eventually he became his master's voice and ear. Galton's scientific curiosity was tempered by social distance even if, for the sake of accuracy, it must be said that he later made much linguistic and ethnographic progress *malgré lui*. He could not help but realize that without command of the language he was without a language for command. "It is hardly possible," he noted, "to amuse and keep them in order without a ready command of their language" (1891, 60). Early on in the narrative he took a cavalier attitude when he remarked: "Few interjections, twenty or thirty substantives, and infinite gesticulation, are amply sufficient for a dexterous traveller to convey to an intelligent native his views and wishes on a marvellous variety of subjects" (31). Later he found occasion to regret his limited abilities (see, for instance, 63–64); he even came close to acknowledging the epistemological significance of language as a source of knowledge not otherwise attainable.

When traveling in Ovambo country he spoke of plans to compile a vocabulary so that he could "learn something more than I could observe of their manners and customs" (138). Incidentally, his vocabulary project met with active opposition. The Ovambo quickly realized that his interests were not limited to linguistic matters.

Finally, at one point Galton made some remarks about the detested Damara language which could be called linguistic in the strict sense. These included an observation that anticipated Evans-Pritchard's often cited locus classicus about terms for cattle: "The vocabulary [of the Damara language) is pretty extensive; it is wonderfully copious on the subject of cattle; every imaginable kind of colour—as brindled, dappled, piebald—is named" (118). As if to make sure that he did not get carried away with admiration, he added: "It [the Damara language] is not strong in the cardinal virtues, the language possessing no word at all for gratitude; but on looking hastily over my dictionary I find fifteen that express different forms of villainous deceit" (118).

This was by no means all that Galton had to say on the subject of language. He described complex multilingual situations (1891, 74, 157, 167), language borders (159), and the use of patois, probably pidgins or vehicular varieties (73); and he actually brought back from his trip grammatical sketches and several vocabularies.[8]

Savages and Subjects

To speak with Africans, directly or through interpreters, is one thing; to describe their languages and thereby select, codify, and dictate means of communication and command, is another. Yet another matter is the conceptual encounter with strange peoples. Stereotypes and images are formed which inform and direct relations, irrespective of, and often against, experiences made in naive, unreflected interaction. Galton's account contains ample evidence that his capacity for open, unbiased relations was limited by intellectual and social prejudice. He found most natives simply unappetizing, "filthy," and "disgusting" (50). Once he noted his reactions to a war dance thus: "I never witnessed a more demoniacal display; their outrageous movements, their barking cries, the brandishing of assegais, and the savage exultation of man, woman, and child at the thought of bloodshed, formed a most horrible scene" (55). But to dwell on his prejudices is not really interesting. We are reading his *Narrative* with a view of discovering how an anthropological or proto-anthropological perspective was formed. What we are looking for is the process by which he conceived and changed his conceptions. He may have been full of Victorian bigotry but it is to the credit of Galton's accuracy and frankness that his account provides the material from which we can reconstruct how, in his mind, the African native was transformed from a savage into both a political subject and a scientific object.

Let us go back to Galton's narrative and meet him again at the outset of his overland journey. Rebellious Boers made impossible his original plan to travel directly north from Cape Town. Instead, he chartered a sailing vessel and reached the coast of Southwest Africa at Sandwich Harbor, south of Walvis Bay. There he had his first encounter with the inhabitants:

In the morning we saw some savages about, and brought the schooner as close in shore as seemed safe, about one-third of a mile from the storehouse, and at midday the captain, the new Missionary [who had traveled with him from Capetown], and ourselves landed. A row of seven dirty, squalid natives came to meet us. Three had guns: they drew up in a line and looked as powerful as they could; and the men with guns professed to load them. They had Hottentot features, but were of darker colour, and a most ill-looking appearance; some had trousers, some coats of skin, and they clicked, and howled, and chattered, and behaved like baboons. (10)

It is no accident that this sounds like a page from Captain Cook's journal. We must remember that by 1850 a modern scientific outlook on other human beings was not yet established. Evolutionary thinking was in ferment but Darwin's *Origin of Species* had not been written yet. It is doubtful that more was intended than a dramatization of strangeness when Galton compared his first natives with baboons. At any rate, although he depicted them with attributes suggesting their animal nature—coats of skin, howling and chattering—he took care to note trousers and guns which spoiled the image. There is no other hint in his account that he regarded Africans, in the manner of later anthropologists, as close taxonomic or functional relatives of our animal ancestors. With the disarming innocence of his upper-class mind he occasionally mentioned them in one breath with domestic animals: "Besides our ride-oxen, we had one ox packed and one loose; three sheep and two Damaras" (38). Or: "I there obtained some valuable additions to my stock of oxen. . . . I also hired a black waggondriver, Phlebus, who knew nothing of his own language, but had been a trained Hottentot and Dutch interpreter." (73)

All in all the impressions Galton reported from his first encounter with "savages" differed little from those noted by travelers in the eighteenth or earlier centuries.[9] Only in the sentence that concludes the passage quoted above do we get a foretaste of the systematization of otherness on which anthropology's claim to be science would be based in the latter half of the nineteenth century: "This was my first impression, and that of all of us, but the time came when, by force of comparison, I looked on these fellows as a sort of link to civilisation" (1891, 10). Even though he mentioned the magic words "comparison" and "link," Galton was still unencumbered by rigid evolutionary methods. He continued to observe and to register his impressions in an unsystematic fashion. Thus he reported later: "In the meantime we had ceased to stare at the strangeness of our new friends, the Damaras" (47). Only on one other occasion did he insinuate something like a borderline of humanity, albeit once removed. When he "caught" his first Bushmen he reported that these hunters and gatherers were considered savages by their African neighbours. Significantly, he referred back to his own first encounter: "These people were thorough Namaquas in feature but darker in colour, exactly like the Walfish [Walvis] Bay people" (95).

When Galton spoke of the "link to civilization" this corresponded to an intermediary phase succeeding the first encounter. Relations still needed to be established, openness and friendliness were a matter of prudence; in fact, depending on circumstances, as we know from other travelogues, close human bonds were sometimes created to the point that the European began to question his mission. That did not happen to Galton who saw to it that the distance he wanted to keep from Africans was never endangered.

Predictably, we find among his conceptualizations the Enlightenment topos of the superior savage. He acknowledges their outstanding skill in tracking (20); their superior physique which makes them "magnificent models for sculptors," adding that "in personal appearance, these naked savages were far less ignoble objects than we Europeans in our dirty shirts and trousers" (60). Although he debunked the myth holding that "early to bed and early to rise is the rule among savages" (67) he still maintained that "a black can bear anything" (137).

Most of the stereotypical images eventually dissolved and gave way to attitudes formed in the practice of daily interaction and to categorizations dictated by the goals of incipient colonization. Galton's stylized report of his arrival on the shores of South West Africa should not make us forget that, far from discovering new territory and peoples, he moved in a sphere in which British rule was already established, albeit precariously. He came with a passport and letters from the Cape government (see Pearson 1914, 219, 220) to a region troubled by endemic cattle raids, tribal warfare, and resistance to European penetration.[10] Although he was only twenty-nine years old at the time, he acted with authority, arrogating to himself the right to judge and punish. He had natives beaten and intimidated (14f., 96, 129) and eventually expressed his conviction (citing a Portuguese traveler) that "if Africa is ever to be thoroughly explored the only way to do it is in company with a well armed force of men (natives of course)" (101). In the last paragraph but one of his book he counted among his accomplishments the following: "I had to break in the very cattle that were to carry me, and to drill into my service a worthless set of natives, speaking an unknown tongue" (192).[11]

Exercising authority was not limited to physical force. Galton saw himself entrusted with a political mission to restore law and order and he carried out his task with his guns, his diplomacy, and an astonishing capacity to profit from internal strife among the leaders of ethnic groups and factions. He bullied, literally, the famous Jonker Afrikaner into submission by riding his ox into the house of the Nama leader. Then he drew up a code of laws that seems to have been accepted, and for a while established a Pax Galtoniana in the area (75; see Pearson 1914, 227–28 for the text of "Galton's law").[12] He also realized what would eventually become the main concern of colonial regimes: the necessity to transform agricultural and pastoral Africans into wage earners capable of "steady work" (105). He knew that to impose power and rule demanded sophisticated knowledge of native character and custom. This is the point where the transformation of savages into political subjects and their conceptualization as scientific objects converge. While he commanded and bullied, Galton never ceased to observe and theorize. He looked into native notions of time, measure, and number (81, 107, 112, 167), made quick but astute analyses of their economic system (162), and at one point even summarized his ethnographic knowledge of the Damara under the rubrics of a conventional monograph (114ff.). Most important of all, he prepared what was to become a classical topos of ethnology and colonial rule: the recognition of, and stress laid upon, differences among native populations. Idealized agriculturalists—the Ovambo who live, according to him, in a well-organized state, have plenty to eat, and can count—are contrasted with maligned pastoralists such as the Damara; the Ovambo and Damara as pure Africans with the Namaquas, as he calls them, who are of mixed African and European descent; and all of these with the Bushmen, hunters and gatherers and true savages. Thus he paints a tableau that would have delighted evolutionists and structuralists.

In Galton's narrative there is as yet little that could be counted as "scientific" racism; when he admires the physique of the Ovambo and finds among the Hottentots the "felon face" characteristic of bad character in England (1891, 75) this is still in the style of the eighteenth century. Nevertheless, by his broad characterizations he laid the foundations (a) for further anthropological theorizing with regard to variation among "savages"; (b) for explanations of variability in natural terms, such as heredity, rather than in moral or political terms; and (c) for the construction of scales of nearness/remoteness from civilization that could, and would, be translated into schemes of "native policy." In fact, Galton formulated the essentials of such a scheme of differential treatment when he said: "I should feel but little compassion if I saw all the Damaras under the hand of a slave-owner, for they could hardly become more wretched than they now are, and might be made much less mischievous; but it would be a crying shame to enslave the Ovampo" (140).

Observation and Imagination

Cultural relativism, the doctrine we associate with modern anthropology, was foreign to Galton's thought. Not for a moment did he relativize, on grounds of principle, his own superior station or that of his nation. He did not doubt that in encounters between cultures the terms were laid down by the Europeans, who held them to be universally valid. Occasional statements in *The Narrative* that sound relativistic are not derived from an axiomatic theory, they simply show that Galton had some compassion and imagination. For instance, after reporting, with outrage, on the practice of "negrohunting" among the Hottentots he checked his indignation:

But we must not be too hard upon the negro and Hottentot morale on that account, or we know little what fearful passions exist in our own European minds until they are thoroughly roused . . . many an instance may be found along the distant coasts of this wide world where a year or two has converted the Saxon youth, who left his mother all innocence and trust, into as diabolical and reckless a character as ever stabbed with a bowie knife. (179f.)

Galton could put himself in the place of someone else, although this seems to have been easier for him in Ovamboland than in other regions. Of his trip there he tells us: "I felt ill at ease . . . because I was no longer my own master. Everybody was perfectly civil, but I could not go as I liked; in fact I felt as a savage would feel in England" (127). Later he extended this when he found that Ovambo, like Englishmen, were under the "sway of fashion" (see 129–30), or when he imagined what traveling Europeans must look like to Africans (133). In the appendix, that is, many years later, he even expressed understanding for Ovambo resistance, again appealing to imagination (198).

 The absence of cultural relativism also shows up in his reports on concrete interaction, what we would nowadays call field research. Value judgments are not axiomatically excluded; Galton struggles with the contradictory demands of his own personal and cultural background and those dictated by the pursuit of science. Rather than hiding his own feelings and preferences under a veneer of disinterested objectivity, he expresses them. He is saved from solipsism because he brings imagination to observation and irony to his scientific seriousness. At least that is how I interpret the famous passage in his account that first aroused my interest in him and will finally explain the title of this chapter.[13] One day, on a mission station in Damaraland, Galton met some of the Hottentot people who had came to this region together with the missionary. It turned out that the station interpreter was married

to a charming person, not only a Hottentot in figure, but in that respect a Venus among Hottentots. I was perfectly aghast at her development, and made inquiries upon that delicate point as far as I dared among my missionary friends. The result is, that I believe Mrs. Petrus [the lady in question] to be the lady who ranks second among all Hottentots for the beautiful outline that her back affords, Jonker's wife ranking as the first; the latter, however was slightly *passée*, while Mrs. Petrus was in full *embonpoint*. I profess to be a scientific man, and was exceedingly anxious to obtain accurate measurement of her shape; but there was a difficulty in doing this. I did not know a word of Hottentot, and could never therefore have explained to the lady what the object of my foot-rule could be; and I really dared not ask my worthy missionary host to interpret for me. I therefore felt in a dilemma as I gazed at her form, that gift of a bounteous nature to this favoured race, which no mantua-maker, with all her crinoline and stuffing, can do otherwise than humbly imitate. The object of my admiration stood under a tree, and was turning herself about to all points of the compass, as ladies who want to be admired usually do. Of a sudden my eye fell upon my sextant; the bright thought struck me, and I took a series of observations upon her figure in every direction, up and down, crosswise, diagonally, and so forth, and I registered them carefully upon an outline drawing for fear of any mistake; this being done, I boldly pulled out my measuring-tape, and measured the distance from where I was to the place she stood, and having thus obtained both base and angles, I worked out the results by trigonometry and logarithms. (53–54)

Is this just a tall tale? I am assured by those who have some knowledge of the matter that measurements of that kind are impossible to take with a sextant. Be that as it may, it is certainly true that Galton liked the anecdote and applied considerable literary polish to it. This shows when we compare the text quoted with an earlier version (and offers an example of the use of diaries or letters in writing travelogues):

I am sure you will be curious to learn whether the Hottentot Ladies are really endowed with that shape which European milliners so vainly attempt to imitate. They are so, it is a fact, Darwin. I have seen figures that would drive the females of our native land desperate—figures that could afford to scoff at Crinoline, nay more, as a scientific man and as a lover of the beautiful I have dexterously even without the knowledge of the parties concerned, resorted to actual measurement.

Had I been proficient in the language, I should have advanced, and bowed and smiled like Goldney, I should have explained the dress of the ladies of our country, I should have said that the earth was ransacked for iron to afford steel springs, that the seas were fished with consummate daring to obtain whalebone, that far distant lands were overrun to possess ourselves of caoutchouc—that these three products were ingeniously wrought by competing artists, to the utmost perfection, that their handiwork was displayed in every street corner and advertised in every periodical but that on the other hand, that great as is European skill, yet it was nothing before the handiwork of a bounteous nature. Here I should have blushed, bowed and smiled again, handed the tape and requested them to make themselves the necessary measurements as I stood by and registered the inches or rather yards. This however I could not do—there were none but Missionaries near to interpret for me, they would never have entered into my feelings and therefore to them I did not apply—but I sat at a distance with my sextant, and as the ladies turned themselves about, as women always do, to be admired, I surveyed them in every way and subsequently measured the distance of the spot where they stood—worked out and tabulated the results at my leisure.[14]

Victorian Science Victorious! This story is hilarious and at the same time a poignant evocation of the plight of anthropologists. We are moved by curiosity, awe, and desire when we meet people who are strange to us in appearance and comportment; and when we avoid encounter this is probably due to disinterest, contempt, and disgust. Anthropology has specialized in bringing these feelings under control. Control is achieved by superimposing measurement, evolutionary scales, structural abstractions, and what not, onto such elementary data of experience as an imposing behind (which, transformed into an anthropological fact, is recognized as a case of "steatopygia"). Documents such as Galton's narrative highlight the precariousness of our superimpositions and take us back to a period before our discipline had become terribly serious. They should be read again as a healthy antidote against being too impressed with our own accumulated scientific lore. Anthropology, at least that part of it which deals with living cultures, needs to be remade with every ethnographic confrontation; it needs irony, imagination, and, *quod erat demonstrandum*, the benefit of hindsight.

Curios and Curiosity

When the chips are down, we talk of objects as we reflect on collected art from the Congo. Their mere presence in our museums is food for thought. Exhibitions make that food into a cuisine; like a cuisine, exhibitions need critics as well as consumers. Not being a certified expert on nor an ardent visitor of museums, I must ask for indulgence when in these notes I dare to make pronouncements about collecting objects I have not seen, let alone touched or smelled, but only read about. Furthermore, I am not only going to talk about objects "once removed," as they exist in written reports and a few illustrations. I shall be concerned, as it were, with objectness itself. No *Ding an sich* looms behind this approach, just an attempt to understand a few of the conditions that had to be met in order to make collectible objects out of things.

How I came to ask such a question requires some introductory remarks regarding the larger project for which I have been preparing myself. After that I shall formulate my general understanding of the role of collecting in ethnography. I then turn to my sources and note some observations on expeditions and markets, as well as on object collecting and ethnographic knowledge. I will end with a conjecture on what made curios turn into Art.

The Larger Project: "Ecstatic" Ethnography[1]

For years I have struggled with epistemology *tout court*—the Kantian "conditions of possibility" of anthropological knowledge. I don't believe for a moment that I have exhausted the topic, but as I found myself adding more and more written sources to my ethnographic research, I began to feel the need for a kind of historical epistemology. I wanted to understand the historically determined and therefore changing goals, conditions, explicit rules, and implicit assumptions of emerging specialized knowledge about other cultures and societies. This is a vast area which I tried to limit in time and space by concentrating on the period of exploration and early ethnography in Central Africa (ca. 1850–1910).

Because I have a polemical mind I began by debunking a myth: The notion that the practice of knowledge gathering/production that was part of Western imperialist expansion was guided, only or mainly, by the methods of natural history, such as observing, measuring, collecting, classifying, and describing. This was (is?) a powerful myth because the immensely popular story it told of the quest carried out by the intrepid explorer and traveler served to justify the practices of exploration and scientific travel as intrinsically rational, that is, as not guided by obviously ideological or doubtful moral motivations. Only "sport"—essentially big game hunting for the hell of it—was considered an admissible diversion from the labors of research.

Exploration and scientific travel had elements, aspects, and conditions that were anything but rational in the sense of being self-controlled, planned, disciplined, and strictly intellectual. There was a dimension to that practice of exploration and early ethnographic investigation that I call "ecstatic." By this I mean everything that corrects the image of the self-contained observer who contemplates from a distance, calmly records, and objectively reports. Much of what there was to know, and what explorers actually got to know, could be gotten at only by their being outside, if not beside, themselves.

When one begins to look for it one quickly realizes how much knowledge of the other—at the time and in the area to which I limited myself—was conditioned by preconceptions and prejudices, as well as topoi such as cannibalism and other forms of savagery. All of these were brought along and hardly controlled by their carriers. Gathering of knowledge was also affected by many circumstances that tend to be over-looked: illness—most often reported as fever—and its treatments such as alcohol, opiates, and other drugs; fear and fatigue; sex and its suppression or sublimation; physical violence and brutality.

Notice that all of this involves the *body*. Acknowledging the body's role in African exploration leads one to pay attention to other, less somber mediations of knowledge that, nevertheless, are what I called ecstatic: the experience of music[2] and dance, the appreciation of pomp and circumstance, in short, of all sorts of "performance" that more often than not marked early encounters between Africans and explorers/ethnographers. We should add to this list food and drink creating or impeding conviviality and, above all, the significance of *objects* in establishing relationships, objects that create (or fail to create) conditions for communication. These objects included presents, trade goods (commodities), weapons, and all sorts of things from camping equipment to phonographs.[3] And there were of course collectibles ("curios," in English reports), that is, objects apt to arouse curiosity in the field as well as at home, or to serve as mementos and as proofs of having been there. It was as mediations of what I called the ecstatic aspect of ethnographic knowledge that objects figured in my study. Here I shall concentrate on their collection as part of ethnography.

When the book was still a project I began my reading, or rereading, of sources from the end of the period I planned to cover, namely the first decade of this century, and with two well-known figures: Emil Torday (with Melville William Hilton-Simpson), and Leo Frobenius. A third traveler, Samuel P. Verner, will be mentioned only occasionally.[4] They represent the end of a line of development that ran from explorer to professional traveler, to traveling professional anthropologist. Most of the quotations will come from their published reports.

Collecting Curios and Doing Ethnography

So far, my reading of the sources and of at least some of the secondary literature has led me to formulate the following basic assumption.

Collection of objects (some or most of which later became classified as African art) was the most important concern of early professional ethnographic research, perhaps not in the hierarchy of scientific or political values, but certainly in terms of the logistics of travel: acquisition of trade goods for barter; decisions on routes, stops, lengths of stay, and time spent on negotiating sales; labeling and cataloguing of articles; packing and shipping; and other expenditures of time and energy, including inquiries related to function, meaning, and context of use.

The importance of objects is usually attributed to the fact that expeditions and travel in general were financed by museums. There is some truth in this, but for Torday, Frobenius, and Verner, this needs qualification. T. A. Joyce, Torday's collaborator on several major publications, notes in his obituary of Torday that the latter's expedition to the Kuba was the first to be sponsored and financed by the Royal Anthropological Institute, "but owing to the strong opposition of certain members of the Council (on the grounds that the Institute was a publishing organization, and not concerned with field-work), the offer was withdrawn, and the expedition was sponsored by the British Museum" (1932, 48). In Frobenius's case, museum sponsorship came only after the fact. When he discusses the financing of his 1904–6 travels in the Congo Free State he mentions grants from foundations, personal gifts, his own funds, two thousand marks from Mrs. Krupp for weapons and hunting gear, as well as goods donated by about a hundred major German manufacturers. After completing the expedition (and evidently before publishing his report) he received funds from the ethnological museum in Hamburg which bought (part of?) the collection (see Frobenius 1907, v–vi).

That so much of early ethnography focused on collecting objects is not sufficiently explained by its institutional support in the metropolitan countries. There were other reasons that made objects the target of undertakings that defined themselves as contributing to scientific knowledge.

First, early traveling ethnographers operated in economic and political situations in which contact with other cultures was crucially linked to exchange and circulation of trade goods, that is, of commodities in existing (sometimes emerging, sometimes expanding) markets. In other words, travel (involving access, movement, communication) and economic transactions were not only means but also aims of exploratory expeditions. They were to demonstrate to rulers, investors, and the European public at large the potential of Central Africa as a target of imperialism. Although much of their content is descriptive of populations and their customs, none of the reports I am considering here announces itself as "ethnographic." Frobenius uses a subtitle designed to give scientific weight to his travelogue, but it is "Inquiries and Observations in the Fields of Geography and Colonial Economy." In the perspective opened up by such guiding interests, it was a stroke of genius to make a commodity of that which only facilitated the major goal and to sell objects obtained in trade transactions as collectibles in Europe. In sum, there is a way of showing the importance of object collection almost deductively, as deriving from the logic that governed exploration and early ethnography.[5]

Second, there were of course also epistemological, methodological, and aesthetic reasons for assigning to objects the central place they occupied in early ethnography. Objects became objects of desire, not only because they offered prospects of profit but because they were, to use an expression coined by Claude Lévi-Strauss in connection with myths, "good to think"—good to label, classify, judge, attribute, serve as evidence, in short, for carrying out all those operations by virtue of which information becomes knowledge. For many kinds of information gathered by explorers (for instance, astronomical, meteorological, horographic, and hydrographic observations, and zoological, botanical, and mineralogical specimens) systematic frames of knowledge already existed, capable of assigning specific tasks in great detail. Aside from contributing to evolutionary narratives and filling out lists of armchair queries, ethnologists were expected to put their discipline onto empirical foundations. Such a task meant that they often had to formulate their questions, as it were, after they had encountered answers. Palpable, manipulable objects were well suited to this kind of paradoxical undertaking; each of them was the answer to a question yet to be asked. Lack of time, of linguistic competence, and of advanced techniques of recording, combined with the vicissitudes of travel, severely limited the accumulation of "hard" social and cultural data. Collecting material tokens of other cultures permitted the establishment of a record that could be transported in space as well as in time. After all, the future destined for collections of objects was to serve the appropriation of the African past.

Expeditions and Markets

Chronologically, our sources lead us to concentrate inquiries into the politics and economics of collecting in the Congo Free State in the first decade of this century. Frobenius traveled roughly between February 1905 and May 1906. This overlapped with Torday's stay but there is something suspiciously unclear about the chronology of Torday's travels as it appears in his published writings. At any rate, Torday and Frobenius met on May 19, 1905, while the former was a Compagnie du Kasai agent, presumably hired to procure rubber and doing some collecting and ethnography on the side. Incidentally, from reading Torday's *Camp and Tramp* it is impossible to tell that he was an agent of the Compagnie du Kasai (although he does mention that he was employed by the Comité Spécial du Katanga before 1904).

Geographically these travelers covered a vast area, including forest as well as savanna, along the Kasai river and its tributaries (the old divisions known as Kwango, Kasai, and Sankuru, north of the Angolan border). The populations gave or were given names that changed even as exploration was in progress. In modern terms, the major groupings were chiefly the Kuba and related groups, the Yanzi, Yaka, Lulua, Luba, Tshokwe, and a host of smaller units. For us this tangle of labels is significant mainly as one of the forms of chaos into which order was to be brought by means of the collection of objects.

I should like to introduce our protagonists through a few quotes.[6] These will show, albeit obliquely, that the year 1905 was indeed a season for collecting and that collectors were beginning to define themselves (and their activities) vis-à-vis each other.

First, here is what Torday has to say about meeting Frobenius and his companion, the artist Hans Martin Lemme:

I was informed by the captain of the *Marie* that I was to be honored with a visit from a distinguished personage, a very great man indeed. He was coming down by the next steamer, I was informed, so some four and twenty hours before I began my preparations. I took out my gun and brought down a couple of birds. Then I went into my kitchen, and with my own hands I prepared various dainty cakes, knowing full well how much a European who has been deprived of his ordinary fare appreciates such luxuries. In due time the steamer arrived. Two exceedingly Teutonic looking gentlemen stood on the deck. One of them was as fully armed as Tweedledum and Tweedledee; his cartridges filled at least four pockets and his waistbelt, and his armory consisted of a revolver and a gun, with other weapons in the background. I went on board and invited him and his companion to lunch. After consulting two watches, he deigned to accept my invitation. We went up to the house and found that the cakes and other *hors d'oeuvres* were ready. Before we began our meal a man of the village came up to me, and begged me to reassure the foreigners he and his fellow-villagers really had no bad intentions, and it was quite safe to lay aside the paraphernalia of war. Fortunately my visitor did not understand.

My refreshments were greatly appreciated by my guests, especially as they had, according to their own account, just quitted a land where snakes and monkey were the only food obtainable. They had, in fact, just come from Michakila, where ordinary mortals find abundant supplies of goats, fowls, and pigs.

They inquired on how long I had been in Africa, to which I replied by saying that I had been in Kongo [the region around Torday's post] about a month. The martial gentleman was good enough to give me some advice as to the rules which it was necessary to observe if I wished to enjoy good health, as he had spent fully four months in the Congo. I accepted his suggestions with gratitude and humility. It was only after a flow of words, uninterrupted for ten minutes, that the captain remarked that I had spent more years in the Congo than my nestor had spent months, and that possibly I already had some knowledge of the questions on which he was laying down the law.

Years later I read a book, published by the very same traveller, in which he described how he had fired a village, how he had tried a new rifle on the inhabitants, and how he had flogged a woman who had displeased his servant. Later still I learned that he had gone, on the pretence of scientific research into an English colony, and had there robbed the natives of their most sacred relics. Well, perhaps it was better for him and for me that I did not know then his real character; there might have been trouble in store for both of us.

What is to be deplored most with people of this kind is that they bring undeserved discredit on their profession and on their country, and I needs must state that he was not a typical scientist. (1913, 74–76)

It is both easy and hard to recognize the great Africanist Leo Frobenius in this caricature (and I see no need to defend a person who showed himself in many respects a despicable character even in his own writings, see Fabian 1992). Nevertheless, this dogmatic gentleman had just prior to the meeting with Torday noted down the following reflections that show him in a different light:

For a scholar, grown up with his studies at home, the first months during which he begins the work of exploration in Africa are decisive. It is the time when he must settle accounts between expectations he brings along and the facts. Theory and practice struggle with each other and in the first months of African explorations he lays the foundations for later intensive and comparative work. (Frobenius 1907, 176)

Later on the same page Frobenius describes the meeting with Torday during the few hours when his steamer stopped at Kongo:

At that time, a curious fellow was staying there. He very kindly sent a splendid roasted bird to the steamer for our lunch. Besides working as a trader he had ethnological aspirations of the English kind and he kindly deigned to introduce me to the necessary anthropological theories. He was the real Congo type: Hungarian by birth, an Englishman by education, a writer by profession, presently a rubber trader in the Belgian Congo. But, all in all, apparently a capable man. (1907, 176–77)

There are discrepancies between these texts that could be submitted to a close reading. It is more important to note that the disagreement between these two largely self-taught men over theories, methods, and ethics documents how much the professionalization of ethnological travel had advanced at the turn of the century.

There was at least one other major expedition traveling through the region. Frobenius met its "manager," a Mr. "Werner" (1907, 249). This must have been Samuel P. Verner, known as the importer to the United States of a group of pygmies for exhibition.[7] Frobenius notes his convivial relations with Verner. On June 5, 1905—a few weeks after his meeting with Torday—he welcomes him as a guest at a dinner party (186). Later he visits Verner at his "station" near Ndjoko Punda (at Ndombe?), a steamer stop on the Kasai where they share a meal and some palm wine (249). As far as I can see Frobenius says nothing derogatory about Verner. These feelings, however, were not mutual. Verner was convinced that

Frobenius—"nominally commissioned to make ethnic collections for the Berlin Museum"—used these activities as a cover for his real assignment which was to gather intelligence for the Germans on the economic potential of the region.[8]

Apart from adding an entertaining Rashomon touch to our story these diverging reports definitely dispose of any simplified ideas we may still hold about the political and academic innocence of object collecting in the Congo around the turn of the century.

In the Beginning Was the Market

The ethnographic expeditions we are considering here were conceived, sponsored, and organized as collecting trips that were buying trips. Because we call what eventually got to museums or private owners "collections" we don't think twice when we refer to the activities involved in assembling objects as "collecting." In fact, during its long history (Pomian 1990) collecting acquired many connotations and became fraught with unreflected ideological presuppositions. Semantically, collecting has an aura of innocence—just picking up things that are there for the picking. As collecting, the acquisition of objects evokes the leisurely pursuits of connoisseurs on the one hand, and the disciplined filling-in of taxonomic pigeon holes carried out by naturalists, on the other. The latter, apart from advertising its scientific legitimacy, also suggests epistemic analogies between gathering specimens "from nature" and assembling tokens of culture. How much there is wrong with this analogy has been the object of many a critical disquisition in anthropology. What is considered less often is the fact that, in the situations we are looking at, both kinds of collecting were always mediated by, among other things, political and economic relations. Perhaps it is not always easy to demonstrate that power and the market were involved in botany and zoology; there can be no doubt that almost all ethnographic objects were acquired by transactions that may have included "gifts" but mostly involved sales and hence the prior constitution of objects as goods, if not commodities.[9] Commodification—at least some form of it—is not so much the result of collecting as its prerequisite.

A test for this assertion is provided by cases where, in the midst of "brisk trade," individual owners negated (or suspended) the commodity character of objects, either by refusing to sell them because they were currently "in use" for their magical qualities or by insisting on giving them away as presents. Because such refusal to sell was, as far as we can tell from the reports, incidental and exceptional it cannot be taken as evidence of a prevailing traditional premarket frame of mind. A better candidate for such an explanation would be an incident reported by Hilton-Simpson. Once again the context is a "roaring trade in curios" (1911, 168), this time among the Tetela:

> The people, as a rule, were perfectly willing to sell their belongings (at their own price!), and only upon one occasion did we meet with a Batetela chief who declined to sell curios. . . . [Instead, he said] that he would allow his drummer to perform for us while we sat at dinner in the evening! This honour we declined; we had all the native music we required when in the forest without accepting it as a favour from the chiefs. Very often upon our arrival in a village the local natives would organise a dance, in which our porters . . . used to take part. (1911, 176–77)

The clash of views that occurred here was most likely not one between premarket and market orientations but simply between different conceptions of what constitutes an object.[10] There are numerous instances that document how firmly African objects were, in the minds and practices of their users, embedded in performance. Here is just one observation noted by Hilton-Simpson: "The local Basonge chief [at the Kasai Company factory in Batempa], having heard of our presence and our desire to purchase articles of native manufacture, came in one morning bringing a large number of interesting objects for sale, and accompanied by his professional dancers and orchestra" (1911, 35).

Just how conscious Africans were of the market aspects of collecting is illustrated by incidents where ethnographic objects appear to be contrasted with the chief commodities of the time, rubber, slaves, and ivory. Such incidents may at a first glance appear to weaken the case for the commodity character of ethnographic objects. But, as I read them, the contrast is established among objects of the same kind and therefore confirms our observations on the presence of the market as an economic institution as well as a cognitive frame.

Hilton-Simpson reports one occasion when the Torday expedition was introduced to a Pende chief by an agent of the Compagnie du Kasai, a certain Bombeecke. Bombeecke informed the chief of the expedition's intentions, insisting that they were big hunters but adding "that we wished to purchase all manner of object such as the natives had never previously had an opportunity of selling, and that we had not come in search of rubber, a commodity with which he well knew the Bakongo would have nothing to do" (1911, 284).

The key to this observation is that the Kongo refused to be drawn into the rubber trade because they resisted control by the Congo Free State; and they presumably thought that trading objects should be avoided for similar political reasons. Earlier in the book, Hilton-Simpson had already noted a case that points to political motives, albeit leading in the opposite direction. The Bambunda, he tells us, were not eager to sell objects and were "extremely reticent upon all matters connected with their tribal customs and beliefs" (1911, 266). Instead they wanted to sell rubber which in this region served as a currency. Torday and Hilton-Simpson nevertheless tried to prevail upon Chief Mokulu, with the help of some presents, to see to it that his people put up objects for sale (he mentions "carved wooden cups, embroidered cloth, weapons, &c."). Mokulu stalled and repeatedly asked for more presents, but "whenever we mentioned the subject of curios to him, he simply laughed and looked at us with a twinkle in his eye, and not one object could we buy in his village" (268).

Hilton-Simpson went on to say that he and Torday should not have given Mokulu presents in the first place. "[We] speculated, and lost; and I think that Mokulu was far more pleased at the knowledge that he had cheated us than he was with the goods we had given him" (1911, 269). Later, among the Bapindji at Bondo village, Torday paraded his famous clockwork elephant. The chief wanted to buy it and Torday, hopeful of obtaining some unknown fetish in return, began negotiations, but these were broken off when only ivory and slaves were offered (270–71). The point is of course that Torday counted on his toy elephant being classified as a fetish, thus making it an object that could be bartered against another of its kind. The Africans (who may or may not have been ready to sell the object desired by Torday) preferred payment "in cash" over barter.

The market did not only become operative when objects were actually bought. The "currency" or trade goods an expedition carried largely determined its course and success: where to acquire the goods destined for purchases, how to transport them, how much of them to acquire; what populations to contact; the need to protect all this walking capital with weapons, which entailed the need for ammunition and paramilitary escorts); the logistics of packing, transporting, conserving and shipping acquired objects—all this occupied by far the largest part of the time economy of these expeditions and their leaders.

It is not surprising that Africans met these buying expeditions as sellers, something that did not fit the image of savages who might "barter" or incidentally part with their objects but were not expected to have mercantile ambitions. Let me quote a few examples from the many that can be found in the reports of Torday, Hilton-Simpson, and Frobenius.

In *On the Trail of the Bushongo* Torday recalls one situation where he had stepped up his buying for the British Museum among the Bushongo/ Kuba. He gives some detailed anecdotal information about the market, including the operation of such classical principles as supply and demand: "Trade was brisk for a few days, and some Bushongo who had held back their treasures in the hope of rising prices were now disposed to sell them at a discount" (1925, 201). Hilton-Simpson reports a remarkable situation illustrating the role of specific trade goods. Among the Kongo the expedition had run out of iron bars and knives. European cotton textiles proved useless because the paramount chief had issued a "decree announcing that any one of his subjects found wearing material of European manufacture would be instantly put to death" (1911, 310)— a remarkable case of economic-political resistance to European intrusion. Finally, the following passage from Frobenius provides concrete and explicit illustrations of several of the points made so far:

Slowly the tall sons of the Lukengo State approached and offered their ethnological stuff [*ethnologischen Kram*][11] for sale. I had sent my people into the country to invite the Bakuba and they came. But when they sell, the Bakuba are truly the worst Greeks. They begin by asking prices that are unheard of and they don't bargain much. Then someone brings the same object and haggles over it in such

a way that the ethnologist needs all his patience and passion for valuable collections in order to endure this ordeal. But in order to be able to acquire more I first
had to pay higher prices and initially had to shed much blood. (1907: 238–39)

The Curio Market Was Part of the World Market

It would be wrong to entertain idyllic or heroic images of the early
traveling ethnographers as connoisseurs of fine and interesting objects, as
if scientific pursuits and esthetic judgments could have existed outside of
a context of political economy. Both Torday and Frobenius (and to a
lesser extent Verner) traveled, acquired their trade goods and much of
their knowledge about markets, made their contacts, and bought objects
in regions that made up the sphere of influence of the Compagnie du
Kasai, an agency set up for the "collection" of rubber. The extent to which
populations were drawn, through rubber and other commodities, into
the world market determined their accessibility for the ethnographer-col-
lectors. Both Torday and Frobenius confirm rather than invalidate that
observation whenever they point to their success in contacting populations that, so far, had resisted the Congo Free State and Compagnie du
Kasai.

Torday was of course a rubber collector before (and while) he collected for the British Museum. Commercial intelligence gathering was
quite likely Frobenius's ulterior purpose.[12] But even more to the point is
that others had, before them or at the same time, recognized the world
market potential of ethnological collectibles. Torday, Frobenius, and
Verner were not only competing against each other.

At a place in Compagnie du Kasai territory called Bena Makima,
Frobenius came into conflict with a company agent who doubled as a collector of objects (and may even have acted for the Compagnie; the affair
was never sufficiently cleared up): "Mr. Oeyen was a passionate collector
of ethnological objects and sent these for sale to Europe. . . . With my
similar enthusiasm for ethnological objects I was getting in this gentleman's way. When, naturally, I paid for the things whatever the value was
they had for us Mr. Oeyen very soon declared that I was spoiling the
prices" (1907, 202). This led eventually to open, violent conflict. Oeyen

claimed that he did his collecting for the Compagnie du Kasai. He beat up Frobenius's porters, some of whom deserted, and closed his station to Frobenius. His superior, a certain Cassart, intervened and promised to settle the conflict, but this remained no more than a promise. The same thing happened when Frobenius took his complaint all the way to the "direction générale" of the company in Europe (202–3).

Collecting as a Political Activity

Because the presence of the state in this area was still very tenuous (after twenty years) other agencies, such as missions, traders, and the parastatal companies, arrogated to themselves political, that is, coercive judicial or military functions. Expeditions could not but follow that pattern although, as we shall see, they differed in the means. The early collecting of objects was backed up by the exercise of some kind of authority and often by real force.

Torday prides himself on never having had to use force.[13] Nevertheless, he took political initiatives and responsibilities as a matter of course. When he traveled among the warring Yanzi, for instance, he spoke of his expedition as being on a "peace mission." He acted as a peacemaker and political broker, much as Francis Galton had done fifty years earlier and with more success, when he single-handedly imposed his "pax Galtoniana" on rival groups in what is now Namibia (see the preceding chapter).[14] Torday stated that all colonization is "in itself an injustice" (1913, 243). His tact and compassion, and his willingness to understand the other side on its own terms, certainly make him an exceptional figure. He nevertheless profited from "the powers that be." Hilton-Simpson acknowledges that his expedition traveled under the protection of the government, represented by troops who were always in the proximity of his route (1911, 115–16).

Frobenius, because he was personally a rather violent character and perhaps because he could not be sure of protection by the Congo authorities, used force and coercion whenever he felt they were needed. He was proud of his "police troop," a uniformed private military escort of twenty men carrying modern rifles, and he marveled at the sense the natives had for weapons (see 1907, 193–94). He freely administered beatings when he did not get his way, especially when he met with insubordination or refusal to provide porters and provisions for his expedition.[15]

Finally, collecting was also political in the sense of international politics. Our three protagonists each represented the interests of a different nation: Germany, Britain, and the United States.

Commodification and Distinction

To insist on commodification being a prerequisite for ethnographic collecting does not mean that ethnography is being equated with trading nor, for that matter, that curios were a commodity like any other. Collecting African objects was distinguished from rounding up supplies of rubber. Why that should have been so cannot be explained in market terms alone. While collectible curios were being produced under the very eyes of the collectors they nevertheless regarded them as a nonrenewable resource. Once, when Frobenius was forced by the rains to stay in one place, he observed Africans of his expedition carving objects. Some of these he bought if he considered them good enough (1907, 83). But almost in the same breath he lamented the corruption of African crafts under European influence. It is as if attestations of threatened tradition and almost vanished originality were required as the finishing touches on the patina of collected objects.

If curios were, unlike rubber, a commodity of distinction because threatened by extinction, this did not remove them from the sphere of markets and commodities. Scarcity, real or manufactured, increased demand (and of course production). Still, from the beginning, authenticity was only interesting if it was backed up by quantity. After all, if you want to create and maintain a profitable market for unique pieces you must keep them in steady supply.[16] At one point, Frobenius, not bothered by the contradiction it implies, ends one of his laments about the disappearance of traditional crafts with the (prophetic) proposal to train Africans and "get a steady supply of products from these schools onto the world market" (1907, 235).

I also think we are entitled to surmise that African owners and producers of curios recognized links between authenticity and scarcity as being important to their customers. Some cases of refusal to sell, or to sell at a given moment, may have to be interpreted as market-guided behavior. In fact, one may even get second thoughts about what exactly happened when Torday convinced the Kuba to part with their royal statues. He took the king into his confidence, we are told, and "he pointed out how many of the native arts were dying out" (Hilton-Simpson 1911, 193). When the king agreed to sell the statues, Torday counted this as a major feat of persuasion and was convinced that he had acquired something uniquely valuable. But from everything we know of African conceptions regarding these and similar objects—and much of that can be learned even from our sources which were written from a rather different perspective—it is unlikely that for the Kuba these carvings could have had the status of unique objects doomed to disappear when their material embodiments decayed or were lost due to some other circumstance. Who was outwitting whom in these deals? Economically the answer seems clear (and is getting clearer with every decade that passes)—but intellectually, culturally, esthetically? Even the political implications are worth pondering. After all, Torday reports that one of the arguments that convinced the king was that the statues would be exhibited in the British Museum. The ruler must have interpreted this as a way to establish a real presence of Kuba political power in one of the centers of imperialism.

In fact, the situation was even more complex. Both Torday and Frobenius knew that it was not political domination as such that doomed traditional culture to disappearance, but the expansion of a market that was to have its local effects largely as a labor market. Hence the topos of depicting African workers in towns as degenerate, uprooted, inauthentic, and ridiculous, and opposing all this to the nobility of traditional culture embodied in genuine objects.

In other words, the hunt for the disappearing object was to a large extent an ideological construct that served to camouflage gross commercial and often doubtful political aspects of collecting. In the sources I am examining here, the collectible objects shared their essential quality with the object of anthropology at large: they were deemed doomed; although present—otherwise they could not have been bought—they were really past. That was what constituted their scientific interest.[17]

One final question to be asked concerns the limits of collecting—not the ones imposed by the limits of buyers' means to buy or the sellers' willingness to sell, but some sort of restraint that we would today qualify as ethical. As far as Torday is concerned, a concern with tact and respect for African values pervaded his reports. Frobenius usually cannot be credited with such qualities, yet even he acknowledged limits. Here are two interesting instances. In one case, a young man whom he asked to sell his *kiteki* (a protective object) answers: "Go away, Tata Boka [Frobenius's African name]. Leave the *kiteki* alone. What am I going to do when my wife gets sick? . . . Who wants to think of a museum in such a case?" (1907, 59). In another case, Frobenius walked through a village and saw a carved door that aroused his interest. He was told that in the hut behind that door a woman was dying. Rather sanctimoniously he stated: "And the ethnologist's mania for collecting [*Sammelwut*] stops at the door of death" (59).

Curios and Curiosity: Object Collecting and Ethnographic Knowledge

Object and Method

The fact that ethnographic collecting as exemplified by Torday and Frobenius was embedded in a market and conditioned by commodification does of course not mean that it was devoid of intellectual significance. After all, our travelers did think of themselves as ethnologists. Frobenius, for instance, stated that the market was not just a circumstance of collecting, an opportunity or a nuisance as the case might be: "The scholar concerned with ethnological problems must in these countries be practical and pay attention to commercial problems. . . . The point is not whether one buys dear or cheap, but rather whether one is able to gain access to the natives and actually obtains the object (1907, 358; see also 355).

The transaction itself is important but objects, despite commodification, remain objects. As such they are products of objectification, that is of processes in which complex ideas are given material existence. In the ethnographic situation—where we strive to understand other peoples' intellectual life without having direct access to it—objects, much like language, are mediations of knowledge (see on this chapter 1). Both our protagonists were aware of this. As a matter of fact, when we get the impression that the collection of objects came first, and only then the collection of ethnographic information, we cannot be sure what dictated that order of preference—the market conditions we outlined above or certain theoretical views regarding the nature of anthropology (epitomized by the fixation on objects characteristic of "diffusionism"). Or is this a moot question? Should we perhaps see in the latter a reflex of the former—anthropology mirroring the circulation of commodities?[18]

Among the uses to which objects were put right on the spot, before they were shipped to the sponsoring museum, was to serve as proof (or disproof) of cultural and historical connections. Already at the beginning of his trip, Frobenius anticipated his later "morphological" method when he derived the cagey personality of forest people from their using the bow and arrow and contrasted this with the open aggressiveness of savanna dwellers who used the spear (1907, 80). At the time we are dealing with here, establishing ethnic boundaries, and migration routes, determining "races" and their degrees of mixture (or purity), locating centers and peripheries of diffusion were urgent tasks. This was not merely an academic problem; the state and the big companies needed such information in order to establish administrative units and boundaries and, above all, to plan labor policies (regarding potential recruitment, location of production sites, etc.). Both Torday and Frobenius observed that the colonial agencies had succeeded in creating Luba ethnicity with the help of criteria that defined people as actual or potential wage earners in the emerging colonial economy.[19] Both men helped to explain resistance to colonial rule among certain populations, for instance, by demonstrating a Bushongo-Kuba cultural sphere whose principal common identifiers were art and material culture.

Objects and Knowledge

Although it is easier to tell from Frobenius's account than from Torday's, both aspired to scientific knowledge. They claimed certain privileges (or made excuses for strange behavior); they set the terms of getting to know the natives, convinced that their intrusive curiosity was sanctioned by science. The scientist's or naturalist's stance was most easily maintained with regard to objects one could point to, acquire, and later manipulate, examine, compare, store, ship, etc. By projecting his own image of such object-oriented science onto the African, Frobenius (taking another contradiction in stride) actually reveals this image: "I studied this point thoroughly, first theoretically, then long enough practically. . . . Trading in ethnographic stuff is, as it were, the highway that leads us to a community of interests and to agreement with the negro. One should never forget that the negro is a thorough materialist and a positivist of the worst kind" (1907, 355). We get a rare glimpse of the semantics of collecting when he expands on this statement and reports the expression "'Tshintu' (Sache der Eingeborenen [thing of the natives])" was their term for a collectible (357).

That object collecting was part of his methodological strategy becomes clear whenever Frobenius is able to do what one may call stationary ethnography. This is how he describes his work at Luebo where he took a fairly long break:

Many a small column of my messengers roamed the country under the well-tried direction of old people. Their task was to call the natives together and to get them to bring along their sacred stuff, their knowledge of religious matters, and other things. Nengengele and Palia Messo were the leaders of these small enterprises, as a result of which black citizens almost daily hurried to come to us. But I also had other people who served as touts [*Schlepper*][20] in order to attract knowledgeable men. (1907, 351)

Objects and Objectivity

While material objects were most easily studied objectively, matters were different, or should have been different, with other kinds of knowledge that demanded linguistic competences and, above all, participation in performances and thereby submission to rules governing such performances. Torday and Frobenius knew that almost everything they collected was embedded in contexts that involved performances or actions.

Yet again and again one gets the impression that these ethnographers wished that all of culture came in the form of "curios." It is now that we recognize one of the functions of that concept; it allowed material objects to be separated from their often equally material context.

When modern critics denounce the decontextualized form of earlier collecting they seem to have in mind mainly the separation of material objects from cultural, that is, symbolic or ideological contexts. But the more thorough separation that had to be operated by those who pioneered ethnographic collecting was the separation of the material object from its material embeddedness: from sound, movement, smell, space, time and timing, and so forth.

As ethnographers the early collectors sought to create situations where they could observe and record without being involved (that is, without being part of the context). Before ending *Camp and Tramp*, Torday states that "having told what I had to say about the natives, I shall now give them a chance of speaking for themselves" (1913, 269). He remarks on the importance of authentic folklore and says that the texts that follow were "overheard when I was a concealed witness of their talk round the campfire" (270). While this eavesdropping is not at all characteristic of Torday—he sought the company of Africans and tried to engage them in conversation—it does reveal his occasional desire to be a detached scientific observer.

Limits on interaction and involvement were set by this stance but also by the time economy of exploratory expeditions. A story, myth, proverb, genealogy, or some other kind of text could be bought rather quickly. Transactions of this kind are too numerous in our sources to be reported here. They presupposed, of course, another kind of commodification—that of knowledge and information. As in the case of objects, this was a process that involved both the ethnographers and their African "informants." When Torday set about to collect a Yaka vocabulary he devised an ingenious procedure:

In order to stimulate public interest I provided myself with a packet of sewing-needles; and when I asked in Kimbala the Bayaka name of some object, the first man to give it received a needle; if, however, he told me a wrong word, he had to surrender one of those previously earned, and the reward went to the man who corrected him. Thus I accumulated my vocabulary at a cost of about twopence (1913, 145).

Waiting around until information came along for free was seldom possible. Incidentally, this explains perhaps the emphasis on rituals as privileged objects of ethnographic description. Rituals were events, or action sequences, short enough to be observed. But note that it took Frobenius almost nine months to see his first masked dancer in action (1907, 256).[21] By that time he had sent collections home that needed, in one case, a caravan of sixty-seven porters. He had by then also completed substantial parts of the manuscript of his published report.[22]

Curios and Objects of Art

To be exact, Torday described himself as buying "curios"; Frobenius did not buy *Kuriositäten* but *ethnographischer Kram*. Torday identified objects either by general labels, or descriptively; Frobenius pretended most of the time to base his classification of objects on native terms (at least as regards the principal objects of desire—statues, fetishes, fabrics, and so forth). Both traveled with artists who, among others, prepared skillful renderings of collected objects. But neither Torday nor Frobenius were inclined to call these objects art. In view of the fact that the esthetic reception of things African seems to have been in full sway in the metropolitan countries, certainly by the time our sources were published,[23] this is rather surprising. What about the aesthetics of collection?

Both traveling ethnographers were liberal in pronouncing judgment on relative quality, beauty, and authenticity, with regard not just to objects but also to music and dance, speech, bodily appearance, and village architecture. In fact, distinction—the demonstrated ability to tell one culture from another, one expression from another, and to see all this arranged in a hierarchy—was a fundamental instrument in establishing intellectual control.

Torday, who collected the pieces that are now considered the most exquisite, mentions "arts and crafts,"[24] but both the plural and the juxtaposition are significant. The same goes for statements by Hilton-Simpson such as the following: "Music and dancing are the arts in which the Basonge chiefly excel, and we were unable to find any traces of the carver's art to compare with the specimens we were later to secure from the Bushongo" (1911, 36). The word "art" may be used ironically, when he tells us of the Bankutu that "with the exception of the building of huts, the only art that has been developed . . . is the art of killing their fellowmen by stealth" (133). Frobenius did speak, not so much in the text but in captions to illustrations of carved cups and pieces of "velvet," of *Prachtstücke der Kubakunst*, splendid specimens of Kuba art.[25] But he too classified certain objects as *Kunstgewerbeartikel*, craft articles (1907, 248).

On the whole, it is clear that what Torday and Frobenius collected did not evoke to them Art with a capital A. Yet both ethnographers took first steps in that direction when they distinguished styles (although not actually using the term, as far as I can see) or pronounced on degrees of purity (when they regretted European influences). A clue, however, may be taken from the fact that both Torday and Frobenius grow eloquent and somewhat solemn when they link the production of certain objects to political structure, especially the Kuba "royal court." My hunch is that the transformation from curio to object of art began (but may not have been completed—for that took processes in the metropolitan countries) when the mechanism of distinction mobilized political and ethnic categories, that is, when the products of certain groups only (people near the court, or certain ethnic groups of "nobility") were praised as pure and refined. Aesthetics and politics meshed. There is an interesting corollary to this. Frobenius makes a lot of the fact that the "Baluba" are great storytellers and talkers but not great producers of exquisite objects [!] (see 1907, 197–98). Because the Baluba are consistently depicted as the most "uprooted" among these populations his observation fits ideas regarding authenticity which he and Torday shared. In the logic of ethnographic collecting, they express the very first premise discussed earlier: objects are collected that are doomed to disappear because they really belong to the past—a past in which the peoples of Africa had to be placed if the schemes of science and imperialism were to make sense.[26]

But this can be read as a verdict only if we were to forget how we started: Objects were to be appreciated as mediations of "ecstatic" knowledge. They remain "outside" of shallow rational schemes, even a hundred years on, and challenge us to step outside of self-complacent views of history, that of Africa as well as that of our disciplines.

Time, Narration, and the Exploration of Central Africa

Time and Anthropology

Time and discourse are the domain of philosophers, historians, and theoreticians of literature. When anthropologists address these topics, they are expected to deliver comparative material, illustrating the ways other societies and cultures have with time and its representations. Such material exists and has been surveyed, and there are colleagues who are more competent and would be more eager than I am to entertain and perhaps enlighten scholars from other disciplines with examples.[1] I am reluctant to do this, not only because I have no special expertise in the study of other conceptions of time, but also because I think that ethnographies of time would be no more relevant to theorizing about time and discourse than, say, ethnographies of initiation rituals, of marriage arrangements, or of the rotation of crops in subsistence agriculture. The reason for this, though perhaps not obvious, is elementary: Anthropology's findings pose the same problems that philosophers, historians, and literary critics address when they think about representations of time. Put somewhat differently, anthropological knowledge is part of the problem, not its solution.[2] Temporality and narrativity, representations of time in a discourse that is condemned (or privileged) to tell stories, have concerned and characterized anthropology even during its most "modern," that is, purportedly "synchronic" (or achronic) phase.[3]

What I will have to say about time and narration is not derived from coherent *tableaux* of thought about time in other cultures. My starting point is the need to come to grips with contradictions between ethnographic practices and anthropological discourse that have kept me preoccupied ever since I had my initiatory fieldwork experience. Foremost among them have been unresolved tensions between, on the one hand, the necessity to share time with our objects of study, a condition of interactive and communicative research, and, on the other, a long-established, persistent tendency to deny, when we write about them, coevalness to the very same people whom we study. To the extent that anthropologists failed to confront this tension they established anthropology as an allochronic discourse: With the help of semantic, syntactic, and rhetorical devices, the researched have consistently and strategically been presented as belonging to times other than that of the researcher. These strategies include "technical" vocabularies, uses of tense (the ethnographic present) and pronouns (predominance of third person and elimination of first and second persons), as well as topoi (research themes such as religion, magic, kinship . . .) and the choice of literary genres (such as the monograph privileging comment over story).

While this argument, formulated in *Time and the Other* (1983), was received as self-destructive critique of my discipline by some, and as salutary postcolonial deconstruction of anthropological discourse by others, I was soon made to realize that the book fell short of achieving what I asserted as its aim: to show how the fundamental contradiction arises from, and how it might be resolved in, our practices of research and writing.[4] Here I should like to continue this project of exploring implications of *Time and the Other* by bringing together certain observations on discursive ways with time at the beginning of modern anthropology. They were made on the corpus of travel narratives reporting on the exploration of Central Africa that was presented in the preceding chapter.[5]

A widespread opinion, if not a myth (frequently stated in histories of anthropology before the historiographical breakthrough of the sixties) held that anthropology became an academic discipline when scientific discourse replaced narration—when, to put it simply, the monograph replaced the travelogue. That development, it has been asserted, was, if not brought about, then completed somewhat later, by intensive, stationary fieldwork taking the place of travel. Today, this view is under attack from several directions. Improved knowledge of the history of our discipline shows that travel never ceased to be part of ethnographic research, certainly not when it came to field work in faraway places, required as initiation to the profession (Stocking 1992, chap. 1). Not only that, travel has been rediscovered as a practice and a figure of speech appropriate to postcolonial conditions and to global circulation of culture (Clifford 1997). What remains to be done is to debunk the myths of exploratory travel and to clarify what kind of practices exploration involved. How was knowledge produced en route, and how were experiences and knowledge represented in the literary form of travelogues? From my own attempt to do this I came away with three conclusions. First, geographical exploration, as it used to be called, was driven by a mixture of reason and madness. Second, knowledge produced by exploration was different, but not different in kind, from what has counted as ethnography in modern anthropology. Third, the explorer's travelogue representing such knowledge was a complex literary form.

In the light of these findings I would now like to interrogate our nineteenth-century sources (including a few that were published in this century but before World War I) about time and narration.

Travel and Narration: Walk a Crooked Path, Tell a Straight Story?

In "scientific" travel it is not movement that is being explored; exploration is carried out through movement. Similarly, the travelogue is never a simple description of travel but a narrative of experiences, events, and observations as they occurred or were made during travel. It is safe to say that travel is, perhaps less in popular perception but certainly as a subject of academic research and reflection, above all associated with the appropriation, indeed, the "conquest," of space. Hence the interest in studying travel writing as representation of space (Mondada 1994). But what about travel and time?

There is a general connection, asserted already at the time when our sources appeared, between travel and history. Travel makes exploration "happen"; exploration makes of travel an "event." Some such idea must have been behind an otherwise rather odd designation of two of the earliest travelogues in my corpus. They are called contributions, not just to the discovery but to the "history of discovery of Africa."[6] Is this just an instance of the usual woolly confusion between history and historiography? Does it mean that travel was sensed to belong to history and accounts of travel to historiography, also called history? One thing seems to me beyond doubt: there was not a single author covering the period and area I selected who did not think of, or hope for, his travelogue *making history* in the sense of influencing the course of exploration (and of conquest and occupation that were soon to follow). What I asserted earlier about travel making exploration happen can therefore also be said about the travelogue as narration. Telling the story of a journey was an integral part of the actions that produced a (hi)story that could be told, and both, narration and travel, enacted political and economic schemes. It was in their capacity as representatives of nation-states (almost all the writers were prone to patriotic effusions in their travelogues) that the explorers wrote reports that could count as history as opposed to the stories told in other tales of travel.[7] Conversely, when explorers departed for Africa they took along, as it were, narrative scripts for their travels.

Changing gears, I should like to move now from general reflections, made from a distance, to taking a closer look at the documents at hand. However, this is a move—and that was one of the disturbing insights suggested by my recent study—we need to prepare first by demystifying exploratory travel in Central Africa. From childhood reading, popular literature, cartoons, comic strips, and films we all collect certain images of explorers and exploration that are lodged in our minds: Heroic men, making purposeful journeys, lead caravans of native porters through the wilds. We bring these images to our reading of travelogues. We expect stories of heroic deeds accomplished while moving through time and space, told by a narrator who is also the hero and who translates control of events and peoples as well as purpose and direction of travel into a narrative that is controlled, purposeful, and (literally) straightforward.

Visual images that condense ideas (or ideologies) of scientific travel and the literary form of travelogues reinforce each other, and this may account for the tenacity of the myth of exploration. Confronted with reality or, to put this more cautiously, with historical information culled from travelogues, little or nothing remains of that myth. To begin with, travel itself was anything but continuous movement. Due to any number of reasons and necessities that ranged from negotiations with local powers to bad weather, most of the time an expedition took was spent stationary. Travel could, therefore, not have been experienced as continuous, relatively speedy movement through time. Speed and setting records for covering distances were a preoccupation of some travelers (and a prominent feature of first reports in the press) but on the whole, most of them waited around rather than rushed through their journeys.

Similarly, notions of travel as the most efficient and shortest trajectory from points of departure to points of destination must be abandoned. The expeditions of the period, including those that could be counted as journeys of discovery, hardly ever, and never for any great distance, left the trodden path. They followed existing, sometimes circuitous routes of trade and communication. Even leaving aside unforeseeable physical obstacles and political events and the vagaries of a tropical climate, the distances that could be covered depended on long-established habits (often on local organizations and enterprises) that determined all important aspects of the logistics of travel, such as recruitment of porters, procurement of provisions and trade goods, tolls, and payments for crossing rivers. At all times and under any circumstances, control over the personnel of a caravan was a precarious matter; all expeditions were plagued by revolts and desertion. Many leaders of expeditions resorted to physical violence (an option made possible by the superiority of their weapons). While it is true that, during the period covered by our sources, an encompassing and explicit regime of mental and physical tropical hygiene was already established, all of the explorers some of the time, and many most of the time, suffered from incapacitating diseases and traveled under the influence of alcohol, opiates, and many kinds of medication. Fits of rage,

bouts of depression or manic activity, attacks of loneliness, sexual deprivation (or excesses), minor but persistent sores, and harassment by
insects, vermin, and the occasional marauding predator further contributed to a general loss of control that leaves the image of the explorer
as the efficient agent of science in shreds.

What comes to the fore when the shreds are removed is a reality full
of intellectual, moral, and political complexities. This should disabuse us
of any notion that narratives of exploration were simple stories, telling
what happened, when, where, and to whom. It is even less plausible to
assume—given the messy reality of travel to Central Africa—that the
travelogue was, as it were, the natural form in which the experience of
exploration could be represented, perhaps because of a mimetic relationship between a journey and a story. Conversely, the travelogue could not
have become a tremendously popular genre and at the same time an early
form of scientific (geographic, anthropological) discourse had it simply
mirrored exploration.

Because the reality of travel was so complex it is unlikely that a full
understanding of travel narratives will be achieved by any single narrato-
logical line of inquiry that could be followed. Strategic choices must be
made and the route I will follow from now on is one that served me earlier when I formulated a critique of fully developed anthropological discourse by examining its uses of time. Much can be discovered when we
look at the explorers' ways with time. Narration, as every one knows, is
suffused with time. Written narratives of exploratory travel that are, in
the sense we spelled out, also exploration *as* narration should therefore
have much to tell us about temporal practices that contributed to the
emergence of both colonial discourse and anthropology.

Anthropological Knowledge and Literary Form

That experience and narration, life and writing life down, or
research and "writing up," are distinctive activities, usually separated
from each other as consecutive or alternating phases, is an idea we probably all hold with varying degrees of conviction. It is also a myth, not
unlike (and, in the case of anthropology, not unrelated to) that of the

intrepid explorer. The latter depicts exploratory travel as a thoroughly rational enterprise; the former makes of writing a mere instrument that can be used with more or less skill but is not otherwise part of the production of knowledge. Critical reflection on the nature of ethno-graphy, of "writing culture" (see Clifford and Marcus 1986), has today reached unprecedented sophistication and there is little left of a misconception that was held during anthropology's modern phase: There are few anthropologists who still think that writing is theoretically and epistemologically irrelevant. To assert this involved deception and self-deception. True, most major figures and authors of ethnographic classics claimed scientific authority based on the quality of their research and the validity of their findings. But there can be no doubt that they owe their place in the anthropological canon also, and perhaps mainly, to the quality of their writing.

Even the much celebrated practice of intensive, local fieldwork demanded by the British school as the only "method" appropriate for the theoretical agenda of functionalism can, with the benefit of today's critical hindsight, be regarded as a set of rules and principles governing the literary form of the scientific monograph, considered superior to the travel narrative. To suggest that functionalism was but a literary style and field research a practice enacting a scientific script, much as exploratory travel enacted imperial scripts, would have been unheard of at the time because modern anthropology had, as it were, bought its scientific respectability at the price of disavowing its literary nature. No such taboos existed during the period I examined. Reflections and observations offered by the authors of our travelogues were seldom naive about the epistemological significance of writing and literary form; often they anticipated insights we now credit with being distinctly postmodern critical achievements.

A first example I should like to quote comes from the three-volume report on the German Loango Expedition of 1873–76 (Güssfeldt, Falkenstein, and Pechuël-Loesche 1879).[8] It is, incidentally, the only work in our corpus that called itself a *Reisewerk*, a travelogue, on the title page. Dr. Paul Güssfeldt defends this designation in his preface to the first volume. The narrative form, he argues, is the one adapted to the present state of knowledge; as long as knowledge is still weak, its presentation must "lean on the means by which it was acquired" (no pagination [ii]). By implication, Güssfeldt asserts the possibility of a kind of knowledge strong enough to do without the literary props of a travelogue. But he is still remarkably free of what I called self-deception; he knows that the knowledge travelers produce cannot be "demonstrated" ([ii]), not even in the sense of being simply displayed, but must be *accounted* for by *recounting* (in narrative sequence, as is clear from the context) how it was gained.

The statement just quoted is in marked contrast to a reflection offered a decade later by an explorer who was less aware than Güssfeldt of the epistemological significance of literary form and more confident in his scientific accomplishments. The author is Dr. Richard Büttner, member of the German Congo Expedition of 1884–86. Significantly, his remarks were not made in a travelogue but in a long, rubricated (that is, quasi-systematic) report published in the bulletin of his sponsoring organization. "I find myself constrained," he says, "to set aside the external form of presentation and to deliver essentially a simple compilation of observations and statements. So as not to report unimportant matters, I must often disregard temporal connections; to avoid repetition, I need to lead the reader in medias res and refer him to earlier publications" (*MAGD* 5, no. 3, [1889]: 168–69).

The point of Büttner's statement seems to be this: Scientific relevance is, if not gained, then improved by separating the important from the unimportant. This is an operation that requires disregard for "temporal connections," occurrence in lived time, and elimination of repetition, that is, of redundancy, a feature that lived experience and its presentation in nonscientific forms (such as dialogues and narratives) have in common. Put in technical terms he did not know, Büttner signals tensions between syntagmatic and paradigmatic presentation, between the narrative and the monograph as literary forms. With Güssfeldt he shares the conviction that the monograph is a scientific ideal to strive for. He also gives us a clue to the crux of the matter, which is a problem writers of travelogues faced in the past and ethnographers have had to struggle with ever since: what to do with time ("temporal connections") as a dimension (or condition) of the production of knowledge? Must time be represented, and if so, how? Our travelogues have some interesting answers.

Clocks and Diaries

Scientific travelers had two daily obligations that kept them concerned about time. Especially during the phase of geographical exploration, the *drawing of maps* was at once the most important task among the explorers' assignments and the most important form of representing knowledge. Accurate timepieces and an accurate calendar were needed to calculate positions with the help of astronomical observations and to measure distances covered during movement between one place and another. A few among the explorers were trained topographers; many had acquired the basic techniques (such as using the sextant) as part of their army or navy training. Contrary to what one might expect, the result of these presumably most objective, scientific ways with time were, on the whole, rather dismal. Chronometers and other instruments deteriorated due to the climate and the vagaries of transportation; travelers often did not keep to observation schedules because they were incapacitated by illness or accidents and in some cases lost track of time to the point they were off the calendar by several days. When their notes and sketches reached metropolitan countries, expert cartographers found reasons to be dissatisfied with the data; topographic observations on entire areas had to be declared virtually useless.[9]

Another assignment and daily chore was to keep a log or diary. As attested by almost all the travelers—and much like keeping time with the help of chronometers—nothing was simple and straightforward about this task. It was beset with problems and complexities that occasioned some of the most penetrating reflections about the production of knowledge and its representation in writing. Foremost, and frequently commented on, were the difficulties explorers had with fitting the diary (and any other writing, such as making ethnographic and linguistic notes, or recording readings from instruments) into the time economy of travel. The German Max Buchner expresses this kind of frustration when he exclaims: "If only I had more time and was not so terribly tired when I have the time! My traveling apparatus [*Reiseapparat*] absorbs too much of my capacity for work" (*MAGD* 2, no. 1 [1880]: 49). Almost daily, explorers were made aware of a profound contradiction (one of many, in fact): Travel as a means always threatened to cancel the purpose of their enterprise. There can be no doubt that most of them wrote against, not with, the flow of time; in order to record what happened daily, they had to take "time out" from the quotidian.[10]

To judge from what authors report in their travelogues, the diary was anything but an elementary sort of chronicle. True, occasionally entries like "June 30. Nothing happened," found their way into the final account, but even these entries expressed the need or pressure writers felt to signal their commitment to a daily task which they perceived as staying in touch with, or being on the lookout for, history. This—the role the diary had in keeping its writer in touch with reality—incidentally, throws some light on the nature of what in modern anthropology was to be called keeping "field notes." Far from being mere recording of data, writing field notes (or, nowadays, conveying them to electronic memory) qualifies as historiography.[11]

There was, of course, more to the diary than its being a representation of daily struggle with time. Our questioning reaches a new level of complexity as soon as we consider another, seemingly elementary, fact. Although many authors may not have kept diaries (and may never have written much of any sort) before they traveled as scientific explorers, their general education and exposure to nineteenth-century culture could hardly have left them unaware that the diary was an established literary genre with its own rules and constraints.[12] Anthropologically speaking, even at its lowest level (lowest in the sense of being an activity that travelers carried out "closest to the ground"), travel writing was culturally mediated. It can furthermore be assumed that authors knew that, in their culture, the diary had an ambiguous status. In phrases like "travel diary," often a synonym for travelogue, it was designated a public genre; at the same time it counted as an intimate, deeply private, and sometimes secretive genre. The diary was a depository not only of events but of thoughts, insights, feelings, and confessions. Private as it may have been thought to be, as a form of writing, and as an important assignment given to travelers, the diary always called up, and was called upon by, public genres. Explorers faced the paradoxical demand to base the scientific objectivity of their accounts on an activity—keeping a diary—that could not have been more subjective in the sense of requiring individual experience and individual efforts to represent that experience. And when we look for the

"condition of possibility" of such a practice we come—though not necessarily on the route just traced—to lived time. Without days, *jours*, or
Tage, a diary, *journal*, or *Tagebuch*, could not be kept. Which may sound
self-evident, if not silly, until one realizes two things. First, such daily
writing was considered a matter of survival, part of an explicit regime of
mental and physical "tropical hygiene." Second, as documented in our
sources, decisions to incorporate or not to incorporate diary writing in
the travel narrative were among the most frequently addressed and
reflected-upon problems of what I called elsewhere "presence and representation." It is this critical standard by which discourses as accounts of
scientific exploration and modern ethnography must be measured: Can
they produce knowledge whose representation does not depend on the
elimination of the presence of acting persons and events (in short, of history)—that is, of "the means by which knowledge was acquired," as
Güssfeldt put it?[13]

Time, Truth, and Reality

Our (and the explorers') observations on the diary as a way of maintaining presence and, indeed, assuring survival help to dispose of yet
another obstinate myth peddled in anthropological lore. This is the mistaken idea that the travelogue needed to be (and was) replaced by scientific writing because it was a purely narrative genre. Narration was,
according to this view, by its nature predestined to turn ethnographic
reporting into fiction, if not outright fabrication.

Through the centuries, many travelogues may have fit this image;
the travel reports selected for our study do not. In fact the generic designation "travelogue" itself can only be upheld if we acknowledge that the
travelogue was a mixed genre. An attentive reading of these accounts
reveals the history of their composition: Breaks, abrupt transitions, unex-
plained juxtapositions—all of them sometimes announced by the
author—keep the process of writing, indeed the writer's work, visible in
ways one will not find in event- and subjectless scientific prose. Especially
interesting among such breaks are some that signal—if an analogy with
the linguistic notion of code switching is allowed—genre switching. Like

its linguistic counterpart, this literary practice could have gotten established to the degree that it characterizes our corpus only as a kind of competence, not as a failure to control literary form.[14] Recent work in linguistics (for example, de Rooij 1996) shows that code switching may shade into style switching, necessitating interpretations that must go beyond strictly referential (or instrumental) aspects and consider pragmatic and rhetorical motives. Especially the latter suggests connections between practices of code switching and features of speech and oral delivery, among them one that may be called timing—the "right" moment in the flow of oral or written delivery that can become constitutive of what is being communicated. In these practices we have another discursive representation of time that is as yet little explored except in studies of poetry and oral performance. Genre switching, far from being just a symptom of uncontrolled "mixture" or intentional "collage," belongs to what has been called the poetics and politics of ethnographic writing.[15]

I mentioned breaks and discontinuities as evidence for process. Several fault lines mark the geology of the travelogue. Perhaps the most conspicuous is one that runs between discourse/history and commentary/story (a contrast authoritatively identified and analyzed by Benveniste 1971 [1956] and Weinrich 1973).[16] It would be tedious in this context to enumerate the many indicators that separate the narration of travel from ethnographic description (often small monographs covering most of the expected rubrics) or from disquisitions on various aspects of natural history. More interesting are the ways in which authors foregrounded separation. Some alternated between modes of representation on the level of chapters or sections. Others made breaks between narration and description corresponding to the actual stop-and-go, or rather go-and-stop, of exploratory travel. Here is an example from Joseph Thomson's travelogue:

> Having entered a new country, and among different people, we may now profitably take a retrospective glance at the country we have passed through, draw isolated facts together which may have been lost sight of in the narrative, and present a condensed view of the whole. (1881, 1:132)[17]

Aside from the lines separating narrative and description, many other cracks are visible on the surface of the travelogue. They set apart historical summaries, anecdotes of remarkable events, hunting tales, occasional poetic effusions or philosophical reflections, intertextual asides (references to, and quotations from, other travelogues, sometimes for polemical purposes), and intratextual flashbacks and anticipations, all of this interspersed with lists, comments and tables, and captions for illustrations. It is, then, not surprising and always interesting to note instances where authors themselves felt the need to point to major breaks, to prepare transitions that readers would otherwise have felt to be too sudden. As far as I can see, these explicit, visible traces of the work of composition expressed several concerns. One of them simply involved coherence and readability. Another was to show authority and command over disparate material presented in the travelogue. A third concern was to assure oneself of one's bearing during the literary voyage, especially since this might also be needed to give credence to the literal voyages that the travelogues represented.

Coherence and correspondence may of course also count as epistemological criteria, and this is where our discussion can focus again on the explorers' struggle with time and the extraordinary role the diary played in shaping their discourse. Let me introduce what is at issue by quoting from a travelogue that qualifies itself as a *Tagebuch* (diary) in the title but is in fact a composite of modes of presentation much like the other sources in our corpus. Paul Pogge, traveling for the German Africa Association, had this to say about the diary form:

So as not to weaken the presentation of the historical course of my journey, I gave preference to the diary form instead of dressing up my experiences in the form of a coherent narrative. For travelers who progress toward the interior [of Africa] on the same route or one nearby, this, the diary form of presentation, seemed to me the most instructive. (1880, v)

Pogge's statement parallels the one by Güssfeldt, quoted above. He shares the latter's concern for matching knowledge and literary form but seems to go one step further when he suggests that narrative coherence may do a disservice to the accuracy (or instructiveness) of representations of travel. His alternative is not systematic description, the scientific monograph marked by the absence of the ethnographer as a narrator or acting subject, but the most subjective (in the sense of subject-bound) form of representing scientific travel, and he proposes the diary form in the name of greater accuracy and realism.

Pogge was a modest man who liked to style himself a simple "farmer and hunter," but his statement should not be dismissed as idiosyncratic and rather naive. Other authors made similar choices and gave similar reasons for letting their diaries tell the true story. I believe that this has a bearing on the question of ethnographic realism as a feature of modern anthropology. Unlike their successors who saw in the ethnographic monograph the most appropriate and realistic representation of knowledge, these explorers did not believe that eliminating experience-near writing would endanger the scientific credibility of their accounts. The point I would like to make here is that the very subjectivity of the diary form assured recognition of lived time as a condition of the production of knowledge *and* of its discursive representation.

This proposition can, as it were, be tested on a feature typical of the sources I examined. In many instances we find authors contradicting themselves, either in statements of fact, or in their explanations and conclusions, and often in both. In other words, the basically narrative superstructure of the travelogue, unlike the monograph, preserves traces of a learning process, hence of the historicity of knowledge production. My thesis is that this happens because, and to the extent to which, writers relied on their diaries when they composed their travelogues. They did not feel the need to eliminate contradictions because this would have amounted to eliminating time (they would have said "reality") from their discourse. The following statement by Coquilhat confirms several of the points just made:

From here on, I'll follow my diary rather than keeping separate the elements of each subject. Day-by-day notes have the advantage that they let the reader live with the author, because the reader sees not only the sequence in the chronology of events but also the succession of groping about and making progress in the work of the pioneer and in the information he collects. (1888, 215)

Becker offers a similar, but also interestingly different, reflection when he insists that the *vrais canevas*, the true composition, of his book was furnished

by the notebooks to which I consigned, every evening, the big and small events, as well as the joyous and sad impressions of the day. After the fact, I augmented them with some retrospective memories. Ordinary, daily facts I connected intimately to ethnographic and anthropological considerations which the reader skips all too often when they make up the content of special chapters breaking the order and movement of the narrative. (1887, 1:xix)

Few authors were as explicit as Coquilhat and Becker, but I can quote the following three examples that have references to diaries as their common element. The first is a statement by Pogge. In a passage of his travelogue marked "September 30, day of rest because a porter is sick" he reports on problems he has with maintaining discipline in his caravan:

Kind words and admonitions don't help at all; scolding is quite useless. All they'll do is laugh at me. (These words I wrote into my diary, which makes me realize today that at first I really had a hard time getting along with my porters.) (1880, 75)

Example two comes from Hermann Wissmann. Toward the end of his travel account (published at a time when he was already active as a colonial officer in German East Africa) he has this reflection:

So far the European has not been competing with the Arab; to the contrary, the Arab only profits from travelers and missionaries. Therefore their relationship is still tolerable. But once the Arab realizes that the European, with his superior means, is about to wrest trade away from him, that relationship is going to change. This is what I wrote then into my diary, without any premonition how quickly my assumption was to become reality. (Wissmann et al. 1889, 281–82)

Finally there is a passage from Leo Frobenius where he begins by praising a Belgian colonial agent for his success in educating his Africans and then adds:

But of course these are experiments that can be conducted only when the European has complete control of the Negro, that is, when they relate to him as children to their father and when both parties communicate spiritually, not just through language. I wrote this in my diary on March 7, 1905. Today I would say that M. Mignon was a kind and trusting man, certainly too trusting when it came to educating the Negro. (1906, 55)

In all three instances the authors first incorporate portions of their diaries in their travel narratives but then seem compelled to leave the time of the narrative and confront it with knowledge or opinions they hold at the moment of writing. What they achieve with this move—apart from commenting on or correcting certain passages—seems to me to be a literary gesture using the diary to anchor their writing in real time and history.

Exactly how the travelers used their diaries to compose their travelogues varied a great deal and cannot always be reconstructed from the finished text. Most explicit are of course cases where quotation from the diary is announced. But even then, how faithfully the diary was copied is a question we cannot answer with the material at hand. In other cases, passages, often substantial portions, in these travelogues have the outer appearance of a diary (entries preceded by noting place and date) but we cannot be sure whether these passages actually were copied from diaries. It is not to be excluded that the diary form, with its acknowledged closeness to reality, was sometimes used as a stylistic element in writing that relied on sources other than a diary. We also have at least one example in our corpus where it becomes difficult to maintain a clear distinction between keeping a diary and writing the travel narrative. This is Leo Frobenius who traveled in the Congo between January 1905 and May or June 1906. His 468-page travelogue was published by 1907. In other words, he must have done his daily writing in a form that permitted him to return with a more or less finished manuscript. Time pressure was a constraint under which all authors worked; after all, exploration was part of an international race during the Scramble for Africa. "I have been compelled to finish the work as rapidly as possible," writes Thomson in the preface to his travelogue, "and therefore to confine myself to a large extent to the simple narrative" (1881, 1:xi).

Conclusion

Travel narratives from a time when Central Africa was a target of European exploration just prior to its becoming occupied and colonized were the sources of this attempt to address the topic of narration. I approached the task, not as a literary expert, but as someone who read these sources as documenting the beginnings of habits and practices of research and representation that are still part of his discipline, anthropology. Taking, as most of us do, narration as a discursive presentation of time, I examined ways in which narrators who were travelers experienced and talked about time—as lived time, as time to be kept and measured, as a scarce resource or as an emptiness to be filled, but above all as history, that is, as action whereby travel became the enactment of an imperial script.

Much of what I had to tell came in the form of negative critical statements addressed to the myth of exploration as heroic quest, the myth of exploratory travel as purposeful movement, and the myth of anthropology having overcome its traveling past. A lot of rubble has to be removed before mining the sources yields results. Among the findings that I brought back from my journey into travelogues is, first of all, the realization that the travelogue was a complex genre and that the authors of the travelogues in my corpus—most of them young military men, with a few physicians and scientists—had a surprisingly clear and sophisticated ideas regarding the representation of scientific travel. At times they expressed positions regarding writing and knowledge production that anthropology (re)gained only after taking its "literary turn" some time in the mid-seventies.

I must confess that I started out with the expectation that, complex as the genre may be, I would find the relationship between travel and narration in travelogues rather unproblematic. This proved not to be the case when I faced the diary, foremost among the "means of production" of travelogues. After considering the general information on the use of diaries that can be culled from the sources and after taking a closer look at a number of explicit statements I am, to continue my confession, unable to state concisely what should be concluded. Tentatively, I would posit that the relationship between diary and travel narrative was not one of, say, material and finished literary product. Their diaries, some of our authors seem to affirm, gave them a position against narration whenever they saw a danger that their account might be taken as just another story. Recourse to the diary allowed them to affirm their authority by affirming their presence in real time and space. But a dialectical conception of narrative and narration is required to understand why the same authors who had recourse to their diaries when it came to asserting the reality of their enterprise would also tell their readers that simple narration was the best way to convey the reality of their experiences (and hence to judge the validity of the knowledge of Africa that they reported). The need to appeal to a higher instance, for a place of refuge from the narrative—perhaps this is what Lourau (1988) has in mind when he places the diary *hors texte*—seems to me to fit a realistic picture of the ethnographer's predicament.

Which brings me to a final remark on narration and ethnographic realism. What makes ethnographic accounts realistic (in either the literary or the epistemological sense of the term) is neither the narrative form nor any isomorphism between travel and narrative, but rather the possibility to take "time out" from an account with reflexive statements (and remembrances, an aspect I had to neglect to keep this exercise from getting even more difficult than it already is). Such stepping outside the narrative gave the readers of travelogues at least a glimpse of how an ethnographic account is made. The nonnarrative monograph had no provisions for such checks on reality and fiction. In this sense, the accepted "scientific" literary form of ethnographic representation was more fictive than the travelogue. Narration may save ethnography, but only as a practice that can be negated by recourse to those records of our ways with time that exist as diaries of field notes.[18]

9

Remembering the Other: Knowledge and Recognition

Die Intelligenz ist *wiedererkennend.*
Intelligence is *re-cognitive.*

—W. F. Hegel, *Enzyklopädie der philosophischen Wissenschaften*

The main importance of *recognition* as the link between ideology and iconology is that it shifts both "sciences" from an epistemological "cognitive" ground (the knowledge of objects by subjects) to an ethical, political, and hermeneutic ground (the knowledge of subjects by subjects . . .). The categories of judgment shift from terms of cognition to terms of re-cognition, from epistemological categories of knowledge to social categories like "acknowledgment."

—W. J. T. Mitchell, *Picture Theory*

Memory and identity have been topics of much recent writing and debate.[1] In this chapter, I shall address what I think is at issue from an angle that may at first not appear to be obvious (except to anthropologists and historians who have worked in societies outside Europe): memory and alterity. It should not take much arguing, though, to realize that tying memory to identity inevitably leads us to thinking about memory and the experience of alterity. What, I want to ask, is the role of remembrance in the production of knowledge about other cultures and societies? Must we, and if so, how can we, "remember" those who are strangers to us?

I shall begin with some findings from the same study of early ethnography that served as background and source in the two preceding chapters (Fabian 2000). Here I want to concentrate on the part exploration had in an enterprise that has been crucial in European experiences and constructions of alterity. But before I get to this I should like to formulate, very briefly, some instructions for use. I shall retrace a trajectory of reflection, and much of what I will have to say is evocative (when I quote texts, for example), exploratory (when I argue for focusing on the *re-* in *recognition*), and limited (when I make claims regarding the significance of my findings for a critique of anthropology). In my understanding, the documents I adduce are exhibited not as proof of preexisting propositions but as part of the route I traveled before I reached my conclusions.

As I examined the published reports and travelogues a central issue began to emerge.[2] Ethnographic knowledge other than of the most casual and superficial sort demands *recognition*, a kind of acknowledgment that must be given to human beings who are subjected to inquiries. Upon reflection it turned out that recognition may include acts that can be qualified as remembering. Recognition encompasses more than memory but, as I hope to show, thinking about memory in contexts of recognition allows us to sharpen our inquiries and to counteract certain dangers of overextension that are inherent in the current boom of memory (and identity) studies. Such dangers loom whenever a concept is in vogue, and that goes perhaps for recognition as much as for memory. The moment to be wary comes when memory, for instance, turns from an idea directed critically toward quasi-mechanical conceptions of society and culture into a so-called regime or system. As a result, memory's creative, often subversive potential will no longer be recognized as a phenomenon, and as a concept, memory may become almost indistinguishable from either identity or culture. This melding may happen when scholars from other fields seek to give coherence to practices of memory by having recourse to an anthropological concept of culture.[3] A similar observation could be made about Marc Augé's anthropological reflections on knowledge and recognition (1998, chap. 5), the most congenial treatment of the topic I have found in recent writing (especially when he insists on pairing recognition with misrecognition). When he states that recognition comes in "universes" and "systems," and when he says that "the only relation obtaining between universes of recognition is mutual nonrecognition" (86), this signals to me the danger of closure that may deprive the concept of its critical and subversive function (which is not to say that closure does not occur in situations anthropologists study, such as the practices of Ivory Coast prophet-healers which Augé analyses in the same chapter).

My own proposal to introduce recognition into our thinking about knowledge and alterity was not inspired by the philosophical debate about multiculturalism and the politics of recognition which will be mentioned later. I was intrigued, rather, by observations I made in reading accounts of early ethnography, observations that, in my view, are still relevant to our current practices. Conversely, when I later argue that these practices may be understood with the help of the concept of recognition, I do not think for a moment that philosophy has, as it were, been waiting for us with ready-made solutions for our ethnographic problems. What philosophers have to say about recognition may be useful to anthropologists; the particular twist I would like to give that concept here may make it resistant or irritating to participants in the current philosophical debate about multiculturalism.

But first I must show what caused me to think about recognition when I read reports on the exploration of Central Africa. I will quote and comment on some remarkable pronouncements, beginning with one that can serve as an epigraph for the first section of this chapter. It was made by Joseph Thomson, a young Scotsman traveling in East Africa in 1878–80, when, foreshadowing Europe's imperial gaze, he looked at an African landscape with recognition.

Explorers on Recognition

We get a delightful view, which might well remind us of our own Scottish land, in its character of hill and dale, clear sparkling stream, open glade studded with stately trees, and cultivated field. Let us take a commanding position, and look about us.

—Joseph Thomson, *To the Central African Lakes and Back* (1881)

When we ask how explorers went about producing knowledge of Central Africa, we find that, on the whole, preexisting images, preconceived ideas, and prefabricated theories (lodged in their memories) served them to make sense of strange sights and of stories they recorded about strange beliefs and practices.[4] Just how much perception was determined by expectations can be seen, for instance, from varying reactions to cannibalism, a pièce de résistance of scientific anthropological explanation up to this day. With few exceptions, each explorer found what he expected— as we might expect. However, when we compare different reports and explanations, we find considerable divergence with regard to the empirical basis on which travelers pronounced their generalizations about eating human flesh. Some simply reiterated age-old myths and platitudes about cannibalism; others went beneath the surface and permitted their minds to get challenged, and often boggled, by seeking a common human ground for understanding such patently inhuman practices. The very least that can be said is that these efforts make us rediscover that sense and knowledge must not be confused. Sense or meaning can be brought along; they affirm and support—most of the time ideas or values already held. As Marc Augé puts it: "By a short-circuiting of thought everywhere attested, people desire less to know the world than to recognize themselves in it, substituting for the indefinite frontiers of an ungraspable universe the totalitarian security of closed worlds" (1998, 82). The term *knowledge*, unless it is taken as a synonym for *projection*, should be reserved for insights and understandings that the knower does not already possess and that, when they occur, change the knower. Much has been written about European travelers projecting images and stereotypes onto Africa and its people. It now seems more urgent and interesting to see what our sources can tell us about how travelers derived from concrete situations and experiences a kind of knowledge that changed the knower.

Numerous statements document how travelers constantly struggled with, and often were torn apart by, glaring contradictions between received theoretical or ideological certainties and their own unexpected, disturbing experiences. As I worked through the sources, I became more and more impressed and puzzled by problems travelers had with their intellectual capacity for *recognizing* what they saw, heard, or felt—struggles that produced accomplishments as well as failures. I found the concept of recognition useful and illuminating, especially when I pondered the richness of connotations it takes on if I let it reverberate, as I often do with philosophical concepts, in my native language. Three German glosses for "recognition" come to mind: *Erkennen* (perhaps even *Kennen*), as in "I know this person or object when I see them" (an act of cognition); *Wiedererkennen*, as in "I know this person or object because I remember them" (an act of memory); and *Anerkennen*, as in "I give this person or object the recognition they ask for and deserve" (an act of acknowledgment).[5] Actually, there is a fourth possible way to translate "recognition" that raises important issues in current debates about ethnography. It should at least be mentioned though I will not dwell on it in this context: "recognizing a speaker" is a kind of technical term, part of the rules of order that govern meetings. To be recognized means to be given a voice; giving a voice to the people we study by including so-called native texts and protocols of conversations in our writings has become a preoccupation in much of recent ethnography.

With the three major connotations—*Erkennen, Wiedererkennen,* and *Anerkennen*—in mind, let me now turn first to difficulties explorers of Central Africa had with recognizing others as persons. The more I read, the more appalled and intrigued I became by how little recognition European travelers had for the Africans they met. When positive impressions were recorded, they were rarely maintained; statements of recognition were made with reluctance, frequently to be taken back in the same sentence. An example of this is an observation Hermann Wissmann (later von Wissmann) noted when he reported on his encounter with one of the most impressive East African rulers of the time, a conqueror and serious political player in a game that included Arab-Swahili colonizers:

At Mirambo's I had a most friendly reception (with two bottles of champagne and a slaughtered ox). This, the most important negro I met in Africa, is thoroughly misjudged [*verkannt*, lit. misrecognized] in Europe; I spent three extremely interesting days with this bellicose prince who must inspire respect even in a European. (*MAGD* 3, no. 4 [1883]: 253)

Prejudice, racism, and an obsession with maintaining superiority may account for such twisted, or strained, compliments ("even in a European"). Many similar statements could be quoted. On the whole, Africans quite simply were denied recognition by the very people who, at great expense, often at the cost of their lives, ventured into Africa in order to study, among other things, its peoples. Such denial was in glaring contrast with the fact that it was vital for explorers to *receive* recognition if they wanted to carry out their work. Some knew that a give-and-take was needed for this relationship to work, and said so. But even the Belgian Jérôme Becker, who went farther than most of his colleagues in this respect, eventually defended an outright colonialist position. Toward the end of his travelogue, he explicitly reflects on the need for *reconnaissance* ("recognition" not "reconnaissance"),[6] if he is to maintain his position as the absolute chief of Karema, one of the *stations scientifiques et hospitalières* set up by Belgian expeditions on the eastern shore of Lake Tanganyika. Yet, he concludes that any appeal to *mutual* recognition would undermine his authority and be incompatible with the European's mission as the emissary of a superior race (1887, 2:333–34). Except for the Hungarian Emil Torday who, as far as I can tell, was the only one to condemn colonization as an injustice, and not counting occasional fits of whimsy among others, all of our travelers were convinced that their assignment to produce knowledge was enhanced rather than endangered by maintaining superiority and distance. It was not for them to ponder the epistemological consequences of exercising power by denying recognition to the people they met.

Moving on to recognition as *Wiedererkennen,* one finds in these travelogues another kind of failure, or refusal, to recognize which is even more intriguing. For years, I have told my students, perhaps a bit flippantly, that the kinds of things explorers and ethnographers sought and found in Africa and eventually reported as strange customs, such as spectacular fertility rites, processions, harvest festivals, masked dances, and whatnot, could in the last third of the nineteenth century also have been found less than ten miles outside Oxford or Cambridge, and certainly in the villages around Berlin, Brussels, or Vienna. If this view is even half correct then it is striking how little *déjà vu,* recognition as remembrance, was expressed when explorers made notes on the demeanor, speech, daily work, seasonal worries, and so forth of African peasants. Of course, logic demands that we note the possibility that such things simply were not part of the memories that would be shared by the middle-class urbanites who became explorers and professional anthropologists. However, at least one traveler in my sample, the German physician Willy Wolff, realized, and dared to spell out, the serious consequences that such forgetfulness could have: "When comparisons are made with other races, especially with the white race, the negroes usually are not matched with the majority of the other people, the rural population. Generally, most of the travelers and writers have in mind their own person and social class when they make comparisons" (Wolff 1889, 197).

If failure to remember was the rule, exceptions indicate that there was nothing inherent in Africans that prevented explorers from recognizing the familiar in the strange. Consider, for instance, one of the admittedly rare flashes of humanity that our travelers cared to record, showing how such recognition could be given, without much reflection, on a existential level. This is how Wissmann described a meeting with an African woman:

[She had something] that made us forget that we had before us just a half-clothed negro woman from the savage interior, something that unconsciously made us behave toward her as to an elderly lady from our home country. The feeling of contempt, which the European often has when he first deals with savages, soon disappears; one no longer notices the people's nudity, and one also learns to distinguish faces, something that is very difficult in the beginning. . . . (Wissmann 1889, 151)

There are other instances where travelers gave evidence of recognition on a more theoretical level. I found a passage documenting recognition as *Wiedererkennen* early in Wolff's travelogue, when their ship is passing Dahomey on its way to the Congo. Wolff observed some "Fetischpriester," (fetish priests), working their magic to protect the boats that had to cross the dangerous surf that prevented larger vessels from anchoring close to the coast. "I am firmly convinced," he says, "that these people have the same success as the processions that in many regions of Europe are supposed to pray to heaven for rain or otherwise favorable weather" (1889, 35).

Similarly, the Belgian Camille Coquilhat expressed *recognition* in this observation about drinking parties he saw on the banks of the Congo: "These drinking conventions sometimes take on gargantuan proportions and in that case, instead of ending like a scene in a picture by Teniers [the Flemish genre painter], they often finish with squabbles that degenerate into bloody fights" (1888, 267). Notice that this statement conforms to a pattern we noted earlier: Recognition may be stated ("comme une scène d'un tableau de Teniers") only to be taken back in the same breath. Were the Flemish drinking scenes Teniers had in mind always as peaceful as they were made to appear in genre painting?

Among exceptional signs of recognition are some "comparative" observations made by two German travelers. One of these observations comes again from Wolff, and concerns the custom of administering the poison ordeal to those who are accused of having caused the death of a person: "Terrible as this custom may at first seem, this Vehmic court is by far less grisly than the witch trials that were fashionable among us for such a long time" (1889, 52). Richard Böhm makes essentially the same point when he qualifies African practices of pursuing sorcerers as expressive of a primitive stage of development because they resemble what "we" have left behind (1888, 92). Such moments demonstrate that comparison can be made to work in two directions: identifying and distancing. Wolff expressed solidarity with, while Böhm set himself apart from, Africans. Interestingly enough, on other occasions both authors use the same formula to designate similarities they see between African and European practices (past, in Böhm's case, present in Wolff's). They call what Africans do "ländlich-sittlich," literally "rural-ethical/customary," that is, acceptable by the standards of a rural society (Böhm 1888, 69; Wolff 1889, 54).

Whereas it seems that explorers usually suppressed recognition (as remembrance) with regard to persons, practices, and institutions, they would frequently recognize familiar features in the African countryside. With the consistency of a topos, re-cognition as remembering is evoked in countless descriptions of the physical environment (which thereby turns into a recognizable landscape). Because such "memories" are so frequent, one is tempted to overlook the fact that their implications for the theme of recognition may vary a great deal.[7] I am certain closer analysis would reveal other differences, but here are examples that suggest a major distinction among superficially similar observations.

On many occasions Paul Pogge, the German explorer of the route to the Lunda capital, recorded landscapes (but also flora and fauna and even implements), stating that they are "very similar to the north German [landscape]" (see 1880, 102, 114). The climate in Musumba "resembles that of north Germany but is less hot" (130). Frogs call at night and their croaking reminds him of "the sound one hears the frogs make in the ponds of north Germany during the season of beautiful summer nights. . . . Indeed, the nights in Inchibaraka resemble the beautiful June nights of north Germany" (180). Throughout the book he localizes recognition when he invariably adds *nord* to *deutsch*. For the native of Mecklenburg this is a compliment; it expresses a specific, highly personal kind of recognition with a message encoded also in reference to his *Heimat*, the part of the world where he grew up, hence to something that touches on his identity.

A different kind of remembering of (features of) landscapes may be qualified as cultural rather than personal; it is aesthetic, artistic, often literally picturesque. Such mediations of memory—sometimes several layers of them—are documented in the following examples. Böhm and Paul Reichard, members of the German East Africa Expedition, traveled down a river where they encountered many *maçáka* (Swahili *chaka*, clump of trees). One day they passed some "that, with the grotesque forms of their towering trees, reminded one of Doré's illustrations of Dante's *Inferno*" (*MAGD* 3, no. 3 [1882]: 213). Becker, describing nature returning to take over an abandoned village, tells us that the scene reminds him of the growth that "covers the remnants of castles in Alsace or the Rhineland . . . it is Life itself singing above Nothingness" (1887, 1:204), an instance of "romanticizing" in the strict sense of the word. He also tells of his German colleague Dr. Emil Kaiser who was critically ill with fever and had himself carried onto a hill he had named *Venusberg* (after one of the "Seven Mountains" near Bonn, with or without a Wagnerian *double entendre*? [2:197]).

Finally, a most intriguing example of this topos is reported by Richard Büttner, a member of the German Congo Expedition. His caravan came to a village in mountainous country: "The village, although located at a high altitude, is surrounded by mountains that are still higher. Kornelius insisted that one of them resembled the Pilatus [a mountain near Luzern in Switzerland]" (1890, 125). This passage gets its poignancy from the fact that Büttner's companion "Kornelius" (Cornelius Bardo) was an educated African from Ghana who had been to Europe and now, in a part of Africa that was new to him, used his memories much like the European travelers. Incidentally, the episode shows that the travelers exchanged and sometimes debated images of recognition.

That recognition could also become appropriation (and then take on a slightly crazy twist) is evidenced in a passage in one of Böhm's published letters to his relatives and friends. He observed that the mountain country of Usagara (in what is now Tanzania) "gives the impression of southern Switzerland. Sometimes the African props make a truly striking impression in scenery that so much resembles European landscapes; the troupes of . . . black warriors, bands of monkeys, parrots, and hornbills don't really fit this frame" (1888, 56).

It was not only landscapes that inspired recognition; the fauna and flora, and even meteorological events, brought up memories ("a real Belgian rain," exclaims one of the Belgian writers). Above all, recognition came into play when travelers described African physiognomies, another source of "scientific" knowledge they liked to tap—occasionally to support their moral judgments of persons, mostly to classify traits and types. All of them associated physiognomy with character, race, and class— faces were qualified as more or less "negroid" or more or less noble. If one added, as it was often done, pairs of qualifiers such as stupid/intelligent, vulgar/refined, honest/shifty, the game of physiognomy had a large number of possible permutations that could be passed off as specific observations. And this is not even counting the fact that physiognomic judgments could be derived also from parts of the face (eyes, nose, mouth, forehead). Nor does it cover confusion and equivocation due to a failure to distinguish between the form of a face (its morphology, one could say) and the expression inferred from the way a face was set or used in communication. Also, many statements about faces are in fact interpretations of gaze (someone looks honest), that is, of intentions and messages expressed in situated contexts of interaction. In other words, physiognomic observations were too varied and confused to support the typifications or generalizations most travelers derived from them.

Especially in instances where remembrance and acknowledgment reinforce each other, recognition entails some form of reaching out. Therefore, it is often not easy to draw the line that separates recognition from projection. The following (admittedly rather exceptional) passages by Coquilhat leave one with an eery feeling of uncertainty—did he rec-

ognize the familiar in the strange, or did he cover the strange with familiar images? Juxtaposed, the two texts I am about to quote offer yet
another example of unresolved contradictions in pronouncements about
Africans. Coquilhat first addresses the notorious difficulties Europeans
seem to have telling African faces apart (see also Wissmann's statement
quoted earlier): They all look alike. Not so, he says; "an extended study
makes [the European] see all the kinds of physiognomy which exist
among us" (1888, 330). As if sensing that he may have gone too far with
this extraordinary admission, he continues with a "toutefois," "nevertheless": "Nevertheless the gaze/expression of the Congolese from the interior generally indicates a certain degree of dissimulation, deceit, and defiance. I know of exceptions to this rule, but only very few" (330). Then,
immediately following this paragraph, Coquilhat treats us to the following gallery of portraits:

To me, the Bangala express a series of well-defined types. Mata-Buiké represents,
under ordinary circumstances, the subtle geniality of a peasant from Normandy,
but when he is preoccupied with something disagreeable, his fatherly face
becomes uncommonly hard. Mata-Monpinza recalls the placid disposition of a
worthy justice of the peace. Mongonga has the rotundity of Roger Bontemps; in
the manner of the well-to-do he deigns to laugh now and then, something that
permits him to show off the beautiful teeth of the unbridled cannibal that he is.
Nyamalembe seems to be smiling and crying at the same time. Mata-Ipéko has
the cold correctness of a public prosecutor. Mata-M'Popo is the good fellow and
libertine. Monpata is a serious and energetic type. Monganga-Doua has seen it
all; his gait is solemn and he carries his head like the holy sacrament. N'Joko is a
thirty-five-year-old dandy, at the same time good-hearted and a family man. Im-
bembé has the distinction of a well-bred plotter. Muélé has the external appearance of a tough businessman. N'Gélé expresses insolence without being conscious of it, etc. As to the women, I easily discover, among the young ones, the
coquettish type, the modest, the cold, the excited, the dainty, the down-to-earth
and, among the old ones, I immediately recognize the fusspot, the gossip, the
harpy, the good housewife, the one who regrets her chubbiness. (330)

At least as far as African men are concerned—all of the persons named in
this text are chiefs or notables he has observed in endless meetings and
negotiations—Coquilhat demonstrates his physiognomic method's
dialectical capacity to make of individuals generic types and, in doing

this, to restore to them a concreteness that enables the reader to relate to persons who would otherwise have remained indistinct cannibal Bangala. To some extent, this even works in his characterization of women; while they remain generic, they are not presented as just one undifferentiated category.[8]

There is another aspect of recognition that can be detected in our sources. In events that produce understanding and knowledge, recognition often comes suddenly (a trait the three kinds of recognition we distinguished earlier seem to share). Torday reports how such an event became for him a kind of conversion experience. On one occasion he had taken a boat ride down the rapids of the Congo river near the later Stanleyville/Kisangani. Here is how he describes what happened to him:

I think those seconds were the most glorious of my life and it came as a revelation to me that these negroes, for whom I had had the contempt that many a civilized man feels towards savages, were giants compared to me, and from that moment my heart went out to them. I do not mean to say that I was aware of this sentiment at once; all I really felt was the admiration that no man can withhold from the strong and the brave; and as with women pity is often the first step on the path to love, with men admiration leads to sympathy and friendship. (1913, 29)

That recognition (as *Erkennen*) comes suddenly (in "seconds") and that it may be irresistible evokes the notion of "involuntary memory," that is, of recognition as *Wiedererkennen*. Usually it is associated with Proust and Baudelaire; here I would like to quote a passage I happened to come upon recently when I read Paul Auster's *City of Glass*, part of his *New York Trilogy*. It is about a father remembering his child:

Every once in a while, he would suddenly feel what it had been like to hold the three-year-old boy in his arms—but that was not exactly thinking, nor was it even remembering. It was a physical sensation, an imprint of the past that had been left in his body, and he had no control over it. (1992, 5)

For reasons that will become clear presently, two things are important in the kind of remembering recorded (or imagined) by Auster: it is involuntary in that the subject cannot control it and it is, as it were, a bodily function. Among our travelers, Ludwig Wolf reports bodily, physical effects of recognition he observed when he met a group of Kuba who (he assumed or was told) had never before seen a European or a riding ox. Notice the double layer of interpretation in this passage: Wolf can ascribe the meaning he gives to the reactions he describes because he *recognizes* them—even certain gestures that presumably were not part of his cultural repertoire—as responses to experiences that called for recognition.

> Then some of them, speechless with wonderment, covered their mouths with their cupped hands; others, holding their spears, aimlessly ran back and forth; while a woman stared at me with an expression of utmost surprise, forcefully pinching herself in her abdominal folds so that the pain she inflicted on herself was mirrored in her face. (Wissmann et al. 1891, 227)

Control and bodily function are also involved when we speak of denying or suppressing recognition of alterity. The enterprise of exploration as well as the exercise of scientific observation to which most explorers were committed were supported by a regime of "tropical hygiene." Explicit rules (set down in manuals and instructions) and implicit norms saw to it that European travelers protected themselves at all times, physically and mentally, against the environment, the people, but above all against any involuntary reactions, sentiments, passions, and memories that might cause them to lose control.[9]

This is perhaps also the moment at least to mention related issues such as alterity and smell, standards of cleanliness, fear of touch, the view of miscegenation as contamination and pollution, and associating skin color with moral qualities. That all these perceptions, reactions, and beliefs affect recognition of others (and that many of them are embedded in involuntary memory) hardly needs pointing out. In fact, inasmuch as it is out of control—because it befalls us or just happens—recognition (including, I would insist, the kind that is part of ethnography) is a matter of passion rather than action. Consequently we may have to distinguish between suppressing and refusing to give recognition. Only the latter seems to be addressed in the civilized discussions of intercultural politics of recognition we will look at in the next section.

At this point I should dispel an impression I do not want to give with texts like the quotation from Torday, namely that most pronouncements that are relevant to the topic of memory and recognition in the production of ethnographic knowledge are of a personal nature. The battle for recognition that was started by these early colonial encounters had dimensions that transcended personal motives and capacities. Under cover of scientific exploration, travelers were sent out to collect information about economic resources and political structures and, wherever possible, to secure national interests by preparing conditions for the eventual occupation of territories. They did this by extracting treaties and concessions, often exploiting and manipulating local tensions, and, above all, by proving that their expeditions could get past barriers that African, Afro-Portuguese, and Arab-Swahili merchants and political rulers had put up to prevent Europeans who operated from the coasts from getting direct access to resources located in the interior of the continent. Still, these economic and political objectives (sold, incidentally, to the European and American public as a campaign against slavery) were mediated by actual contacts that were made by persons whose immediate tasks involved the production of knowledge about Africa and its peoples. All the travelers whose writings I studied experienced contradictions between the pursuit of knowledge and conquest; many had a surprisingly clear grasp of their predicament.

Conditions of ethnographic research changed when colonies were fully established (though less dramatically than was often assumed) and then again when direct colonization was replaced by postcolonial absentee imperialism. But there are as many reasons today as there were a century ago to ponder the epistemological significance of recognition and its denial. What this involves I would now like to elucidate further by taking a brief detour through current philosophical thought.

Philosophers on the Politics of Recognition

Recognition, as a gloss for the German term *Anerkennung*, has been a topic of philosophical reflection inspired by Fichte and Hegel.[10] Through the writings of Frantz Fanon and Jean-Paul Sartre it became a topos in the critique of colonial oppression. For "radical" social scientists of the sixties and seventies, the master-slave chapter in Hegel's *Phenomenology of the Spirit* or, more often, its interpretation by Kojève (1969), was a canonical text, read and discussed in seminars and taught to undergraduates as an introduction to dialectical thinking. In anthropology, *dialectical* signaled a current that made the critique of naive scientism in our theories and practices of research a central concern (there were similar efforts in sociology, psychology, political science, and history, although—remember—the preferred adjective for these currents was *phenomenological*). In the American context, probably because it was prepared for this by philosophical pragmatism, the reception of critical theory as formulated by the Frankfurt School led to calls for "reinventing anthropology" (Hymes 1974a), rallying those who demanded that critique had to go beyond collective expressions of guilt and remorse that dominated the so-called ethics debate of the period. Critique, it was realized, had to address our practices of knowledge making, that is, the epistemology of our discipline, from ethnographic methods to the construction of anthropology's object. This movement ran its course but not, as is now widely recognized, without giving the decisive impulse and many of its central issues to the so-called postmodern turn that continues to dominate theoretical debates in anthropology.

In the postmodern climate that anthropology shares with many other fields, the concept of recognition, together with recourse to Hegel, has reemerged in attempts to come to grips with pressing issues posed by multiculturalism, feminism and gender studies, and the strife of ethnic identities (Taylor 1992, 1993, 1994, Huntington 1998). As far as I can see, philosophical reflections and theorizing on recognition, though they may be said to be about politics of recognition, are primarily addressed to ethics, that is, to devising universally valid theories of the good life (where the "universe" in *universal* is often the nation-state).[11] As Axel Honneth, inspired by Hegel, Habermas, and G. H. Mead, put it, the task is to define "the structural elements of ethics that can be abstracted normatively from the multitude of all specific ways of life with a general view regarding how self-realization can be made communicatively possible" (Honneth 1994, 276; my translation). In his comments on Hegel's *Realphilosophie*, Honneth at one point offers an opening for thought about recognition in the sense of re-cognition when he states that the fight for recognition is not aimed at simply hurting or overpowering the other; the aim is "sich dem Anderen gewissermassen wieder zur Kenntnis zu bringen," "to get, as it were, known again by the Other" (75). This *wieder*/again is the re- in recognition. But connections to memory or remembering are not further pursued, and when Honneth later speaks of the fight for recognition as "in Erinnerung . . . rufen," "recalling, reminding," this is qualified with a "nur", "only" (79), as an act that is secondary and hence not really constitutive of recognition.

Not surprisingly, Honneth is most interested in the phase of the battle for recognition from which Hegel derives the institutionalization of *Anerkennung* in systems of law that provide the foundation of civil society. Inasmuch as this is posited as a necessary element (by Hegel and to some extent by Honneth), there would be no way to interpret the colonial encounter, the initial *Kampf um Anerkennung,* "fight for recognition," as an open process. Explorers and Africans did not meet, as it were, in a natural state of Hobbesian struggle; but neither was there a common ground of *Recht,* of institutionalized legitimacy, between intruders and intruded upon. There were good reasons for the many forms in which colonial regimes tried to camouflage their true intentions which were *verbrecherisch,* "criminal," a concept central in another text by Hegel, his *System der Sittlichkeit* (see Honneth 1994, chap. 2). Colonial powers claimed universal rights or pretended to act within existing legitimacy when they appointed "traditional" chiefs in order to establish indirect rule (often revealing "tradition" as a potentially hypocritical notion).

Honneth, though he acknowledges Hegel's influence on Fanon and Sartre (1994, 249–51), is not concerned with struggles for recognition outside the institutionalized ethics and legitimacy of what he calls *Gesellschaft,* "society," although it is clear that he has the nation-state in mind. His aim is to show that a theory of recognition as a "grammar of social conflicts" (thus the subtitle of his essay) can and should be the core of a "a normative, yet substantive theory of society" (259). For my taste, this comes too close to a Durkheimian moralization of social theory, the functionalist elegance of which is regarded by many anthropologists too high a price to pay for the losses it entails on the side of cultural and historical difference and specificity. Right now, nothing seems to concern critical intellectuals, liberals, neoliberals, conservatives, and many who were once engaged in radical projects, more than the loss of society's (the state's?) moral authority. They lament the disappearance of values on all levels, from communitarian and national to global (forgetting in the latter case that it is not certain either that there ever were global values that could disappear or that a global context can ever be one of shared values).

What troubles me about theories of this sort is that their overwhelming concern with ethics, rights, and laws may once again endanger the unfinished epistemological project of a critical anthropology. "Substantive" ethics, if it is not to become the worst kind of ethnocentric righteousness in the guise of supposedly universal principles, needs to be grounded in knowledge of the ways of life that often are other than those shared by the inventors of ethical systems. Obtaining such knowledge is not primarily a matter of ethics. If anything, producing knowledge of others who do not subscribe to our "systems of values, norms, and beliefs" (as we used to call it) is anthropology's continued raison d'être in this so-called postcolonial era.

If I had to make a choice, I would side with the Enlightenment view of the problem. Ignorance and moral weakness may contribute equally to messing up the world; but our chances of doing anything about this are better when we attack error and ignorance. I also believe that this must be anthropology's choice. Anthropology's task is to produce empirical knowledge of others *and* to address the question of the possibility and validity of such knowledge, a question that is not answered by invoking consensus in a community of scholars. This is why anthropologists can go along with, say, Rorty (1980) and Taylor (1995) when they reject epistemology understood as an ultimately metaphysical foundation of all possible knowledge. Anthropologists must part company with them when they seem to suggest that communitarian consensus as such suffices to legitimize practices of inquiry. To repeat a point already made (and in this chapter exemplified by those initial encounters that took place in the course of "exploration"): Such a consensus simply cannot be assumed in the study of others except at the price of relapsing into a positivist stance. As I see it, anthropology cannot do without an epistemology that, rather than providing foundations, consists of critical and public reflection on every step and level of knowledge production, with "the public" including our own societies as well as those we study.

I have tried to make my contribution to this task by exploring conditions of possibility of ethnographic inquiries across cultural boundaries. I argued that they rest on intersubjectivity, created and expressed by language, dialogue, and joint performances (see chapter 1), all of them involving the sharing of time and hence *recognition of anthropology's subjects as coeval.* In a book and several essays I exposed a history of denying recognition (Fabian 1983, 1991a) and I tried to write ethnographies that do not hide what I called their conditions of possibility (most recently Fabian 1996). In my current thinking about recognition as re-cognition and its role in the production of knowledge about others I see the following arguments emerge.

To recognize those whom we study as coeval participants in communicative exchanges is a decisive step away from ethnographic research conceived as natural history or as an operation following the rules of positivist science. Recognition is a condition that makes communication possible but—and here is the point where we inevitably are led to ponder Hegel—it is an agonistic relationship; it involves participants in confrontation and struggle. Recognition is not something that one party can simply grant to the other; *Annerkennung* is not doled out like political independence or development aid. Recognition may be defined by legal rights, but in situations in which ethnographers usually work, it is achieved through exchanges that have startling, upsetting, sometimes profoundly disturbing consequences for all participants.[12]

Awareness of this has been expressed in much thoughtful writing about anthropology's collusion, theoretical as well as practical, with Western imperialist and colonialist expansion. The better examples of such critical writing (those that go beyond crude and global indictments of anthropology as an imperialist science) have made us aware of the role of power and authority in research as well as in the presentation of our findings.[13] If anything, this trend has given us a more realistic understanding of our practices. But if we look at the effect such critical awareness has on our practices, we have no reason to be complacent about the current state of our discipline. Somehow we seem to be caught in a paralyzing bind between often bewildering postmodern strategies of "power-free" research and experimentation with new genres of writing, on the one hand, and efforts to find post-positivist foundations for scientific objectivity, on the other.

As I see the situation, one way to avoid postmodern escapism with its gratuitous celebration of "multivocality," as well as a new objectivism often characterized by calls to rally under the flag of "globalization," is to stand by recognition as a central issue *and* to avoid new closures, which, I think, are inevitable if we are too quick to construe new systems of universal ethics. Instead, we should travel farther on the road opened up by thought about re-cognition and adopt what is valuable in the current fascination with memory and identity. When we seriously consider the "re-" in recognition, and when we concentrate on recognition as an epistemological problem, we may be able to avoid the kind of positive thinking about identity (see chapter 5) that seems to characterize the philosophical trend of thought about the politics of recognition referred to earlier—a positivity that derives from accepting without much debate the nation-state or ethnicity as given frames of the debate.

Recognition and the Politics of Ethnography

Indépendance, cha-cha, tout oublié.

(Independence, cha-cha, all is forgotten.)

—Song by Joseph Kabassélé (ca. 1960)[14]

One of the conclusions I took away from the study of early ethnography was that knowledge of others is gained through communicative practices that require that both sides be able to transcend the confines of their cultures by reaching a common ground, or by traveling, as it were, back and forth between the grounds on which they stand. Put like this, communication across cultural boundaries becomes a problem of identity that can only be conceived in dialectical terms. Identity must be maintained because action needs an agent; it must be abandoned because no action, certainly not the kind of action intended in exploration and ethnography, could take place if identity were rigidly maintained. This apparent contradiction is resolved as soon as identity—and its recognition—is thought of, not as a property or state, but as a process. Except in limit cases that may be pathological, human beings everywhere (as individuals as well as collectivities) must be presumed to be engaged in identity-forming (hence identity-changing) activities and processes. This makes identity, of self as well as of other, a precarious matter and may be the reason why in Western thought, if we may use this summary notion to cover a vast variety of individual and collective processes, conceptions of identity (including the concept of culture) stress the necessity of control, spawning defensive measures of self-affirmation and often aggressive ways of presenting others as different.

The point I tried to make with examples culled from writing about African exploration is that recognition as re-cognition, that is, as the mobilization, or the "suffering," of memories that are at the core of personal identity, seems to be the cutting edge in relations with others that have a chance of producing knowledge. In *Time and the Other* I said something to this effect: In order to be knowingly in each other's presence we must somehow share each other's past. To put this provocatively, I am convinced that only when self and other get to a point where they begin to "remember the present"[15] will they be drawn into a process of mutual recognition based on the kind of knowledge that changes the knower and that by the same token re-constitutes his or her identity.

It may be said that I am playing it rather loose when I let myself be guided by connotations of "recognition" which are not obvious to those who do not care to follow me in the game of retranslating this Hegelian term into German. However, it is not etymology but reflection on anthropological practices that argues for thinking *Erkennnen, Anerkennen*, and *Wiedererkennen* together. The greatest gain to be derived from such an approach may be this: Put in the context of recognition, memory can be significant as an epistemological concept. This is not limited to, and should not be confused with, the meaning memory may have for cognitive scientists. But neither is the sense I gave to the term in these reflections on memory and alterity—and that may be even more important to point out—the one that has produced so much recent writing on places, regimes, and arts of memory. Remembering the Other quite simply (though there is nothing simple about the acts it involves) serves as a formula expressing the insight that the production of knowledge about others is based on perceptions that are transformed into memory such that they get us—remember the epigram by Mitchell—from cognition to recognition (and the other way around) because they involve us in identity-changing and identity-constituting relations with the subjects of our inquiries.

That is not all there is to ethnography. It would be silly to propose a sort of radical "commemorative" ethnography with the same naivete that one may find in certain calls for a communicative or dialogical ethnography, as if the panoply of scientific methods based on observing, measuring, classifying, and typologizing accumulated by our discipline during its history could simply be abandoned. But forays into the depth of thought about recognition may help us to discern between what has a chance of being productive and what, in our arsenal of procedures, should be marked for the junkyard.

Africa's Belgium

Introduction: Possessive Memories

The conference where I presented a first version of this chapter was called "Belgium's Africa." I took the possessive form in the title to express, above all, an interest in an intellectual appropriation of Belgium's colonial history by current African studies. When I speak of appropriation, I assume a direction of regard (from Belgium to Africa) and I have no illusions about the many connections, the many forms of admitted or silent complicity, between scholarly attention and what has been called the imperial gaze. This is not only a figure widely employed in critical discourse.[1] As we shall see, gaze is (or was) a reality in Belgium's Africa, observed with striking accuracy by its objects, the Congolese. The question I should like to ask in the reflections that follow is: Would it not be possible to take a fresh look at relations between Belgium and the Congo by reversing the gaze? Of course we cannot do this literally; I am not a Congolese and I cannot assume the other's gaze. Still, what I cannot do literally I may be able to do at least vicariously, by interpreting *témoignages* and documents I found dispersed in various studies I conducted in the past.[2]

Pioneered, in the field of African art, by Lips's *The Savage Hits Back* (1966 [1937]),[3] depictions of the colonizer in the plastic arts, in early painting on dwellings, and in contemporary popular paintings have received attention in recent years. As evidence for active, creative African response, they often served revisionist interpretations, rejecting the notion that colonization was endured merely passively. But depictions of the colonizer are not limited to visual images, and even in visual images references to the colonizer may not be recognizable without knowledge of the discourse that is articulated visually. There is much more to Congolese experience with, and images of, Belgium than certain stereotypical responses that can easily be detected and have been circulated by generations of colonials.

Before I go about substantiating this statement, I should briefly indicate some difficulties and limitations affecting any attempt at critical understanding by someone who, being neither Belgian nor Congolese, is an outsider to both parties in one of the most violent and intricate chapters of modern colonization. I must place my work in a context of interpretations and evaluations, as well as of firm beliefs and deep emotions.

Social scientists began to formulate retrospective and comparative theories of the colonization of Africa a generation ago.[4] Several characteristics were named as typical of the Belgian approach: its "Platonism," its paternalism, its triad of powers (government, companies, missions), and its distinctive hypocrisy. Platonism (the designation adopted by Hodgkin [1956]) was "a vision of the totalitarian unification of human ideals and utilitarian aims, the rigid stratification of society, and the pyramid-like distribution of access to goods and power."[5] Paternalism, though certainly an attitude not limited to Belgian colonization, was thought to have reached its most thorough form in the Congo (Onwumelo 1966). The power triad was rehearsed in most writing on the colonial Congo, usually with a glaring absence of attention to critical diversity and conflicts within each of the agencies involved. Hypocrisy, a term circulated more often informally in oral exchanges than in written analyses, was— again according to my recollections, not so much a moral judgment applied to individual colonial agents as a social characterization. It referred to the resolve of the essentially bourgeois class that determined Belgian colonial policy to live with unresolved contradictions; it was a quality of Platonism put into practice.

Deeper, and drawing on a history longer than that of such social-scientific figures of thought, is a layer of emotionally charged images and concepts that are apt to challenge and confuse the outsider. There is a certain kind of sentimentalism that has suffused Belgian-Congolese relations from the beginning and continues to do so in postcolonial times. On the side of the colonizer, this would come up again and again in invocations of heroic patriotism in carrying out the *oeuvre civilisatrice* (shared by Flemings and Walloons alike), of unselfish love of the natives, of the common destiny of Belgium and the Congo, even of an intimacy that excludes outsiders. Intimacy also served the colonized to think of colonial relations as gendered, as love and hate between man and woman (whereby, as we shall see, the roles were interchangeable). Related to this emotional complex are the many, often ineffable, shared habits of speech and conduct, styles of education and administration, standards of bourgeois respectability, influences of Flemish popular religiosity, and whatever else may have been part of a "colonial culture" whose reality we are only now beginning to appreciate and critically analyze.[6] I'll be the first to admit that the sense of ultimate failure that befalls anthropologists who have given much of their time and energy to studying a culture and to communicating their knowledge to others may also be experienced when we try to understand what was Belgian-Congolese about the colonization of the Congo.

And as if social science stereotypes and ineffable shared habits and sentiments were not enough to make us wary, things become further complicated when we deal, not with reality as it is "out there," but with memories of events, persons, and experiences; memories, furthermore, not as they are preserved in unique private recollections, but as they are shared and publicly expressed and documented. Such memories may simply be suffered; often they are mobilized in order to overcome suffering. They are involved in processes of identity construction; they are about positing a subject (a nation, a community) which makes history and to which history happens. It is not hard to predict that, as Belgian society moves toward coming to grips with its colonial past (somewhat in the fashion of German *Vergangenheitsbewältigung*), prodded by outside critics or not, it will have to confront the memories of those with whom it shares a past. Then it will find that Congolese have made remarkable efforts toward gaining shared understandings of their history.

Memories, Crude and Fine

Colonial experience was consigned to memory by the colonized ever since Belgium explored, occupied, and claimed the Congo as a colony. There were stories and songs, visual images, dances and theatrical performances. Few among these early expressions were documented as such.[7] I don't know of any comprehensive effort to collect such documents for the Congo before the postcolonial era. Two of the sources I will be using (the *Vocabulary of the Town of Elizabethville* and Tshibumba Kanda Matulu's history of Zaire) draw on oral transmission of memory, and are somewhat extraordinary in that they were written or painted; a third source will be ethnographic work with popular theater as performed by the Groupe Mufwankolo in Lubumbashi.[8]

It's a Bitch, Being Colonized

I begin with a chapter from the *Vocabulary* (the division into paragraphs is my own).

XXXIX. WISDOM AMONG THE SOLDERS

1. There was true wisdom among the SOLDIERS. In the old days we saw the government agents walking barefoot, and the police too. Thus the Belgians clothed the legs of the soldiers with gaiters, but the feet were bare. Then they had a cap, a belt, and a nightstick with which to beat the people. These were called Matracs [matraques].

2. Now, [the soldiers'] wisdom appeared in the war of Kenya. [In] this war, when the soldiers went to Kenya, their leader, their [sergeant] major, expressed regrets before them here at the station of E/ville. It was in the afternoon. He said: You, Colonel, and you, Bwana Maron Alphonse, listen to the story of a man who had a dog as his wife. This Bwana himself wanted the dog to be his wife. Truly, the dog agreed with this Bwana to be his wife. And, truly, they sinned. Then this man's dog got pregnant and gave birth to a child. This Bwana did not stop laughing when he saw that his wife, the dog, had given birth to a child that was fully human. It had a human appearance compared to his mother, the dog.

3. So this Bwana slept in the same bed with his child. The dog, on her part, thought: I, the dog, gave this Bwana a child and he will respect me. But there this poor dog was wrong. Everyday, this Bwana and the dog's child ate at

one table. So this mama went on thinking: I love this Bwana. This Bwana, on his part, did not think so.

4. Now, one day the dog tried to sleep in the bed of her lover, this white man. Truly, when this Bwana found her there, he chased his wife, this dog, away at once. He cursed her saying: Looo! What kind of a curse falls on me, the human husband, from this wife, the dog [who wants] to sleep with me in [my] bed. What does this mean, brothers? On that day, the poor dog was patient enough to think: perhaps this human husband of mine forgot who I am.

5. So, some other day his wife, the dog, saw this white man's boy [servant] lay the table. Lady dog told the boy, don't lay two places today, you must lay three. Truly, this boy thought to himself, perhaps another white man will visit us today. This boy laid the table for three persons, which is to say, three plates. Then it was time for this Bwana to come home and there he met his wife, the dog. She had already sat down at her husband's, the white man's, table. So this white man beat this poor dog.

6. And the poor dog asked him, why do you beat me? Her husband answered, because you are an animal, I am a White, a human being. Then the dog told him: Loo! Be cursed, child of dead wood [a curse]. Are you no white man if you don't mary a wife of your color? I have this child I myself gave birth to. How come you and my child sleep in one bed? And you eat with this child of mine, the one I myself gave birth to, at one table. Now I, the child's mother, am an animal in your eyes?

7. Listen to this Premier Sergeant Major, how he gave an example to the Whites, the Belgians. The meaning of this fable was: Among the Whites there were those who loved our wives and our children. But they did not like to eat with us, nor to sleep with us in one bed. Only with our women they liked to eat and to sleep. This is the fable which this Premier Sergeant Major told the Belgians when they left for the war of Kenya. And the dog's child, that is the Mulatto; [her] mother is the wife. Now, for them, the mother of the dog, that's us. The child is the wife who lives with them in one house and eats with them.

8. That is the fable this Premier Sergeant Major gave to his Bwana Colonel and to Bwana Governor Alphonse Maro[n]. And he said, we fought the war of 1914 until the war ended in 1918. Ever since, we the soldiers have worn shorts and [gone] barefoot, without putting on shoes. And we sleep in tiny houses, like latrines. But from this day on, as we are leaving for your war, we want to be certain that we will no longer be beaten with a stick. This is now impossible. And we demand, be it in this or the next war, that, as a white man can have a war command, so can a black Sergeant Major. And if we get out of this war and come back here we don't want to wear shorts any more, and gaiters and go bare-

foot without shoes. We cannot accept this [any longer]. And we want to see decent housing.

9. This is why you see that the soldiers nowadays have all these things. On that day, at the station, the Whites lamented and their madames ground their teeth. They themselves cried and shed tears. And all of us—there was not a person who went [to the station] without a pack of cigarettes, or some bread, to give to those soldiers who went to war. This is the story of the war of Kenya. (Fabian 1990a, 115–18)

Comment. One possible position to take on this kind of text (certainly the most tempting one) is to assume that it hardly needs interpreting of, or arguing about, its manifest message. Clearly, the story is an allegory of Congolese response to the Belgian colonial rule. The general mood of the feelings expressed is familiar. We have come to expect complaints and recriminations from countless similar stories and, even though we may sympathize with the colonized, we are tempted to file this account away in that vast category of "reactions to conquest." Now, I would like to contend that nothing, including prejudice and bigotry, is a greater obstacle to confronting colonial, in this case Congolese, memories than this kind of embracing as already familiar what in fact challenges our capacity to understand. The challenge is to take this kind of document not only as a token of reaction, not as the image of a state of mind, certainly not as a generic and folkloric response, but as a *protocol of action*, as a *script for performing memories*. To indicate this emphasis on action and on the (often artful) crafting of shared recollections, I shall call these practices "memory-work."

We can bring out the pragmatic structure of this text when we ask: What is being communicated, how, and to whom?

The centerpiece, the most visible and, as I argued in Fabian 1990a, falsely familiar, feature is the fable of a man and his wife. However, this particular instance of the genre has some features one would not expect in the usual animal story. The narrative mixes human and animal protagonists (in this case a domestic animal). This, as far as I can tell, is uncommon, but the most salient break with animal stories from the "traditional" repertoire occurs when the metaphorical animality of one of the actors is itself made a topic by being rejected (paragraph 6). This transports the narrative from the world of exemplary stories to that of actual human relations. This is a fable that denies being a fable; a metaphor that negates a metaphor affirms a reality.

Furthermore, the fable is framed by the account of an actual event. The location is specified, a speaker is identified, and so are the people to whom he addresses his story (paragraphs 1–2). Of special interest is a seemingly minor detail, the naming of the governor of Katanga (1941–45), Amour Maron, whose first name is here given as Alphonse. There are intertextual reasons for this. Maron was the government representative who confronted and brutally broke the miners' strike of 1941 at Elisabethville. In the *Vocabulary's* account of that event he is also called Alphonse. That makes what he did even more heinous. We are told that the first person shot by Maron himself was a Congolese, a certain Alphonse, with whom the governor "had an understanding" and—this is a cultural thing that "goes without saying"—to whom he should have been tied by the special relation of friendship that is expected to exist between namesakes.[9]

The fable is embedded in history. Not only that, both the fable and the historical anecdote are again in turn recollections (those of the author of the *Vocabulary* and/or of his informants or sources). They state facts of colonial experience (such as denying footwear to soldiers [paragraphs 1, 8–9) that made the storyteller utter recriminations on the memorable occasion here described.

Finally, the text is a chapter from a history of Elisabethville, written a few years after the Congo became independent. It was mimeographed and obviously intended for wider distribution. The work was sponsored by an association of former domestic servants (a category, as the *Vocabulary* states, that included all sorts of servants of the colonial regime, among them soldiers). In other words, these memories are recorded by a group that occupied a specific position in postcolonial society and they are used to formulate demands for the future.[10] It is characteristic of the early postcolonial period that the addressee of the demands remains vague; the *Vocabulary* speaks to the political powers in a period of transition from the Katanga secession to a unified Congolese state, but certainly also to the former colonial rulers.

In the text, the presence of the Belgians is required for the story to make sense; this is not a generalizing, moralizing fable that may be understood almost anywhere. Present are also many of the images and figures I listed in the introduction. Colonial relations are depicted as domestic and gendered, only to be revealed as hypocritical and inhuman.[11] Racism asserts itself in the (fulfilled) desire for sexual transgression and in the rejection of the partner who cannot even claim the child she gave birth to as one of her kind (paragraphs 2, 6).[12] In this Bwana's household, eating is denied, and physical violence is the response to the wife's pathetic attempt to get her presence at the common table recognized (paragraph 6). There is not only a moral but also a strong sentimental element in her story that makes it one of unrequited love. Throughout, one senses a desire, and hope, for recognition. In a more literal translation, the last line of paragraph 4, for instance, reads: "Perhaps this human husband of mine forgot on his side to know me."[13] Not immediately obvious, but nonetheless striking, are indications of how far the wife/colonized had been prepared to meet the husband/colonizer: husband and wife eating at the same table, children sleeping close to their parents, were not practices endorsed by tradition. All this willingness to comply and adapt was to no avail. In the end, all that remains for the dog is to curse her husband.

This is but a sketch of some of the features that make the text relevant for this essay (a more thorough treatment would have to include more attention to its linguistic context, to its literary form, to problems of translation, and so forth). Still, I hope to have made clear what I meant by memory as action. Crude as the fable may at first appear as yet another story of Belgium as the victimizer, "Wisdom among the Soldiers" is constructed with a finesse that makes it an interpretive intellectual challenge of the highest order.

Getting "Booked": Exploration and Writing

The "Wisdom among the Soldiers" story distills relations with the colonizer to their experienced essence. It would be wrong, however, to create the impression that African victims worked out the meaning of colonization only in totalizing images of moral outrage—the expected reaction to the traumatic impact that European expansion is supposed to have caused wherever it hit the African continent.[14] The documents we have show that, much like enlightened and critical scholarly studies of imperialism, popular thought and memory see colonization as a complex historical process consisting of more than the exercise of military and moral force.[15] Again and again one is struck by surprising connections popular historians draw between events, connections that at first seem to violate the chronological conventions and schemes academic historiography uses to impose order through periodization. Equally remarkable is their penchant for dwelling on often tiny detail, on objects and anecdotes that become vignettes capable of condensing experiences and interpretations, evidence of an intellectual achievement that is the opposite of creating stereotypes. A favorite of mine, from the *Vocabulary*, epitomizes what I said about returning the imperial gaze: "Behold in your thoughts: The great King [Leopold II] put his hand to his white beard and talked [to himself] looking at the map of Africa" (Fabian 1990a, 67).

With these points in mind, we may now turn to the history of Zaire as painted and told by Tshibumba Kanda Matulu. Though deeply embedded in the collective memory-work that is put into images in genre painting, his work is unequaled in scope and depth. While it certainly draws the grand picture, one of its outstanding qualities is attention to detail. The following fragment is quoted from Tshibumba's narrative accompanying painting no. 6 (in a series of more than one hundred; see Fabian 1996, 24).[16] At the bottom, the picture is inscribed in French: "Already in the sixteenth century Livingstone had met a caravan that came from Katanga village." The background shows a blue sky, empty except for two birds in flight. Below, we see bleak savanna country with the typical vegetation: some grass and small clumps of bushes and a single palm tree, spaced widely apart. A red laterite road cuts diagonally through the foreground from lower left to upper right. Livingstone stands on the road, on the left. He is clad in a white tropical suit or uniform and wears sturdy shoes and gaiters and a pith helmet. His gaze is fixed on the open book he holds in his left hand while he writes in it. A tall African, clad in a loin cloth and wearing bracelets and anklets, walks toward the explorer. In his right hand he carries a walking stick; his left is held up high, showing Livingstone a cruciform copper ingot, or *croisette*. Behind him, another African pulls a four-wheeled wagon loaded with *croisettes*. He does this with the help of a pole and a harness that is wrapped around his upper body. Two other men, one at the back, another at the left side, are pushing the vehicle. The three are clad like their leader. Here is what Tshibumba said about this painting:[17]

In the region of Katanga, Livingstone got to meet people from Katanga. They had come with a shipment of copper ingots from Katanga and were going to sell it in faraway places. And he was amazed to see for the first time a human being different from himself, with a color other than his. But, after all, he had set out to search [for wealth] and so he saw the copper ingots and the copper wire and other things on the cart they were pushing. "Where are they going [he thought] to sell that copper?" He asked them, but they simply had no language in which to communicate. They belonged to different peoples; one spoke the language of his home country, the other his, and so they failed to understand each other.

All right. [Someone] showed [Livingstone] the copper and pronounced the name of chief Katanga. And Livingstone wrote it down in his book. And Livingstone continued his travels; on his way he passed Lake Moero and came to Nguba, where he met black people who were producing salt. Then he arrived in Mulungwishi, and that is where he continued to teach the Protestant religion. Finally, he got tired and rested.

Livingstone in Katanga is one of three paintings in which Livingstone appears; the others show his famous meeting with Stanley and his death mourned by Africans. Within the entire series *Livingstone in Katanga* follows a picture of the discovery of the Congo by Diogo Câo. The intriguing inscription "already in the sixteenth century" repeats poetic licence Tshibumba also took on the Câo painting where an inscription makes Stanley a contemporary of the Portuguese seafarer (Fabian 1996, 22). Here I do not want to dwell on the significance of such chronological "mistakes,"[18] except to point out that as a rhetorical strategy—to depict periods of colonization as contemporary that are "in fact" separated by centuries—they allow popular historians to state that, from the point of view of the colonized, Câo, Livingstone, and Stanley were players in one and the same drama.[19] Tshibumba repeats this rhetorical gesture visually when he shows (again being anachronistic in the case of Câo) all three explorers in identical nineteenth-century colonial clothing (22–25). When I later questioned him about this, he insisted that the travelers' garb was (like) a military uniform. They were hired and paid to do a job, he said (29), and thereby showed—all the colonial heroizing notwithstanding—

the realistic understanding he had of exploration. It is not for him to imagine Europeans penetrating a jungle populated by wild beasts and savages. The painting we are looking at shows Livingstone *standing* on a trodden path cutting through the savanna. The Africans who *walk* to encounter him are engaged in the peaceful and highly specialized work of transporting copper over great distances (later the text also mentions another commodity, salt). I translate the term Tshibumba uses to describe the copper ingots, *mukuba*, pl. *mikuba*, as *croisette*, because that is what the picture shows: small crosses. In Belgian times, *mikuba* also designated the final product of copper mining and smelting: large ingots, no longer cruciform, destined to leave the Congo for treatment and sale in Europe. In his narrative Tshibumba connects "traditional" and modern copper mining essentially as what it was: Europeans "discovered" copper when they broke into ongoing operations. (Other examples of colonization appropriating what already existed would be political processes of state formation, long-distance trade, and Arab-Swahili agricultural colonization). At one point (39) Tshibumba even states that the technology of copper smelting Africans had practiced "since the days of old" was simply taken over by the Europeans, a statement not entirely unrealistic when we remember the very first artisanal operations of the Union Minière around 1906.

But back to Livingstone. The essential role assigned to him by Tshibumba is that of explorer and prospector for mineral wealth. Repeating a device noted earlier (the explorer stands, the Africans walk toward him) the painting here has an interesting iconological message: It is the African who, in a reversal of a gesture repeated in countless images since the age of discovery, holds up the "cross" to the European. The commodity so prominently displayed in the painting is not (yet) the explorer's object of desire for wealth. The *croisette* faces the book. Livingstone is collecting *written*—colonial discourse would call it scientific—knowledge, above all "geographical" information such as the name and location of the village where the copper caravan came from. Albeit briefly and elliptically, Tshibumba also shows his awareness that communicating, being able to exchange information in a shared language, was the foremost practical problem of exploration at that stage (Fabian 1996, 24, 29).

In the other two paintings/chapters of his history that Tshibumba devotes to Livingstone he is depicted as a counter figure to the ruthless Stanley. In the painter's account, Stanley, carrying a gun (Fabian 1996, 25, 29), never actually meets Africans, who always flee from him (a reason that his employer, King Leopold II, instructs him to make contact with Livingstone in order to get reliable information about the Congo [27]). Livingstone preaches the word of God, eventually learns to communicate, and when he dies he is buried and mourned by his African friends (31). Contrast and opposition are also expressed when Tshibumba repeatedly points out that Livingstone represented Protestantism, that is, the variety of Christianity perceived as non-Belgian. This connection is also encoded in his reporting Mulungwishi as the place where Livingstone died, which is factually inaccurate but historically significant. This village, situated on the road between Likasi and Tenke, had been the headquarters of the Methodist mission under Bishop Springer (hence the popular name for the place, *spilinga*, and for Methodist Congolese, *baspilinga*).

Tshibumba leaves no doubt, incidentally, that exploration soon turned into conquest and that this was a Belgian enterprise, even though neither Livingstone nor Stanley were Belgians. The latter, according to Tshibumba, was a Portuguese—another instance of factual error but poetic truth, considering his crucial role in the colonization of the Congo. In Tshibumba's pictorial language, the ambiguous status of Europeans engaged in fighting during the anti-Arab campaigns is indicated by their distinctive tropical dress that makes them look like explorers (Fabian 1996, 34, painting no. 12). The definitive change from exploration to military rule is then encoded in painting no. 13 where the execution of the defeated Arab leaders is commanded by a European officer and carried out by Africans, both in uniforms of the Force Publique, the colonial army (35).

I think these comments suffice to justify the claim I made regarding the subtlety of popular historiology when it employs a method I do not hesitate to call dialectical. It consists of construing the narrative by means of constant back-and-forth tracking between specific detail and totalizing statements and images. Interpretation must follow this movement if it is do justice to the documents. Of course, a further layer or dimension of complexity is added when oral accounts and pictorial representations are joined, as is the case with Tshibumba's history and in

Congolese popular painting generally (Fabian 1996, chaps. 1–3).[20] African memory-work has characteristically been a "multimedia" performance, as we shall see in the next and final section where I consider what and how popular theater contributes to remembering the colonial past.[21] If I end with popular theater this is not to say that the field is covered. Popular music (about which we get to know more in recent years) and popular storytelling (an area that calls for much future research) should at least be mentioned as sources for the study of "Africa's Belgium."[22]

Contested Memories

When I write or speak about the accomplishments of popular historiology I do not hide my admiration. Occasionally, critics find this irritating and accuse me of romanticizing my subject. I think one could do worse, but I admit that such criticism is invited when we appear, often constrained by the circumstances of our presentations, to give attention only to the finished products of popular thought and imagination, such as the texts and paintings discussed so far. Paradoxically, our interpretive exertions, intended to make texts and pictures come alive, may then contribute to their reification and to their, as I am tempted to call it, folklorization: Scholarly analyses often show popular culture that is interesting but has lost its bite. To prevent this from happening is in my view the task of ethnography, and often its most difficult one. What distinguishes the ethnographer from the literary scholar or art critic is that he or she has a responsibility that goes farther than to exhibit and interpret cultural objects/documents. We must not only consider their context and history—in a general way, literary and art critics do that, too—but give accounts that can count as ethnography because they are based on our presence and work among the people who make culture. This presence and work consist of observing, communicating, preparing and collecting documents (in the widest sense of the term), and, as one colleague (I believe it was James Clifford) has put it, "deep hanging out." By this I take him to refer to experiences and sources of knowledge that often, and sometimes only, come to us when we don't pursue them with our research schemes.

In the study of Tshibumba's history of Zaire I have tried to show

how this works and how it can be represented. In *Power and Performance* (Fabian 1990b) I had, as it were, rehearsed this approach in an ethnography of a piece of theater conceived and acted by the Groupe Mufwankolo of Lubumbashi. For the purposes of my argument here I could summarily restate my findings from that study. But I can do better and give a more vivid account by going back to field notes taken when I witnessed the preparations for another play, one that I was unable to record when it was performed. In other words, in this case I will have to report on memory-work without having a finished product before me (other than the notes in my diary which I am now going to follow).

Lubumbashi, June 17, 1986. The scene is an elegant, if a bit seedy clubhouse, the former Cercle Albert, one-time meeting place of the Belgian bourgeoisie that ruled Elisabethville. Now it is called Cercle Makutano, its social activities are modest, and its main attraction is the bar, which seems to be a watering hole for men of the Congolese upper class: university staff, mining engineers, administrators, and businessmen. From my previous stays in Lubumbashi I know many of them and enjoy taking part in their banter and gossip (in French and Swahili). The Cercle is one of the places in town where deals are made, intrigues hatched, and events transformed into memories and stories. For me, this particular evening was to be the beginning of one of the most exciting pieces of research I ever did, unplanned and, in fact, somewhat overwhelming. It began when Mufwankolo and Kachelewa, two old friends from the seventies and still the leaders of their troupe of actors, joined the crowd at the bar. What followed is described in *Power and Performance* (1990b, 3–5, chap. 4). Here is the gist of it: At the time, I was preoccupied with trying to trace the origin, and fathom the meaning, of a cultural axiom that had been quoted to me: *Le pouvoir se mange entier* (power is eaten whole). The three of us talked about it over drinks until it was time to start what Kachelewa and Mufwankolo had come for, one of the rehearsals of their group for which the Cercle Makutano provided its former ballroom.

In the book, I described my excitement when the leaders announced to the assembled actors and actresses that their next play, to be broadcast on television on the occasion of June 30, Independence Day, would be titled *Le pouvoir se mange entier*. The session turned into a veritable brainstorm. The saying was discussed with fervor and in great detail, and individual actors freely contributed their opinions and examples from their cultural background. Then Kachelewa, sensing that the meeting was getting out of control, reminded the assembly that they were there to plan for a play on June 30. Not only that, there was more work ahead. He announced that the Groupe Mufwankolo had been "voted" by the Catholic clergy and members of religious congregations to do a piece on the history of Christianity in Shaba/Katanga, to commemorate the seventy-fifth anniversary of the diocese of Lubumbashi. He began to say it should be a "history from Monsignor de Hemptinne . . . " (legendary and notorious founder of the Benedictine mission in Katanga) when one of the actors cut in, completing the phrase, " . . . to Abbé Kasongo," a reference, elliptic for the outsider, that was greeted with general mirth.

This could have remained one of the jokes and aleatory digressions I witnessed in most meetings of the group, but I soon realized that it marked a point of departure for taking a critical distance to a command performance intended to celebrate an important chapter of colonial history.

Abbé Pius Kasongo was a dissident priest who had become a leader in the neo-Pentecostal Catholic charismatic renewal. He was famous as a preacher and healer who attracted thousands from all walks of life. Defying the archbishop, he lived and conducted his activities at the parish compound in the miners' settlement of Lubumbashi. Quite likely he was holding one of his meetings while we talked at the Cercle Makutano. For the actor who called out his name and for all who were present, Abbé Kasongo represented African defiance and resistance to an institution that, though "Africanized" as far as its personnel and some of its rites were concerned, remained connected to its colonial past.[23] Of course, Mufwankolo and Kachelewa understood what was happening when Kasongo was invoked. They had difficulties controlling the lively exchanges that followed—some actors, obviously with a plot in mind, even began to assign parts. With a reminder that the play should make a "positive contribution," the leaders declared the meeting officially closed. When I left, the discussion and some joking were still going on.

June 19. The Groupe Mufwankolo is back at the Cercle Makutano. More, sometimes heated, discussion about the meaning of *le pouvoir se mange entier.* Finally, Mufwankolo takes the lead and announces that the next task is to agree on a plot for the play and on the casting for the parts. As in the previous meeting—as if this would help to calm the actors—he reminds them of the other play on the history of the Catholic mission, to be performed three months hence. He has arrived late today, coming directly from a meeting at the chancery where the clerical organizing committee has given him "texts" to be followed in composing the play. This is immediately met with heated criticism. The ensuing discussion, somewhat confused and always following several strands, brings out that the actors resent being used for church propaganda. They want to know (and from here on I quote from my notes),

whether the piece can include a) the shady sides of the mission (like last time, the prime example is the pressure exercised when children are to be enrolled in mission schools) [and] b) should one address the phenomenon of many competing religions *and* of tradition competing with Christianity . . . "God was known before the whites came," [someone says]. Most of the older members reject anything controversial: only this history from de Hemptinne to Kabanga [the current archbishop]. Someone says the purpose of the piece is to be *éducatif.* K. (the voice of the dissenters), in his dry manner, throws in: "Educate whom? The clergy?" Mufwankolo finally controls the situation, not with arguments but with one of his brilliant performances. He gives a synopsis of the piece as he sees it. It has a sequence of *tableaux,* separated by *pancartes* [posters] with dates marking the historical period; this is a method they used before when they did a command performance of a play about the history of the Gécamines [mining company]. Listening closely one detects that he does include all the controversial questions, albeit obliquely as invocations of events and scenes—the difference between art and propaganda?

The meeting ends with arrangements for further work.

July 4. Performance, filming, and broadcast of *Le pouvoir se mange entier* are behind us (see Fabian 1996) and the group has come together again to work on the new project. This and that is talked about while Mufwankolo sits aside, taking notes. He then opens the meeting officially with one of his soft-spoken, moralizing speeches in "good" Swahili (of the kind he usually pronounces after the end of a performance). He reminds the group that they are responding to a wish expressed by Monseigneur

[Kabanga]. That does not mean they are in his service. They will work together with the church but what counts for them is that they work as actors. Then he proposes that a committee be chosen to prepare the piece. Everyone will have occasion to express his or her opinion. He also reminds them that the performance will be *séance payante* (a point of importance for actors who usually work without compensation). If all goes well, there are prospects that the piece may tour the diocese.

He must think that this news has calmed down the meeting because he now goes on to describe his vision more concretely. The piece should start with depicting traditional religion. It should show that there was such a thing and that it was good. He evokes the role of ancestor statues, offerings, healing of illness, divination, and prayer. Then should come the arrival of the missionaries, who met people who were naked . . . at which point K. cuts in again: "Is this *histoire?*" Which I take to mean: We don't need narration, give us events we can enact. Mufwankolo is not to be steered away from his chosen course. He goes on to describe the implantation of Christianity, the role of the catechist and the Bible, and also says that it will be one of the tasks of the piece to show the difference between *christianisme ya zamani* (of old) and its contemporary expressions.

This is a cue for one of the actors to go into a rambling speech, quoting Mobutu and denouncing the proliferation of cults and denominations as a *course au pouvoir et au fric* (race for power and money). He gives many examples of the greed of preachers and healers, arguing that most of the churches are fraudulent. The others seem to agree, only to be contradicted by cantankerous K. (more than slightly drunk today) who embarks on the story of his own younger brother, a lifelong drunkard. At one time, this brother fell into a coma that lasted for three days, woke up, announced that he was now a prophet, and never touched alcohol again. He practices prophesy and has his followers but does not do it for money.

One more time Mufwankolo takes up his projected outline of the piece. Again he stresses that the ancestors did have genuine prayer and knew how to pray (enacting the traditional gestures of making an offering). But the *bazungu balikuwa na kitabu*, the whites had the book, and the book had powerful pictures. He mentions confession and the sins Christianity denounced. Some actors, voicing the ever-present critical countercurrent, bring up examples of missionaries breaking the seal of confession.[24] The more cautious and conservative actors reject this as a possible subject, which causes the critics once more to raise objections against the piece as propaganda. The floor is open again and the situation gets dramatic. K. embarks on a tirade against the undemocratic ways the leaders try to run the business of the group. This goes on for a while until Mufwankolo takes control with a speech dwelling on communality and cooperation, a voice for everyone, but also stressing the need to get on with the task. At this point I must leave for another appointment.

July 8. Time is getting short and the group should start rehearsals. Instead, Mufwankolo starts today's meeting again with a *causerie morale* much like the one that concluded the last session. Apparently, his idea of a committee charged to prepare the piece for the diocese makes many actors fear that they will be left out of the business of shaping a play dealing with a history and memories about which they have strong feelings and opinions. F. rises to express these fears. He admonishes the leaders, telling them not to respond to criticism with "sentiments." At the same time he assures them that the group will cooperate and follow their direction. Mufwankolo responds with remarks on the purpose of the committee and then continues to talk about his idea of the plot and outline. F. takes the floor again and draws a picture of mission history that strikes me as more impressive than Mufwankolo's. He suggests they should look for inspiration to historical photos in the archives of the diocese (he probably got the idea from a recent exhibition commemorating the seventy-fifth anniversary of the town). When he is finished, the meeting turns to urgent business. A one-page outline has been prepared. Mufwankolo encourages well-founded comments and, while the actors think about it, he announces the composition of the committee. A schedule for the rehearsals is set and the meeting is closed.

Before my departure from Lubumbashi on July 25, I make several recordings with Mufwankolo of some of the sketches the group performed in the past (he acts all the parts). We also meet twice with one of the senior actresses and discuss what they call the *crise* in the group. But the need to complete my follow-up work on the Jamaa movement prevents me from attending the rehearsals of the mission play that begin during that period.

Postcript, August 22, 1999. A telephone conversation with Dr. Achille Mutombo, who was the archbishop's secretary and the contact person with the Groupe Mufwankolo in 1986, allows me to close the gap caused by my leaving Lubumbashi before the play was performed.[25] Various festivities to celebrate the anniversary took place over one week. The play, called (as suggested by Archbishop Kabanga) *Eglise et développement*, was the final event; it was performed on August 12, in the Salle Familia before a capacity audience and in the presence of Cardinal Malula, two bishops, and numerous other dignitaries. The theme of African religion before the arrival of the missions had a prominent part *and the story about the broken confessional secret was included* (though a bit mitigated; the authorities found the less offensive remains of a goat). The play ended with Mufwankolo alone on the stage, dressed as a priest and blessing the audience. Father Mutombo and others translated for the guests who did not speak Swahili. The play was the first public performance of the Groupe Mufwankolo in years and had a great popular success.

Conclusion

Let me begin by relating this long digression into ethnography to the questions I raised throughout this paper on Africa's Belgium. As I pointed out earlier, "folkorization" is one of the main obstacles in the way of adequately appreciating the work of memory Congolese engage in when they attempt to come to grips with the colonial experience. I also suggested that this effect may be reinforced, though not intentionally, when our scholarly efforts are focused on technical analyses and aesthetic interpretations of texts and artistic creations. Without needing much comment, I hope, my ethnographic notes helped to document the involved, complex, and often subtle intellectual struggle that memory-work requires. Not only that, a glance behind the scenes of the Groupe Mufwankolo reminds us just how much calling up the past is also "remembering the present." Diverging opinions and interests, conflicts that arise from the present situation of the group, including the dynamics that characterize any collective and creative effort, irrespective of the themes and tasks at hand, always mediate the finished product. We may surmise that similar struggle preceded the writing of the *Vocabulary*, and we know much about Tshibumba's extraordinary courage, his doubts and reflections.

I would be satisfied if the three examples I have discussed made a small contribution toward returning the imperial gaze and giving a voice to Congolese perceptions and interpretations of their colonial experience. But in the end, the question will of course be: How is all this significant for the theme of a meeting called to make, as it were, an inventory of scholarly efforts to understand Belgium's colonial past and, thereby its present? It seems to me that the most significant gain in recent years has been a growing awareness, with consequences for theory and method, of the fact that academic scholarship must confront, not just study, the memory-work in contemporary Congolese culture.[26] This, to elaborate on a point already made, means that we take our studies to the level of theory and method in popular memory-work, its literary devices and conventions, its metahistorical reflections, and the political visions and challenges it formulates. It is my impression that many scholars, Belgians and others who have devoted much of their work to Belgium's Africa, now take such a perspective, sometimes implicitly but often also explicitly.[27] It is my hope that it will be maintained, expanded, and sharpened in debates and controversies with our Congolese colleagues.

Not in a Thousand Years:
On the (Ir)relevance of the Millennium

When an editor asks you for a paper on a topic you don't want to write about because you have not given it any thought (and were not planning to), just say No. Don't decline the honor of the invitation with a reasoned No. The editor will grab you by your reasons and tell you that this is precisely what he was looking for: an essay arguing why the proposed topic—anthropology and the millennium—is a nontopic. So, I found myself noting down thoughts about my discipline and the millennium.

I

Anthropology and the millennium is a nontopic because a millennium is a nonevent in secular history. The year 2000 marks a date in a Christian history of salvation. As most histories of anthropology see the matter, for our discipline to emerge, history of salvation had to be overcome, left behind, or at least put aside, by schemes of progress and evolution predicated on nature's time. Natural time knows neither high nor low points, neither important nor indifferent moments. It just goes by. There are those who observed that our Enlightenment predecessors never got farther than replacing the history of salvation with a "mythe-histoire de la raison" (myth-history of reason) (Gusdorf 1973) which, having progress or evolution move from one crucial development to another, is still as teleological as hell or, rather, heaven. Modern scientists have been pledging allegiance to nature and natural time; when they catch themselves at being teleological, they are expected to repent. Postmodern thinkers, incidentally, give rise to the suspicion that they have somehow found a way back to the fold of salvation, and a rather ego-centered, Protestant version at that, when they seek comfort in deconstructive hermeneutics and preach the end of history as a secular master narrative.

Even those who have no taste for musings about science's apparently less than successful efforts to get away from theology must be open to an elementary critical consideration: *This* millennium is not a meaningful date for most people in this world. (Ironically, the creators of global computer technology now must fear Christ's revenge when they face Armageddon, and huge expenses because, being comfortably at home in "the West," they forgot to program the ominous date change when they made us embark on a glorious future of all-encompassing "communication.") Anthropologists, at least, should be sensitive to the political implications of acts and gestures of domination entailed in imposing the Western (but really Christian) calendar on the rest of the world. They should make us think twice before we join the celebrations.

II

I have argued that the millennium is a nonevent; it would be silly to declare nonevents all the activities, festivities, symposia, special issues of journals, and fin de siècle projects such as George E. Marcus's that foreshadow the year 2000. Personally, I have no millennial feelings whatsoever. If, as I presume, I am not alone in this, other anthropologists will use the occasion to renew a critical stance to research practices and habits of thought of our discipline. If an invitation to speculate about our field in the next millennium is heeded, even though a millennium is a nonevent, it can only be understood as a call to assess our present. At the very least, we should not let the offer of prophetic indulgence become an excuse for forgetting the present. Prophets, we might also remember, speak out, or up; they may announce, even warn or threaten, but only rather dubious figures among them actually "prophesy."

III

This should remind us that the millennium has been a topic of anthropological research on messianic, prophetic, and charismatic movements. As someone who has worked in this field (more by planting than harvesting) I might be expected to offer special insights. There is little that can be said briefly enough without embarking on a treatise on "chiliasm and nativism"; thus the title of a study published in 1961 by W. E. Mühlmann, a German ethnologist whose intelligence and erudition did not prevent him from once asking his fellow social scientists to understand that terrible chiliast/millennialist, Hitler, as a charismatic leader. History should have taught us to be wary of attempts to distill meaning from a basically meaningless date or interval that happens to involve the number one thousand.

History continued after Hitler's rather brief Thousand Year Reich, and Mühlmann, who had survived it and its leader, went on to make intelligent observations on millennarianism. Checking my memories of the decades when anthropological research on "movements" was more prominent than it is now, I come up with one thought worth pondering in the present context. What we found in our inquiries was that prophets, charismatic leaders, and their movements can do without a millennium, but that the millennium as a (usually threatening, sometimes promising) idea cannot do without prophets and movements. Which brings us back to the millennium as a source of power. Here I find myself in a precarious position. Back then, when I still accepted anthropology's apparent consensus about culture being above all concerned with shared "meaning," I once said that the anthropologist and the prophet/charismatic leader whom he or she studies resemble each other in that both are trying to make sense of confused situations. It did not occur to me then that this pronouncement might come back to haunt me as soon as power, rather than meaning, took the center stage of theory. All this goes to say that anthropologists who are called upon to bring their special competences as students of millennarian movements to the meaning of the millennium should be diffident about such recognition as specialists. They may find themselves (remember Mühlmann) co-opted by something they cannot, or should not, subscribe to, at least not as anthropologists.

There is another thought that comes to mind even though I can do little more than offer it as a reminder. A powerful current in modern anthropology, inspired by "structuralist" theory, would seem especially vulnerable to some millennialist speculation. In a structuralist vein, one could argue as follows. Precisely because a millennium is such an utterly arbitrary period it is, as a sign, potentially an almost irresistible carrier of meaning. It is the stuff of myths that think us, as Lévi-Strauss once put it in a seductive formulation. Perhaps they do; why else would I be writing about anthropology and the millennium? How do I know that I am not enacting, rather then critically analyzing, a myth?

IV

Having stated my view of the millennium as a non-event, it is perhaps time now to pull back the heavy critical weaponry and make another start with questions such as the following. Might matters not be turned around? Could it be that an effort of collective appraisal is called for because something is really happening in anthropology? The millennium would then just be a convenient peg for changes we observe or wish for. As far as I can see, the "state of anthropology" as the millennium approaches is that there is no state of anthropology. True, certain trends that thought of themselves as postmodern (often forgetful of the issues that critical anthropology had put on the table since the seventies) became so enamored with their discourse that they ended up with a static posture. There was a brief period when many anthropologists, perhaps a majority, experienced the postmodern turn as paralysing and reacted with defensive pleas for returning to "science as usual," meaning to a basically positivist position that seemed to have served our discipline so well in its heyday between World War II and Vietnam. Persisting in a status quo seemed preferable to being immobilized by postmodern navel gazing. They failed to realize that the valuable elements brought about by the turn to language, interpretation, and literary theory were not matters of fancy or fashion but attempts to catch up with radical changes in practices of ethnography, of research and writing. These changes were less invented than dictated by the end of direct colonization. Of course, the proof of the pudding had to be, and was, that these new theoretical positions produced solid ethnographies, rich in information and persuasive in their arguments. Such ethnographies have been published and more are to come, judging from impressive recent first books and dissertations. Added to this must be work inspired by feminist theory, by the (re)discovery of material culture, of the body and the senses, as well as of the "dark" sides of human conduct—evil, violence, and plain madness— aspects that in our more "sociological" period we ignored or swept under the carpet of "deviant behavior." The consequences that all this will have for "culture," our guiding concept, are as yet hard to imagine. Much of current talk about globalization fills, for the time being, the gap between culture predicated on identity, integration, and stability (in short, on social life in a nation-state) and something else whose theoretical shape we don't grasp because its practical, political embodiment has not yet found its form.

All this adds up to an agenda that will keep us busy after the year 2000. It is also a fair guess that the practice of anthropology outside academe will continue to grow, not just as a concomitant of aid and development programs, but in a context of problems that Western and post–Iron Curtain societies have with ethnicity, massive (im)migration, and plain global mobility. Other areas of rapid change—the visual media, the Internet, local and global "popular culture," but also genetic technology and looming ecological catastrophes—have already found their anthropological "specialists," including some who experiment with the idea of anthropology as science fiction.

This rapid review does not amount to a "vision" of anthropology's future. After all, visions and visionaries are in demand only if they come up with images that may be wrong but must be clear. Given the political chaos and the mire of seemingly bottomless pauperization in the regions of the world where most of anthropological research has been carried out, all I am able to envision is that our discipline keeps beating its drums to the tune of a *métissage universel,* the only hope, and a joyous prospect, for humanity.

V

Which (the drumming) brings me to another thought and question. To judge by preparations that are under way all over the world, the millennium will be a huge party. What could be wrong with anthropology joining the fun and having a good time, a break from drab business as usual? Nothing and everything. Nothing, because, as an ardent advocate of performance-centered approaches, I wish that our discipline's newly gained momentum would make us move into the new millennium dancing (the kind of dance Nietzsche dreamed of for a new science; or the one Marx thought we should teach the "petrified relations" in this world). Everything, because most of those whom we have discovered as our dance partners (we used to call them objects of study, Others, with whom we treated as informants) are not likely to be invited to the party; not, I fear, in a thousand years.

Anthropology emerged, less as a science of human nature than as the study of the damage done by one part of mankind to another (and thereby to all of humanity). If that has indeed been our raison d'être during the last century or two, we are not likely to lose it in the next millennium.

REFERENCE MATTER

Notes

CHAPTER I. ETHNOGRAPHIC OBJECTIVITY

1. An exception was the article by Maquet published in *Current Anthropology* (1964). Remarkably for its time, the question of objectivity is here tied to decolonization and the political predicament of anthropology. Unfortunately, in the disciplinary debates of the time, the epistemological concern with objectivity was deflected toward ethics. The term "epistemology" had been used in connection with anthropology in the title of a volume edited by Northrop and Livingston (1964). Epistemology, as a level of critical reflection on which the question of objectivity needs to be discussed, was not a matter of concern in American anthropology. The first panel discussion of "epistemological foundations for anthropology" was convened by Bob Scholte (who had created awareness of such questions in Scholte 1966) and myself at the annual meeting of the American Anthropological Association in San Diego in 1970.

2. Barnes could not avoid, of course, wondering occasionally about differences in these researchers' approaches to ethnography. That these may have been expressive of different literary practices is only hinted at. The term "style" figures prominently in the title of the book but only in one brief passage do we find any discussion of stylistic devices (1971, 259). To appreciate the trajectory that anthropology has completed since, Barnes's book should be compared to another study of the work of three towering anthropologists (Lévi-Strauss is on both lists), Geertz's essay on the anthropologist as author (1988).

3. Habermas 1967, now available in English (1988). I take the fact that this work has been translated as confirmation of my view that the issues it first raised in the mid-sixties are live ones.

4. An issue is "naturalized" when it is postulated to be untouched by cultural, historical, and political specificity. Notice that naturalization is the program in a recent philosophical work on objectivity (Ellis 1990). It is written from a position of scientific realism and discusses at great length the place of ontology in a naturalized theory of truth and objectivity. Objectivity is here opposed to "convention" (88f.), and the adversary is identified as "conventionalism."

5. More than "foundation," *Begründung* connotes not only the spatial image of providing something with firm ground, but also a logical or rhetorical argument (providing the "grounds," that is, reasons for something) and finally an activity rather than a state.

6. The essay was reprinted in Fabian 1991a, chap. 1.

7. The wording of the theses shows that I did not formulate them in isolation from wider currents of thought. As I mentioned briefly, I had encountered phenomenology in the fifties and begun to read critical theory and hermeneutics before the major works became available in English. Equally important was Dell Hymes's "ethnography of speaking" (1964), which has inspired one of the most influential critical movements in recent anthropology. Finally, I drew on a rather private discovery, Wilhelm von Humboldt, especially the introduction to his work on the Kawi languages which remains an inexhaustible source of inspiration (see the most recent English translation of 1988).

8. I am neither able nor willing to give this term a clear axiomatic definition. What it designates is a problem I am struggling with: The notion of objectivity as applied to knowledge of "things cultural and historical" needs to be developed in terms of a theory of *Vergegenständlichung*, that is of the making of all those things that can become the objects of—in the case we are discussing here—ethnographic knowledge.

9. This, incidentally, is an important rule of critical theory. Ethnographic objectivity is not best, or even better, understood if we analyze the anthropologist anthropologically as, say, a stranger (see Jarvie 1969, who does this with the ethics of participant observation in mind). To propose "anthropology of anthropology"—if such a thing is possible without facing the problem of infinite regress—may signal a call for reflexivity; it is no substitute for epistemology.

10. A title search was conducted (in 1990) of *American Anthropologist*, the *Journal of Anthropological Research, Current Anthropology*, and *Man*; the same was done for *Philosophy of the Social Sciences* with the idea that anthropologists might have preferred to address the issue in a journal devoted to philosophy of science. Because the pickings were slim beyond expectations, a title and keyword search ("objectivity," "epistemology") was also conducted of *Sociological Abstracts*, which covers most social science journals and books in the major languages. An unexpected result of the survey was that debates involving objectivity and epistemol-

ogy were alive in archeology (we comment on this briefly) and in feminist stud-ies. In the latter case, my general impression is that there was a development from denouncing objectivity as a token of maleness to proposing that objectivity be given a new and broader meaning by incorporating new insights on gender and knowledge processes. I suspect that there may be much convergence with the general argument of this chapter; see an essay by Mieke Bal (1993).

11. R. J. Bernstein (1983) showed the irrelevance with regard to the objectiv-ity question of such "problems" as ethnocentrism or even relativism. He argued that objectivism and relativism must be left behind as meaningless positions if we want to get to a theory of interpretation that meets criteria of epistemologi-cal objectivity similar to the ones I formulated above.

12. This is diametrically opposed to Peter Novick's finding when he says: "Of all the social disciplines, it was in anthropology that the 'objectivity question' assumed the greatest centrality in recent decades, and where it was most deci-sive" (1988, 548–49). Such a glaring contradiction with our findings can only be due to the fact that Novick let himself be impressed by professions of cultural relativism and perhaps by the ethics debate which was supposed to cleanse the discipline from complicity with Western imperialism. He failed to see that, as an epistemological question, objectivity by and large lingered in limbo.

13. "Correct" refers to the canonical character of a given decision. While it could change through time it was not to be questioned at any given moment in the planning and execution of research. Canonicity is a characteristic shared by a great variety of philosophical positions ranging from naive realism to extreme nominalism. In the more closed and dogmatic cases, objectivity is often equated with canonicity.

14. The handbook by Hammersley and Atkinson (1983), on the whole a rather sensitive treatment of ethnographic "principles in practice," does address issues such as access, presence, and field relations. The authors resolutely opt for an ethnography that is reflexive, and they also seem to reject the separation of knower and known when they say: "There is no way in which we can escape the social world in order to study it" (15). But neither objectivity nor epistemology rate an entry in the index, nor are they discussed in the body of the text.

15. "Natural science" refers here and elsewhere to social-scientific (and some-times philosophical) images that tend to be decidedly premodern—closer to Newton than to Heisenberg. Practicing natural scientists, I am sure, will recog-nize many of the issues I raise.

16. Defenders of a scientistic notion of objectivity cried "phenomenological putsch" in response to our critical efforts (see Jarvie 1975).

17. This observation applies only to a kind of simplified reception of phe-nomenology in anglophone social sciences (one in which, I suspect, Berger and

Luckmann 1966 played an important role). As a member of the board of Northwestern University Press from 1968 to 1972, I became familiar with many serious efforts, such as translations of Husserl and Merleau-Ponty.

18. This account of the fate of objectivity prior to the advent of postmodernism leaves several loose ends: the relevance of the "rationality debate" might be examined, and there is "evolutionary epistemology," not to mention "reflexivity," an issue that would seem to be immediately relevant (see Woolgar 1988). But tying these ends together would inflate this essay without changing the terms and direction of my argument.

19. Whenever I use the term "postmodern" I feel guilty of intellectual laziness. On the other hand, once it is understood that no one expects it to have a clear reference, it is helpful to be able to designate in an indexical manner a critical movement in anthropology (and beyond, of course) that may be rather shapeless but is nonetheless quite visible. As far as postmodern ethnography is concerned, the obligatory reference is Clifford and Marcus 1986. How that turn changed the agenda and direction of questioning could not be better illustrated than by reading side by side the Hammersley and Atkinson text (1983), already cited, and the more recent book by Atkinson alone (1990).

20. The move from production to representation has also been made in the sociology of science (see Lynch and Woolgar 1988). Ironically, while within anthropology "ethnography" as an activity and as a product loses its contours, students of science seem to think that ethnographic approaches are helpful in tackling their problems.

21. *Writing Culture* was followed, only two years later, by Van Maanen's *Tales of the Field*, subtitled *On Writing Ethnography* (1988). Much of what the contributors to *Writing Culture* offered as questions and, perhaps, provocations, is here treated as accepted routine. And as expected, objectivity and epistemology are not among the announced topics.

22. On presence and representation see Fabian 1990c (reprinted in Fabian 1991a, chap. 11).

23. Nor does it simply "impose" categories on reality, as a Durkheimian approach would have it. This point needs to be made in order to avoid possible misunderstanding when (following Herder and Humboldt and, in a later version of the same view, Habermas) I posit that knowing, because it is mediated by language, is essentially social.

24. For logical reasons alone: "Constructing" objects does not describe what is specific to ethnography, a scientific enterprise where people seek knowledge about other people. Also, somewhere extreme empiricism and extreme constructivism meet in their fundamental ontological assumptions. Both must have faith in something that becomes the material for either abstraction or imposition.

25. Although this goes against the beat of the dirges for Marxism that are being sung by those who misunderstand what happened in Eastern Europe, I do think that further and deeper thought about objectivity needs to return to ideas that were developed by Hegel and Marx. There are signs that this is occurring, for instance in Dan Miller's courageous attempt to rethink "objectification" for inquiries that straddle archeology, material culture, and mass consumption (1987). See also the way Komesaroff works "commodity fetishism" into his theory of objectivity (1986, chap. 6).

26. On my own experiences with reading a text from "the other side" see Fabian 1990a and chapter 3 below.

27. This makes opposing ethnography to history questionable. Not only are the two closely related as soon as we take history to mean historiography (more on this in chapter 4), but if what we just said about the role of time is correct, there cannot be contents of ethnography that are not also historical. Conversely, a historian who has participated in the event he describes is not thereby disqualified as a historian.

28. To name but a few references from anthropology, see the account given in Fabian 1983; also Stoller (1989, chap. 2) and Tyler 1984. The general debate about 'ocularcentrism' is of course much wider (see Jay 1986, among others).

29. An evocative and richly documented essay on embodiment by T. J. Csordas (1990) is directly relevant to our discussion of objectivity.

30. Some thoughts along that line, including a reference to *intercorporeity*, a concept introduced by Merleau-Ponty, may be found in Komesaroff 1986, 359. Generally speaking, Komesaroff's study, an attempt to integrate phenomenology, Marxism, critical theory, and insights from modern physics, is the most comprehensive (and most congenial) philosophical treatment of objectivity that I have read while writing this essay. Merleau-Ponty is also invoked by Michael Jackson (1989, 119) one of a small but growing number of practicing ethnographers who seem to share a critical attitude toward visualism. Another is Paul Stoller whose collection of essays (1989) addresses "the senses in anthropology" in its subtitle. Neither Jackson nor Stoller, as far as I can see, feels the need to relate his insights to the issue of ethnographic objectivity. In fact, I read Stoller as rejecting the need for epistemology, when he says that we need no "theory of ethnography" (140).

31. Not to forget, in earlier times, plenty of medicines, especially powerful opiates (as we were reminded, for instance, by Malinowski's diary).

32. I can think of several ethnographies that could be cited as achieving that task: Chernoff's study of "African sensitivity," based on his apprenticeship as a drummer (1979); Steven Feld, who also takes sound as an object of ethnography (1982); and Loring Danforth's account of firewalking (1989). Apart from Michael

Taussig (1987), I know of two German anthropologists of the younger generation who have addressed the epistemic status of knowledge of the Other through mimesis, possession, and other ecstatic forms of experience in comprehensive works (Kramer 1987, trans. 1993; Duerr 1978, trans. 1985).

33. In the decade since I wrote this paragraph I have worked on a study on the role of ecstasis in early forms of ethnography that were part of the exploration of Central Africa. By and large, my findings confirmed the programmatic statements formulated here (Fabian 2000).

34. This has also been the logical fault in attempts to pass off participant observation as a method. If an ethnographer acquires the communicative competences and technical skills that allow him to participate, this will enhance his chances of initiating productive communication. But participation as such does not produce ethnography any more than observation as such.

CHAPTER 2. ETHNOGRAPHIC MISUNDERSTANDING
AND THE PERILS OF CONTEXT

1. At this point, so as to avoid making an already difficult reflection even more complex, I use the terms synonymously. That they may have to be distinguished is a question that can be addressed more profitably after I have provided examples of ethnographic understanding going wrong. In the meantime I must ask for indulgence when I use "misunderstanding" in an undifferentiated sense, covering both "not-" and "mis-."

2. When this chapter was first published I should have mentioned an important exception, an essay by the late Roger Keesing (1989) that examines misinterpretation due to overexotic readings of native texts. More recently J.-P. Olivier de Sardan (1996) has written about ethnographic misunderstandings due to overinterpretation, an example of a thoughtful critical treatment in defense of established rules of empirical research.

3. For acknowledgments to J. Habermas and Dell Hymes see chapter 1. Although the ethnography of speaking forms a background for these reflections, it is not what I am discussing here. Contextualization and (mis)communication in conversations are widely debated issues in sociolinguistics (see, for instance, Auer and Di Luzio 1992 and Duranti and Goodwin 1992) but, as far as I can see, sociolinguistics is not concerned with the issue of ethnographic knowledge production as such. Just as earlier "ethnography of communication" did not give us a method for producing ethnography (just a better understanding of what we were doing), so it is also unlikely that sociolinguistic studies of conversational strategies will provide us with rules for dealing with ethnographic misunderstandings. For an earlier paper in which I discuss a misunderstanding or mistake

that made me rethink "ethnography as communication" see Fabian 1979a (reprinted in Fabian 1991a, chap. 5).

4. For a recent discussion of the problem of context in anthropology see the volume edited by Roy Dilley (1999) in which the first published version of this chapter was reprinted. Context was also addressed critically in an earlier collection edited by R. H. Barnes et al. (1985), especially in the contribution to that volume by Mark Hobart (1985), whose target is the use of context in hermeneutic interpretation.

5. For the sake of the argument, let us omit the fact that understanding is already required in the preceding phase, that of deciding what to record and what not.

6. D. Tedlock's essays (1983) are still the most complete discussion of the matter. My own comprehension of the task is formulated in Fabian 1990b. A most perceptive and comprehensive treatment of "context presentation" in transcribing may be found in Cook 1990. See also the more broadly formulated arguments against naive conceptions of transcription in Mishler 1991.

7. From a recording made on June 30, 1986, at Kawama village near Lubumbashi, Shaba/Katanga.

8. This is not to say that Africans such as Kanyemba are "color blind"— shades and hues of skin color are constantly distinguished and remarked upon. Incidentally, our text contains at least a hint of uncertainty that I failed to notice when I did the transcription. At one point the person is referred to as *ule kama ni muzungu* (this person like a *muzungu*), a Shaba/Katanga Swahili idiom signaling a hedge on the part of the speaker.

9. This is how I understand Bourdieu when he qualifies, or denounces, anthropological structuralism as "hermeneutic" because objectivist (1977, 1–2 and elsewhere).

10. We first met on June 14, 1986, at her home.

11. In Lubumbashi, relationships between the prayer groups and the official church hierarchy have been precarious, to say the least.

12. Note that the following excerpt, although edited to prevent autobiographical detail from distracting from the argument, is translated as faithfully as possible; it's just that faithfulness is not enough when it comes to meeting the challenge of this sort of text. Matters are further complicated by two factors. Mama Régine, although fluent in Swahili, is not very articulate in this language. She resorts to intonation, gestures, and other means to compensate for shortcomings in vocabulary and idiom. Furthermore, our conversation had come to a point where performative elements began to prevail over referential discourse. Both of us worked with allusions, innuendos, and ellipsis; we used phonations

and gestures, changes in intonation, and pauses. The difficulties that such texts pose are dealt with in Fabian 1990b, chap. 5.

13. Reported and analyzed in Fabian 1974 (reprinted in 1991a, chap. 3) under the heading of "testimony." I refer to this essay also for the remarks that follow.

14. And that has been a reason for me not to invoke "pragmatics" as if it were merely another level of linguistic analysis. For the problems I have with (mis)understanding utterances and texts, little seems to be gained by considering pragmatics abstractly.

15. Mieke Bal, to whom I owe this quotation, goes on state: "Context, in other words, is a text and thus presents the same interpretation as any other text" (1991, 6).

16. For a dialectical approach to understanding I find congenial to my own views see Hamacher 1996.

17. Actually, Humboldt does not say "nobody means" the same but "nobody thinks" the same—a nuance that signals his concern with language as activity of the mind rather than as system of significations.

18. I only note, but cannot adequately discuss here, a further complication: In cultural and social anthropology, context, more than other "technical terms," has an evocative, rhetorical, rather than referential meaning. It does not really belong to terms designating the object, or aspects of the object, we study, such as "culture," "religion," "kinship," "economy," and so forth. Nor is it usually part of a conceptual scheme constructed of opposites or contrasts such as structure (versus event) or meaning (versus function). In fact, once anthropology developed more or less holistic approaches to whatever it studies, a call for consideration of context often turns out to be preaching to the converted.

19. Hymes refers to other authors who speak of "context of situation," which I take to imply a view of context *as* situation, that is, as a state of affairs (1974, 20). He points approvingly to Malinowski's use of "context" as something that underlies (again a static notion) acts and events (61). But notice also a shift of meaning when Hymes speaks of the event itself as "context" (23).

CHAPTER 3. KEEP LISTENING

1. The following is a sweeping review of theoretical developments in anthropological studies of literacy, with no pretensions to completeness. No attempt is made to provide an adequate bibliography. Nevertheless, here are some of the works I shall be referring to: Goody 1986, 1987; Gusdorf 1973, part 3; Ong 1958; Schousboe and Larsen 1989; Street 1984; and Vansina 1961 and 1985.

2. Probst makes a similar observation regarding the ways Goody first establishes difference between literate and nonliterate societies and then determines processes of transition from one to the other (1989, 478). Notice that this other-

wise interesting and critical paper treats of literacy and its conditions and consequences by considering only writing (except for one or two formulaic expressions such as "read and write").

3. A notion generalized by Rorty (1980) in his critique of Western philosophy.

4. I want to thank Michael Harbsmeier for calling Schön's study to my attention. Incidentally, the book raises an interesting question regarding the history of anthropology. It is now recognized that one of its origins in the sixteenth century was the so-called *ars apodemica*, which produced a vast body of writing on the method of travel (inspired by Ramist philosophy, see Stagl 1980, or a collection of his essays in English, 1995). A comparable methodologization of reading (documented by Schön) may have had a similar importance for anthropology's ways with texts that became the object of ethnographic collecting. The visualist bent is common to both, or was, up to the time when the "ethnography of speaking" (see chapters 1 and 2) embarked on the critique of structuralism.

5. I may have exaggerated the absence of concerns with reading in anthropological studies of literacy in order to improve my story—but not much. Notice that in Goody's summary of his work on literacy throughout human history (1987) reading does not even rate an entry in the index.

6. Exemplary for this are the proposal by Mary Louise Pratt (1977) to apply insights from sociolinguistics and speech act theory to literary discourse, as well as the works written or edited by Deborah Tannen (1982a, 1982b, 1984, 1985). In literary theory, the writings of M. M. Bakhtin have been influential in ways I cannot even attempt to document bibliographically in this paper (but see Bakhtin 1986 for a first orientation). Both developments may appear as new trends, but an entire discipline, often organized in "Departments of Interpretation," has existed for some time which has approached reading as oral and communicative performance. It has produced theoretical treatises, textbooks, and even its own historiography (see Bahn and Bahn 1970, Bartine 1989, and Thompson et al. 1983, to cite only a few examples for the latter). Aside from the question whether we can learn from Interpretation, the fact that it became professionalized should be taken as part of the phenomenon of literacy.

7. The *Vocabulary of the Town of Elizabethville* (Fabian 1990a), a unique history of the principal town of the mining region in southeastern Congo—Elisabethville, now Lubumbashi—commissioned by an association of former domestic servants and written by one André Yav: a colonial history written by the colonized for the colonized.

8. For further discussion and other examples of grassroots writing in Shaba/Katanga Swahili see Blommaert 1999.

9. Somehow one expects native speakers to guarantee correct transcription. The example of a misunderstanding discussed in chapter 2 (a wrong transcrip-

tion on which both Kalundi Mango and I had agreed) shows such a view is naive. There may be differences in degree, as there are differences in language competence, but in principle all transcribers face the same problems.

10. See, for example, the thoughts on the role of interpreters as interlocutors, with a critical discussion of Owusu's important paper (1978) in Pool 1989, and my own findings on the role of interpreters in the exploration of Central Africa (Fabian 2000, 130–33).

11. Implicit in this observation is yet another set of problems that an ethnography of reading must face: In ways to be determined, the strictures and constraints that are usually ascribed to literacy as writing may also be operative in reading, even in a literacy that is recent and tenuous and comparatively uncontrolled.

12. This is precisely the point made by Michel de Certeau when he qualifies reading as "poaching" (1984, chap. 12). Margaret Drewal of the Department of Performance Studies at Northwestern University brought de Certeau's essay to my attention.

13. That similar conclusions regarding the role of cultural knowledge in reading can be reached by a different route—in this case the performance of school-children in reading-ability tests—was shown by C. J. Fillmore and his collaborators (Fillmore 1982). See also Tannen's remarks on reading and writing as "involvement-focused skills" (1985, 140).

14. It is also the weakness of arguments that see in silent reading an evolutionary achievement that necessarily replaces reading aloud. Historically these arguments do not hold water: silent reading was practiced, albeit exceptionally, in ancient Greece (see Svenbro 1987; 1988, chap. 9), and reading aloud has never ceased to be practiced. Theoretically and methodologically such an evolutionary position goes together with "ocular" theories of reading as the mere decoding of signs.

15. Quoted in Schön 1987, 104–5; the translation is mine.

CHAPTER 4. ETHNOLOGY AND HISTORY

1. A few years ago, David W. Cohen, an American historian of Africa (with an appointment in both history and anthropology) placed his own critical work in the context of a series of roundtables on history and anthropology organized by the Max-Planck Institut für Geschichte in Göttingen, starting in 1978. Six meetings had taken place by the time Cohen wrote his retrospective account (Cohen 1994, chap. 1). Although I met most of the principal participants (David Cohen, Hans Medick, David Sabean, and Gerald Sider, among others) in other contexts, my own work neither led me to contribute directly to these debates

nor did it leave me the time to study the published results with the care they deserve.

2. Bernheim is not cited in any of the histories of anthropology that began to appear in the United States toward the end of the sixties (for instance, Harris, Honigman, Voget, Stocking); even Mühlmann's references to Bernheim's influence on Ratzel and Graebner (1968, 123), and to his connection to Durkheim (168), are curiously perfunctory. My impression that he was cited but not read is based on what I recall when I received my first introduction to ethnology based on the *Kulturkreis* paradigm.

3. One may object that the two are not simply synonymous and that I am changing referents and thereby invalidating whatever argument I am making. My reply is that the issue at hand in this section is the influence of Bernheim; when Bernheim, as we shall see, leads us to Vansina, this also leads us to ethnology as practiced in the context in which Vansina eventually worked and taught, that is, to American anthropology. When I continue, later in this chapter, to speak of ethnology, this is in deference to the mainly German audience I was invited to address.

4. The 1914 edition of his book shows as yet no awareness of Foy's and Graebner's debts to it; when it comes to ethnology, Bernheim refers to Bastian, Ratzel, Waitz, Schurtz, and others.

5. Bernheim touches on the opposition between analogical and dialogical modes of knowledge production in anthropology as discussed in Dennis Tedlock's critique of scientism in anthropology (1983, chap. 16).

6. See Burke 1978 and Ginsburg 1976. Vansina vigorously—sometimes viciously—opposed "Rangerism" as blindly leftist (see Vansina 1994, index under "Ranger"). The victim of such attacks is ultimately a better understanding of relations between history and anthropology.

7. An example of writing based on this insight is Paul Friedrich's "essay in anthrohistorical method" (1986), a book that deserved more attention than it seems to have gotten. Another set of connections—between autobiography, ethnography, history, and archeology—is explored in the extraordinary "chronicles" of Carmel Schrire (1995).

8. See Sahlins 1985 and numerous other writings by him and others; see Friedman 1887 and Thomas 1989 for early critical responses, and my review of the latter (Fabian 1991b), anticipating some of the points formulated in this chapter.

9. See Fabian 1971b, reprinted in 1991a, chap. 1.

10. Analogous revisions are, of course, overdue with regard to ethnography. Elsewhere (in the preceding chapter and in Fabian 1990a, 165) I recall from my own work just how tenacious the conviction can be that "we write and they

speak" even in the manifest presence of literacy among those whom we study (a kind of blindness that, at least temporarily, may have been reinforced by hermeneutic, text-centered approaches).

11. See the exchanges published during the last two years or so in the *Newsletter* of the American Anthropological Association.

12. For this point, albeit made from concern for boundaries between anthropology and cultural studies, see Handler 1998.

13. As just one example of interesting inquiries on the subject of memory I should like to cite a collection of essays recently edited by Richard Werbner (1998).

CHAPTER 5.   CULTURE WITH AN ATTITUDE

1. I reread Adorno's *Negative Dialektik* (1966) for this occasion; his thought has been one of the sources of attitude in my critical work.

2. For a fuller treatment, including some of the concrete reasons that moved me at the time, see the essay on "Text as Terror" (Fabian 1991a, chap. 4, esp. 123, for remarks on negativity and the theory of religious movements in general).

3. See Fabian 1991a, chap. 10 and p. 220; Fabian 1995, 1999b.

4. A decisive step in that direction was made with a thorough revision of that classical taxonomic concept, genre, documented in the essays assembled by Dan Ben-Amos in 1976.

5. For the notorious "German connection" in the history of the concept of culture, see Stocking 1996. Especially the essay by Bunzl (1996) in that volume provides a useful antidote to simplification of that history. Concern with authenticity may in part have been a response to the negative aura of falseness that characterized folklore's emergence as a field of study and is still attached to certain usages of the term (perhaps most strongly in French: *c'est du folklore* can be a devastating comment). See on this Barbara Kirshenblatt-Gimblett's essay on "Folklore's Crisis" (1998, 269ff.). She reminds us how, after it became the name of a discipline, the term eventually served to eliminate or defuse negativity: "The very term *folklore* marks a transformation of errors into archaisms" (298).

6. Far from having run its course, this critical impetus inspired by Dell Hymes is, for instance, just now showing up in post-structuralist France. See the collection of essays edited by Masquelier and Siran (2000) and the radical deconstruction of the structuralist notion of myth by Siran (1998).

7. See Gysels 1996, 13.

8. In local Swahili *bongo* has no plural form I know of; the plural of *hadisi* (often pronounced *arisi*, from East Coast Arabic/Swahili *hadith*) would be *mahadisi*.

9. His stated ideas in this regard can be found in Fabian 1996, Prelude, pp. 3–15, and dispersed throughout the complete protocol of his narrative and our conversations, now available on the Web at http://www.pscw.uva.nl/lpca/, "Language and Popular Culture in Africa."

10. See Fabian 1996, 309–16; also the index under "Truth."

11. Unlike in the book, I here opt for the "stronger" singular, bringing out the juxtaposition.

12. When the manuscript of this book was at the stage of copyediting, a study by Diana Coole came to my attention—a thorough and informative survey of negativity in the history of thought from Kant onward (Coole 2000).

13. See chaps. 1 and 2 in Fabian 1998a, where I present ethnographic evidence for the programmatic statements that follow.

14. An important book sadly ignored in recent debates that fail to reach its critical level (see note 19).

15. Incidentally, here is a question to ponder. Why, given the fact that anthropological theories of culture have been modeled on theories of language, has the capacity of language to negate not been made an issue? I found an exception, following a hint by Hymes (1974a, 136), in an essay by Kenneth Burke (1966, chap. 7). His position is: *"Language by its nature necessarily culminates in the Negative, hence negation is of the very essence of language"* (457; emphasis in the original). And: "The Negative. Perhaps the one great motivational principle that man, in his role as the language-using animal, has added to nature" (469); see also his remarks on negations as conditions of irony (461), and of "uses of metaphor without madness" (462).

16. Awareness of reflexivity in performance does not necessarily lead to considering negativity. Victor Turner, who, as far as I can tell, had no taste for negative dialectics, was among those who recognized connections between performance and reflexivity (see, for instance, 1986, 42, and, with acknowledgments to Barbara Myerhoff, 81). In contrast, in the essay already quoted, Kenneth Burke (1968) sees negation and negativity as an essential element of his "dramatistic"— we would not say, performative—view of language.

17. There is more on this in Peter Berger's broader treatment of humor (1997).

18. For the civil and liberal—and positive—approach to multiculturalism (including some dissenting responses, all of them falling short of Hamacher's radical critique) see Charles Taylor et al. (1994). I also recommend Gerd Baumann (1999) for a lucid, constructive yet critical treatment of the subject based on his own ethnographic work.

19. See Scott (1990) who has to say things about the "work of negation" (ibid.

III–18) I find congenial—especially the way he de-romanticizes resistance—even though he deploys negativity in a more limited way than I would advocate.

20. See the positive, conciliatory, sometimes congratulatory tone in some recent anthropological discussions of the "Fate of Culture" (such as Ortner 1999, which, despite the title, exemplifies positive thought). An exceptionally informative and evenhanded (and definitely positive) essay by Christoph Brumann (1999), arguing in favor of maintaining the concept of culture in anthropology, leads off a special issue of *Cultural Anthropology*. The title—"Writing for Culture"—marks his position against the one taken by Leila Abu-Lughod (1991), and he frequently cites another *CA* paper on the subject by Brightman (1995). On a related critical debate—culture and identity—see the commented articles in *Current Anthropology* 40, no. 4 (1999), and a volume of essays edited by Assmann and Friese (1998). All these sources are also guides to the huge literature on the topic.

CHAPTER 6. HINDSIGHT

1. First edition published by Murray, in London. The Minerva Library edition was the fourth; it seems that the appendix was written by Galton for that edition. The book is not mentioned at all in the article on Galton by F. N. David in the *International Encyclopedia of the Social Sciences* (1968, 5:48–52), which seems to be exemplary for its fate in recent years, although a reprint of the original edition (without the appendix) appeared in 1972. With some insignificant changes, place, geographical, and ethnic names will be used as given by Galton. The principal terms, with modern equivalents in parentheses, are as follows: Ovampo (Ovambo), Damara (Herero, Bergdama?), Namaqua (Nama). Lebzelter quotes Galton writing on the Damara, but under the heading "Herero" (1934, 182).

2. This is a reprint of the 1872 edition by John Murray in London. It contains a brief but informative introduction by Dorothy Middleton. As Karl Pearson, Galton's student and biographer already noted, *The Art of Travel* surprises by the virtual absence of anthropological material (physical as well as cultural); the perspective is strictly geographical (see Pearson 1924, 4). There was thus no overlap with *Notes and Queries*, the anthropologist's field guide published by the British Association. About the latter Galton says: "I had some share in this, but by no means a large one" (1974, 163). On Galton's later influence, via Rivers, see Stocking 1983, 86.

3. And so, apparently, did Charles Darwin. After reading *The Narrative* he writes to Galton (letter dated July 24, 1853—six years before the publication of *The Origin of Species*): "I live at a village called Down near Farnborough in Kent, and employ myself in Zoology; but the objects of my study are very small fry,

and to a man accustomed to rhinoceroses and lions, it would appear infinitely insignificant" (Pearson 1914, 240).

4. See Galton's own recollections and reflections on the matter in his *Memories* (1974, chap. 7, "Hunting and Shooting").

5. The term "spy" first occurs in this meaning in 1974, 101, after which it is used especially in connection with descriptions of the usefulness of (African) women in a traveler's party. They establish informal connections between the expedition and local population. Galton recalls: "It was a system of espionage which proved most effectual" (120; see also 102). This is, incidentally, one of the few pieces of practical advice that found its way into the *Art of Travel* (see 1972 under "Natives' Wives"). Incidentally, Galton noted a few items of reported "intelligence" that are clearly traces of the canon of fantastic elements transmitted through the ages. He cites as credible a report—not solicited, as he is careful to state—of unicorns (173) and another one of a strange people with rigid joints who must feed each other (53).

6. This was Charles John Andersson (1827–67), who published, among other works, a travel narrative titled *Lake Ngami* (1988), in which he reports on his travels with Galton.

7. Galton gives a telling indirect description of the "British" attitude when he compares the two famous discoverers of the sources of the Nile, Richard Burton and J. H. Speke (whom he knew as an official of the Royal Geographic Society): "Burton was a man of eccentric genius and tastes, orientalised in character and thoroughly Bohemian. He was a born linguist, and ever busy in collecting minute information as to manners and habits. Speke, on the other hand, was a thorough Briton, conventional, solid, and resolute" (1974, 199).

8. See Pearson 1914, 216 n. 1, for materials then preserved in the Galton laboratory. An amusing comment on Galton's linguistic competence is made in a letter by Emily Butler, sister of his wife-to-be, Louisa Butler: "He [Galton] has been to spirit rappings and had another conversation in Damara with a deceased chief of that tribe. Is not that wonderful, for Mr. Galton is the only man in Europe who knows Damara. The chief promised to go abroad with him, which is a pleasant look-out, for Loui [Louisa]" (Letter to her brother, May 1853, as quoted in Pearson 1914, 242).

9. Hottentots had become a topos already in earlier travel accounts because, as Michèle Duchet argued (1971, 33), contacts with them were as frequent as they were brief. The clicks in their language were always reported among the traits that made them appear different and savage (see Harbsmeier 1989 and 1994, 210, on the history of travelers' reports on the Hottentot language). Finally, the tableau of the natives on the shore painted by Galton had its predecessors and

contemporary counterparts in perceptions of Patagonians (see Boon 1982, 37–43, especially 40–41, on Darwin's description of his first encounter).

10. He comes back to this in the appendix (1891, 194). In a letter from the field he wrote: "The country here is in the wildest disorder, murdering and cattle robbing are of every day occurrence. . . . A set of lawless ruffians many of whose leaders were born in the Cape Colony do all this . . . " (Letter to W. F. Campbell, M.P., dated December 5, 1850, as quoted in Pearson 1914, 225).

11. This is repeated with small but perhaps significant changes in his *Memories*: "The very cattle that were to carry me had to be broken in, and I had to call into service an indolent and cruel set of natives speaking an unknown tongue" (1974, 149).

12. Hans Vedder, in his history of Southwest Africa, devotes a section to "Der Galton-Friede von Windhuk" (1934, 277–79). The very least that can be said is that Galton's peace had become part of historical lore.

13. I am indebted to Peter Gay for suggesting this title.

14. From a letter to his brother Darwin that Galton dated February 23, 1851, quoted in Pearson 1914, 231–32.

CHAPTER 7. CURIOS AND CURIOSITY

1. The study, which was still a project when this essay was written, has meanwhile been completed (Fabian 2000) and should be consulted for further background, including on the topic of collecting.

2. Perhaps one should put this more generally as the experience of "noise" which in accounts of African travel always seems to mark the beginning, later to be transformed into sounds that are meaningful and evocative.

3. For a most original and incisive account of the exchange of objects in early colonization (in this case of the Pacific) see Thomas 1991.

4. On Torday see the essay by John Mack (n.d. [1990]), written to go with an exhibition of his collections in the British Museum. Hilton-Simpson's account of his travels with Torday (1911) offers us the rare case of an observer observed. However, his account covers only the expedition led by Torday between 1907 and 1909. Verner is a main figure in another contribution to the volume in which this essay first appeared (Schildkrout and Keim 1998, 169–92).

5. As I reread these passages after the publication of the book, I am amazed that I did not explicitly link all this to current anthropological discussion of commodification. Two of the principal contributors go uncited in *Out of Our Minds*, Daniel Miller (1987; but see the reference to his work in Fabian 2000, chap. 1) and, above all, Arjun Appadurai (for instance, the collection edited by him in 1986). On the other hand, the fact that my findings have not been generated by an elaborate theory of commodification may increase their interest. After the

fact, I am glad that I resisted (or did not feel) the temptation to tell the story of exploration and early ethnography as merely a chapter in the history of commodification and commodities.

6. For biographical information on Torday and Frobenius see Schildkrout and Keim 1998 and Fabian 2000 (with further references).

7. On Verner see Schildkrout and Keim 1998 (index), and Schildkrout and Keim 1990, 48.

8. Stated in a letter written much later (1936) and quoted in Gibson (MS). It is more than likely that Frobenius did intelligence work but the Berlin Museum was not the sponsor of his trip. Gibson also notes that Verner "directed Frobenius to the country of the Bena Mbindu (Bindundu) where they expected Frobenius's party to lose its way." Apparently Frobenius was not taken in. He was, incidentally, aware of being suspected as a spy—for the English, or the Free State, or the Germans (1907, 274).

9. Requisitioning, or whatever euphemism may be used for the seizure of objects, is reported by other travelers (see Fabian 2000). Frobenius always speaks of trade; it is however likely that his African "scouts" (see below) were not squeamish about how they got their objects together. For a thorough critique of the notion of "exchange" in connection with objects see Thomas 1991.

10. See MacGaffey's essay in Schildkrout and Keim 1998, chap. 9; notice also that the Tetela chief anticipated Robert F. Thompson's views on "African Art in Motion" by more than half a century (Thompson 1974).

11. Frobenius also uses variants of this expression, such as *ethnographischer Kram*, ethnographic "stuff" ("odds and ends," "bric-à-brac," if not actually "junk") (1907, 355) and *heiliger Kram*, sacred "stuff" (351).

12. To be accurate, information about a potential African labor force was at least as important. Frobenius states this at the very beginning of his book (1907, 2) and later reports amazing experiments in what would now be called applied anthropology of work (chap. 6).

13. At least not in connection with collecting objects. But he did report, for instance, on beating a Muluba who was about to sell his wife as a slave to the Tshokwe (1925, 277).

14. Torday 1913, chap. 10. Torday, incidentally, recalls some personal advice he once got from Galton on dressing up when negotiating with natives (1925, 138–39). Frobenius also reports that his services as peacemaker were sought in a conflict between the Free State and the descendants of Wissmann's friend Mukenge Kalamba of the "children of hemp" (1907, 257; on the children of hemp see Fabian 2000, chap. 7).

15. See especially the chapter reporting on his trip through Pende country (1907, 267–71). He then tells us that once "friendship" was established he could

hardly manage to take down all the ethnographic information and buy all the objects that were offered. Photos of his *Polizeitruppe* are reproduced on pp. 270, 271.

16. How well Africans always seem to have been aware of the supply side of the market—and the doubts that this creates about the recent origin of "tourist art"—has been noted for some time. See, for instance, Richter 1980, 3–4, and especially the exhibition catalogue by Schildkrout and Keim (1990) and Schild-krout's contribution in Schildkrout and Keim 1998, chap. 7.

17. This argument was developed in Fabian 1983, 95–96. The topos of spoiled authenticity/originality is open to yet another interpretation. In the context cited earlier (Frobenius 1907, 83–84) Frobenius thought about instituting certain controls as regards collecting objects. We may have here the methodological prototype of what later was often called "data control." The point is that data control is not aimed at that which is given but at those items/objects that are admitted as data. As an expression of "discipline" it is really control of the objectives and purposes of a scientific activity.

18. Perhaps it is time that the much-maligned diffusionism—which never ceased to be useful so long as the only things to go on were objects and their distribution in space (see Hodder 1978)—should be appreciated historically, especially in histories of anthropology. Was it not an outlook that imposed itself when mercantile expansion set in motion processes of globalization?

19. See also the long passage on this topic in Hilton-Simpson 1911, 72–75.

20. A surprisingly modern term, now used for entrepreneurs specializing in procuring illegal laborers or transporting immigrants without papers.

21. Later he was not above having the greedy Tshokwe put on masked initiation dances for *matabishi*, payment (1907, 327, 331).

22. Frobenius recommended his method of "writing up" in the field (1907, 352) and promised that a more ethnographic volume was soon to follow. It was never published during his lifetime, although we now have an edited collection of his Congo field notes prepared by H. Klein (Frobenius 1985–90).

23. See the contributions by Binkley and Darish and by Mack in Schildkrout and Keim 1998, chaps. 2 and 3.

24. See Torday 1925, title of chapter 19—dating from many years after he had done the collecting.

25. See for instance the illustrations in 1907, 234, 235, 253–56.

26. Torday as well as Frobenius accepted, and contributed to, this colonial image—or rather mirage, because one could not have an image of a population that existed largely as a colonial artifice—of the Baluba as the Jews of the Congo. Torday notes some rather general analogies, such as their being "scattered all over

the Land" (1925, 40). Frobenius obviously relishes the occasion to vent his anti-Semitic feelings. At one point he tries to get a particular "Luba portrait" because it shows a "Semitentypus" (1907, 62). Note, however, that this colonial topos had the effect of classifying, by designating them as "Jews," at least one category of Africans as contemporaries rather than representatives of a savage past.

CHAPTER 8. TIME, NARRATION, AND THE EXPLORATION
OF CENTRAL AFRICA

1. See the critical survey by Munn (1992), a book by Gell (1992), and a collection edited by Hughes and Trautmann (1995).

2. That I could not offer solutions was something I first realized when I was invited to participate in an interdisciplinary exploration of ideas of death and dying and came up with an essay (Fabian 1972, reprinted in 1991a, chap. 9) that made me embark on reflections about anthropology, otherness, and time.

3. Inescapable narrativity was the subject of a paper I gave at a conference on "chronotypes" (1991d, reprinted in Fabian 1991a, chap. 12). There were two other anthropological contributions: Jack Goody (1991) delivered a brief report in the ethnographic vein on time in oral culture; David W. Cohen (1991) offered a critical confrontation between a Western and an African narrative, touching on some of the issues to be raised in this essay. Of course, narrativity is a predicament anthropology shares with other disciplines (Nash 1990). For a recent discussion involving archeology see Pluciennik 1999.

4. In order to make up for this shortcoming, I collected a number of critical essays in a volume (Fabian 1991a) and continued to address issues of time in research and representation in work on performance (1990b), popular historiography (1990a, 1996), and popular culture in general (1998a).

5. Here I bring together and develop with a focus on narration observations made in several chapters of Fabian 2000.

6. *Beiträge zur Entdeckungsgeschichte Afrikas* was a series brought out by the publisher Dietrich Reimer in Berlin. The first two publications, the second in two parts, consisted of comments by H. Kiepert on maps showing the progress of discovery since ancient times (both reprints of articles that had previously appeared in the journal of the Berlin geographical society); and of an account of German contributions to the discovery and exploration of Africa by W. Komer. They were followed by two travelogues, Pogge (1880) and Schütt (1881); only the latter two were included in the corpus I studied.

7. Hayden White's suggestion (1980) that a political subject (such as Hegel's state) is needed before chronicles become history and that therefore there is a political dimension to narratives, or narrativity, may well apply here.

8. The expedition was organized by the Deutsche Gesellschaft zur Erforschung Aequatorial-Africas, a predecessor of the German affiliate of King Leopold's International African Association which was active during the period I concentrated on (see the introduction to Fabian 2000).

9. For more detail on time and clocks see Fabian 2000, chap. 3, section on time and timing. Maps were representations of (traveled) time as well as of space. For those who could read them, they were stories of their making. This may apply even to such decidedly nonnarrative representations as catalogues, lists, and tables—writing, as several authors tell us, that was often done to fill "empty time" during periods of waiting.

10. I believe it was this positioning of the diarist "outside" that inspired René Lourau to oppose, as *hors-texte*, the diary to the scientific account, the *texte*—the point of departure in his extraordinary study of the *journal de recherche* (1988). I thank Bertrand Muller for bringing this work to my attention.

11. On the current state of anthropological reflection on ethnographic field notes see a volume edited by Roger Sanjek (1990) and a guide to writing field notes by Emerson et al. (1995).

12. In order to keep things manageable, I will refrain in this chapter from introducing another complication which consists of the relationship between the traveler's diary and his sometimes copious private correspondence through letters, often addressed to friends and members of his family. These documents contained substantial reports on natural history, geography, and ethnography. Several authors quoted (from) such letters when they composed their accounts; one "travelogue" in our corpus consists only of the explorer's posthumously edited and published letters (Böhm 1888).

13. See Fabian 1990c, reprinted in 1991a, chap. 11.

14. Code switching in the linguistic sense, incidentally, is one generic trait that travel writing and modern ethnography share. This involves practices that may range from the larding of prose in a European language with, in our case, African or Latin terms (the latter in "naturalists'" reports ostentatiously using Linnaean classifications) to quoting phrases, fragments of dialogue, or short texts in an African language. For a study of such practices based on two works, one of which, Becker 1887, is part of our corpus, see Fabian 1985.

15. Thus the subtitle of *Writing Culture* (Clifford and Marcus 1986). On time and discursive versus performative speech see Fabian 1990b, chap. 5.

16. Their ideas inspired one of the arguments regarding the uses of the "ethnographic present" in my *Time and the Other* (1983, 82–86).

17. On isomorphism between itinerary and discourse see Mondada 1994, 378–86.

18. For a somewhat related view of ethnography as narrative see Bruner 1986.

CHAPTER 9. REMEMBERING THE OTHER

1. For a comprehensive and most informative collection of essays on these subjects see Assmann and Friese 1998.

2. The quotations from travelogues in this chapter are taken from Fabian 2000, and some of the comments and thoughts about recognition were first formulated there and in an earlier essay (Fabian 1998b).

3. See, for instance, the highly interesting study by Jan Assmann (1992).

4. How such classifying and typifying memory was put to work when museums displayed the strange objects collected, for instance, by explorers of Central Africa, is analyzed in a paper by Nélia Dias (1994). But this kind of memory—schemes that enable one to put the unfamiliar into familiar categories—is not what I have in mind in the reflections that follow. What I do have in mind will have to be developed with the help of examples selected from explorers' writings.

5. I realize that "acknowledgment" is rather vague at this point. Is it submission to ethical norms, to legal principles or political power, or is it (in Hegelian terms) constitutive of a person's identity? Because deciding which of these aspects should be considered the most important one is part of the problem addressed in this chapter, it would be premature to introduce a more specific notion now.

6. French thus adds another twist to the term. In a way, the contradiction I referred to earlier—between received certainties and disturbing experiences—also arises between carrying out reconnaissance and giving *reconnaissance*. Incidentally, in a title search for writings on recognition (in English, from the Library of Congress catalogue) I got the impression that the largest category of cited books consisted of manuals for identifying aircraft and ships—i.e., manuals of reconnaissance—followed by works on (cognitive) pattern recognition and (political) recognition of governments and countries. Only a handful of entries (out of more than four hundred) seemed relevant to the issues discussed here.

7. For examples other than the ones to be quoted now see Fabian 2000 and 1998b.

8. There is much food for thought about remembrance and re-cognition in the concept of genre as it may be applied when exploring connections between systems of memory and the differentiation of genres in oral and literary discourse as well as in painting. See Fabian 1996, chaps. 1 and 3; also 1998a, chap. 2.

9. The role of tropical hygiene in exploration is discussed at length in Fabian 2000; see also Fabian 1991a, chap. 8.

10. For this section I consulted Axel Honneth (1994), mainly to refresh my earlier reading of Hegel's Jena writings; Charles Taylor (1994, in which the 1992 edition is augmented with essays by Jürgen Habermas and K. Anthony Appiah); and Robert R. Williams (1998), which builds on, and completes, his 1992 study.

Patricia J. Huntington (1998) addresses, from a feminist position, many issues that also occupied me in my recent work, among them the notion of ecstatic subjectivity and asymmetrical reciprocity. Finally, I should like to mention again a radical critique of Taylor's and Habermas's essays (in Taylor 1994) offered by Werner Hamacher (1997) that came to my attention after the previously published version of this chapter was written. It was quoted and commented on above in chapter 5.

11. Taylor (1994) does not contain entries for memory, remembering, or even history, in its extensive (for such a small book) index. Neither does Williams (1998), which is surprising for someone who advocates an intersubjective and processual concept of recognition, a position akin to those taken by Habermas and by Appiah (in Taylor 1994). For Appiah, this is the point where he feels he differs from Taylor and takes his own stand in the multiculturalism debate (see also his review of books by Michael Walzer and Nathan Glazer, Appiah 1997).

12. Much as I learned from Williams about appreciating how multifaceted Hegel's thought on recognition was, the difference of our points of departure— the philosopher who thinks within the horizon of Western philosophy and the anthropologist who must come to grips with the merging of horizons that occurs in the encounter with other cultures—leads me to take a less sanguine view of Kojève's reading of Hegel (Williams 1998, 10–13).

13. See, for instance, the collections of essays edited by Stocking (1991) and by Pels and Salemink (1994, 1999).

14. With this song, Joseph Kabasselé, leader of an African jazz orchestra, celebrated Congolese independence and the country's international recognition around 1960. After the opening line, the song goes right on to remember the leaders and crucial events that brought independence about.

15. I have tried to show that such a notion can be given empirical content in a work on popular historiography (Fabian 1996; see also Fabian 1998a).

CHAPTER 10.   AFRICA'S BELGIUM

1. An exemplary text is Mary Louise Pratt's *Imperial Eyes* (1992).

2. Though even this is doubted by some; see, for instance, V. Y. Mudimbe in his *Invention of Africa* (1988).

3. I have often wondered about the martial tone of this title (at least in English; the German version is called *Der Weisse im Spiegel der Farbigen*, literally "The European Mirrored by Africans"). Did it need the implied presence of a conflict, of a striking and striking back, for these particular objects of African art to be found striking?

4. If I had to cite at least one influential work it would be Thomas Hodgkin's characterization of the Belgian system (1956); see my comments in Fabian 1971, 55–56.

5. Thus my, slightly edited, paraphrase of Hodgkin in Fabian 1971a, 55.

6. See on this concept Dirks 1992, Thomas 1994; also Pratt 1992 on "transculturation."

7. Indirect evidence may be found in Schipper–De Leeuw 1973 and, less focused but probing more deeply, in Kramer 1987. Another line of investigation to be mentioned is the work pioneered and inspired by J. C. Mitchell (1956).

8. The two documents mentioned and my notes come from the sixties, seventies, and eighties, respectively; see Fabian 1990a, 1990b, 1996.

9. See Fabian 1990a, 109, 154 n. 125. Incidentally, the (re)naming of colonial agents of all sorts, a practice that began with first encounters during exploration and has continued ever since, would offer abundant material for a study that could add much to documenting this aspect of response to colonization (but has, to my knowledge, not been undertaken except anecdotally).

10. This is made explicit in the conclusion of the *Vocabulary*; see Fabian 1990a, 128–29, 218–27.

11. As I said before, the gendered relation may be reversed. During the critical period in early 1967, when Mobutu tried to nationalize the Union Minière and the expatriate population experienced harassment by the military and police, I was told that this was but a domestic conflict. A husband (in this case the Congo) quarrels with his wife (Belgium) and may chase her away. Then he realizes the consequences (such as having to restitute the bride-price) and eventually asks her to come back.

12. Psychologists may detect intimations of sodomy (forbidden relations between species) and incest ("sleeping with" one's child) as the kind of deepseated wrong that faults interracial relations.

13. This evokes themes of re-cognition and of memory and alterity treated in the preceding chapter.

14. Examples of a growing literature devoted to overcoming the impact-reaction scheme of colonial history may be found in the work of Jean and John Comaroff (for instance 1991, 1997) and, in a different way, in Nicholas Thomas's study of material culture and colonization (1991). See also Paul Stoller on "embodying colonial memories" (1995).

15. On connections between memory and thought see my comments on the semantics of *-jua*, *-kumbuka*, and *-waza*, the Swahili terms most salient in the documents of popular thought I have been studying; see Fabian 1998, 120–22, and elsewhere.

16. The most striking detail of that picture was reproduced on the cover of Fabian 2000.

17. The text is slightly edited by removing my brief interjections ("Mm-hmm").

18. See on this Fabian 1998a, 87–93.

19. I should mention here that Congolese memories of colonization, to judge from the documents I have been using, are by no means limited to the part Belgians played. Arab-Swahili traders are vividly recalled and so are the Portuguese.

20. I should at this point at least mention the admirable work on Congolese painting published through the years by the historian Bogumil Jewsiewicki (examples are 1992 and 1999, collections of essays where references to his work and that of others can be found).

21. This invites an observation I can only note here: Eventually a thorough treatment of the topic of this chapter would require comparison between Congolese and Belgian memory-work. How much, in comparison, is the latter hampered and prevented from having a broad impact by compartmentalization of media and divisions of academic and popular production of knowledge? A remarkable attempt to overcome such divisions by focusing on an institution, the Royal Africa Museum in Tervuren, is a book by edited by Asselberghs and Lesage (1999).

22. On storytelling see the dissertation by M. Gysels (1996) mentioned in chapter 5; on Congolese popular music, see Sylvain Bemba (1984), Graeme Ewens (1994), Walu Engundu (1999), and Bob White (1998).

23. Pius Kasongo was also an old acquaintance of mine from the sixties when I did research on the Jamaa, mainly in the Kolwezi area. His parents were members of the movement. In the seventies, we met again at the university in Lubumbashi. By then Kasongo had more or less drifted away from the church and was working as a critical journalist (as far as that was possible under the Mobutu regime). When I found him reborn in the eighties, I was collecting material for a study of the charismatic renewal. He refused to cooperate and granted me only one, rather strange, audience. That story remains to be told.

24. In the seventies I had heard a story that had been told in Lubumbashi since colonial times: A certain baba T., a famous prankster, had told a priest in confession that he had killed a white man and buried the body in his back yard. Not much later, the *Sûreté* showed up at baba T.'s house and began to dig up the yard. What they found were the remains of a pig.

25. Mutombo is now pastor of a parish in southwestern Germany and is preparing a second doctorate at the University of Tübingen.

26. See the discussion of relations between ethnology, academic historiography, and popular historiology in chapter 3.

27. I have already mentioned the work of Bogumil Jewsiewicki and his many Congolese collaborators and I should like to recall the influence of B. Verhaegen as mirrored a few years ago in a *hommage* to him (Tshonda Omasombo 1993). Of course, these two references do not cover other significant work (notably by J.-L. Vellut and J.-C. Willame, F. de Boeck, R. Ceyssens, and a growing number of Congolese scholars).

References

Abu-Lughod, Leila. 1991. "Writing against Culture." In *Recapturing Anthropology: Working in the Present,* ed. Richard G. Fox, 137–62. Santa Fe: School of American Research Press.

Adorno, Theodor W. 1966. *Negative Dialektik.* Frankfurt: Suhrkamp.

Agar, Michael. 1982. "Toward an Ethnographic Language." *American Anthropologist* 84:779–95.

Amselle, Jean-Loup. 1998 [1990]. *Mestizo Logics: Anthropology of Identity in Africa and Elsewhere.* Translated by Claudia Royal. Stanford, Calif.: Stanford University Press.

Andersson, Charles John. 1988. *Lake Ngami: Exploration and Discoveries during Four Years' Wanderings in the Wilds of South Western Africa.* Camden, S.C.: Briar Patch Press. (Originally published by Hurst and Blackett, London, 1856.)

Appadurai, Arjun, ed. 1986. *The Social Life of Things: Commodities in Cultural Perspective.* Cambridge: Cambridge University Press.

Appiah, K. Anthony. 1997. "The Multiculturalist Misunderstanding." *New York Review of Books,* October 9, 30–33.

Apte, Mahadev L. 1985. *Humor and Laughter. An Anthropological Approach.* Ithaca, N.Y.: Cornell University Press.

Asselberghs, Herman, and Dieter Lesage, eds. 1999. *Het museum van de natie: Van kolonisatie tot globalisering.* Brussels: Yves Gevaert.

Assmann, Aleida, and Heidrun Friese, eds. 1998. *Identitäten: Erinnerung, Geschichte, Identität,* vol. 3. Frankfurt: Suhrkamp.

Assmann, Jan. 1992. *Das kulturelle Gedächtnis: Schrift, Erinnerung und politische Identität in frühen Hochkulturen.* Munich: C. H. Beck.

Atkinson, Paul. 1990. *The Ethnographic Imagination: Textual Constructions of Reality.* London: Routledge.

Auer, Peter, and Aldo di Luzio, eds. 1992. *The Contextualization of Language.* Amsterdam: John Benjamins.

Augé, Marc. 1998. *A Sense for the Other: The Timeliness and Relevance of Anthropology.* Translated by Amy Jacobs. Stanford, Calif.: Stanford University Press.

Auster, Paul. 1992. *The New York Trilogy.* London: Faber and Faber. (British pocketbook edition.)

Bahn, Eugene, and Margaret L. Bahn. 1970. *A History of Oral Interpretation.* Minneapolis: Burgess.

Bakhtin, M. M. 1986. *Speech Genres and Other Late Essays.* Austin: University of Texas Press.

Bal, Mieke. 1991. *Reading "Rembrandt": Beyond the Word-Image Opposition.* Cambridge: Cambridge University Press.

———. 1993. "First Person, Second Person, Same Person: Narrative as Epistemology." *New Literary History* 24:293–320.

Barnes, J. A. 1971. *Three Styles in the Study of Kinship.* Berkeley: University of California Press.

Barnes, R. H., Daniel de Coppet, and R. J. Parkin, eds. 1985. *Contexts and Levels. Anthropological Essays on Hierarchy.* Oxford: Oxford University Press.

Bartine, David E. 1989. *Early English Reading Theory: Origins and Current Debates.* Columbia, S.C.: University of South Carolina Press.

Bauman, Zygmunt. 1973. *Culture as Praxis.* London: Routledge & Kegan Paul.

Baumann, Gerd. 1999. *The Multicultural Riddle: Rethinking National, Ethnic, and Religious Identities.* London: Routledge.

Beatty, J. H. M. 1984. "Objectivity and Social Anthropology." In Stuart C. Brown (ed.), *Objectivity and Cultural Divergence.* Supplement to *Philosophy* 1984. Cambridge: Cambridge University Press, pp. 1–20.

Becker, Jérôme. 1887. *La vie en Afrique ou trois ans dans l'Afrique Centrale.* 2 vols. Brussels: J. Lebuège.

Bemba, Sylvain. 1984. *50 ans de musique Congo-Zaïre.* Paris: Présence Africaine.

Ben-Amos, Dan, ed. 1976. *Folkore Genres.* Austin: University of Texas Press.

Bender, John, and David E. Wellbery, eds. 1991. *Chronotypes: The Construction of Time.* Stanford, Calif.: Stanford University Press.

Bendix, Regina. 1997. *In Search of Authenticity: The Formation of Folklore Studies.*

Madison: University of Wisconsin Press.

Benveniste, Emile. 1971 [1956]. *Problems in General Linguistics.* Coral Gables: University of Miami Press.

Berger, Peter L. 1997. *Redeeming Laughter: The Comic Dimension of Human Experience.* Berlin: Walter de Gruyter.

Berger, Peter L., and Thomas Luckmann. 1966. *The Social Construction of Reality: A Treatise on the Sociology of Knowledge.* Garden City, N.Y.: Doubleday.

Bernheim, Ernst. 1908. *Lehrbuch der historischen Methode und der Geschichtsphilosophie.* 5th ed. Leipzig: Duncker and Humblot. (Reprinted by Burt Franklin, New York, 1970.)

Bernstein, Richard J. 1983. *Beyond Objectivism and Relativism.* Oxford: Blackwell.

Blommaert, Jan. 1999. "Reconstructing the Sociolinguistic Image of Africa: Grassroots Writing in Shaba (Congo)." *Text* 2:175–200.

Böhm, Richard. 1888. *Von Sansibar zum Tanganjika: Briefe aus Ostafrika von Dr. Richard Böhm: Nach dem Tode des Reisenden mit einer biographischen Skizze herausgegeben von Herman Schalow.* Leipzig: F. A Brockhaus.

Boon, James A. 1982. *Other Tribes, Other Scribes.* Cambridge: Cambridge University Press.

Bourdieu, Pierre. 1977. *Outline of a Theory of Practice.* Cambridge: Cambridge University Press.

Boyarin, Jonathan. 1991. "Jewish Ethnography and the Question of the Book." *Anthropological Quarterly* 64:14–29.

———, ed. 1993. *The Ethnography of Reading.* Berkeley: University of California Press.

Brightman, Robert. 1995. "Forget Culture: Replacement, Transcendence, Relexification." *Current Anthropology* 36:509–46.

Brown, Stuart C., ed. 1984. *Objectivity and Cultural Divergence.* Supplement to *Philosophy* 1984. Cambridge: Cambridge University Press.

Brumann, Christoph. 1999. "Writing for Culture: Why a Successful Concept Should Not Be Discarded." In *Culture: A Second Chance?* special issue of *Current Anthropology* 40: S1–S27.

Bruner, Edward M. 1986. "Ethnography as Narrative." In *The Anthropology of Experience*, ed. Victor W. Turner and Edward Bruner, 139–55. Urbana: University of Illinois Press.

Bunzl, Matti. 1996. "Franz Boas and the Humboldtian Tradition: From *Volksgeist* and *Nationalcharakter* to an Anthropological Concept of Culture." In *Volksgeist as Method and Ethic: Essays on Boasian Ethnography and the German Anthropological Tradition*, ed. George W. Stocking, Jr., 17–78.

History of Anthropology, vol. 8. Madison: University of Wisconsin Press.

Burke, Kenneth. 1968. *Language as Symbolic Action: Essays on Life, Literature, and Method.* Berkeley: University of California Press.

Burke, Peter. 1978. *Popular Culture in Early Modern Europe.* New York: New York University Press.

Büttner, Richard. 1890. *Reisen im Kongolande.* Leipzig: Hinrichs.

Certeau, Michel de. 1984. "Reading as Poaching." In *The Practice of Everyday Life*, 165–76. Berkeley: University of California Press.

Chernoff, John Miller. 1979. *African Rhythm and African Sensibility: Aesthetics and Social Action in African Musical Idioms.* Chicago: University of Chicago Press.

Clifford, James. 1988. *The Predicament of Culture: Twentieth-Century Ethnography, Literature, and Art.* Cambridge, Mass.: Harvard University Press.

———. 1997. *Routes: Travel and Translation in the Late Twentieth Century.* Cambridge, Mass.: Harvard University Press.

Clifford, James, and George E. Marcus, eds. 1986. *Writing Culture: The Poetics and Politics of Ethnography.* Berkeley: University of California Press.

Cohen, David William. 1991. "La Fontaine and the Wamimbi: The Anthropology of 'Time-Present' as the Substructure of Historical Oration." In *Chronotypes: The Construction of Time*, ed. John Bender and David E. Wellbery, 205–25. Stanford, Calif.: Stanford University Press.

———. 1994. *The Combing of History.* Chicago: University of Chicago Press.

Comaroff, John L., and Jean Comaroff. 1991, 1997. *Of Revelation and Revolution: The Dialectics of Modernity on a South African Frontier.* 2 vols. Chicago: Chicago University Press.

Cook, Guy. 1990. "Transcribing Infinity: Problems of Context Presentation." *Journal of Pragmatics* 14: 1–24.

Coole, Diana. 2000. *Negativity and Politics: Dionysus and Dialectic from Kant to Poststructuralism.* London: Routledge.

Coquilhat, Camille. 1888. *Sur le Haut-Congo.* Paris: J. Lebègue.

Csordas, Thomas. 1990. "Embodiment as a Paradigm for Anthropology." *Ethics* 18: 5–47.

Culler, Jonathan. 1988. *Framing the Sign: Criticism and Its Institutions.* Norman: University of Oklahoma Press.

Danforth, Loring M. 1989. *Firewalking and Religious Healing: The Anastenaria of Greece and the American Firewalking Movement.* Princeton, N.J.: Princeton University Press.

David, F. N. 1968. "Galton, Francis." *International Encyclopedia of the Social Sciences*, 5: 48–52.

Derrida, Jacques. 1976. *Of Grammatology*. Baltimore: Johns Hopkins University Press.

Dias, Nélia. 1994. "Looking at Objects: Memory and Knowledge in Nineteenth-Century Ethnographic Displays." In *Travellers' Tales*, ed. George Robertson et al., 164–76. London: Routledge.

Dilley, Roy, ed. 1999. *The Problem of Context*. Oxford: Berghahn.

Dirks, Nicholas B., ed. 1992. *Colonialism and Culture*. Ann Arbor: University of Michigan Press.

Duchet, Michèle. 1971. *Anthropologie et histoire au siècle des lumières*. Paris: Maspéro.

Duerr, Hans-Peter. 1978. *Traumzeit: Über die Grenze zwischen Wildnis und Zivilisation*. 2d. ed. Frankfurt: Syndikat.

———. 1985. *Dreamtime: Concerning the Boundary Between Wilderness and Civilization*. Translated by Felicitas Goodman. Oxford: Basil Blackwell.

Duranti, Alessandro, and Charles Goodwin, eds. 1992. *Rethinking Context: Language as Interactive Phenomenon*. Cambridge: Cambridge University Press.

Ellis, Brian. 1990. *Truth and Objectivity*. Oxford: Basil Blackwell.

Emerson, Robert M., Rachel I. Fretz, and Linda L. Shaw. 1995. *Writing Ethnographic Fieldnotes*. Chicago: University of Chicago Press.

Ewens, Graeme. 1994. *Congo Colossus: The Life and Legacy of Franco & OK Jazz*. North Walsham, Notfolk: Buku Press.

Fabian, Johannes
    1971a. *Jamaa: A Charismatic Movement in Katanga*. Evanston, Ill.: Northwestern University Press.

    1971b. "History, Language and Anthropology." *Philosophy of the Social Sciences* 1:19–47.

    1972. "How Others Die—Reflections on the Anthropology of Death." *Social Research* 39:543–67.

    1974. "Genres in an Emerging Tradition: An Approach to Religious Communication." In *Changing Perspectives in the Scientific Study of Religion*, ed. A. W. Eister, 249–72. New York: Wiley Interscience.

    1977. "Charisma: Theory and Practice." *ASA Review of Books* 3:122–34.

    1979a. "Rule and Process: Thoughts on Ethnography as Communication." *Philosophy of the Social Sciences* 9:1–26.

    1979b. "Introduction." In *Beyond Charisma: Religious Movements as Discourse*, ed. J. Fabian, special issue of *Social Research* 46:4–35.

1983. *Time and the Other: How Anthropology Makes Its Object.* New York: Columbia University Press.

1985. *Language on the Road: Notes on Swahili in Two Nineteenth-Century Travelogues.* Hamburg: H. Buske.

1986. *Language and Colonial Power: The Appropriation of Swahili in the Former Belgian Congo, 1880–1938.* Cambridge: Cambridge University Press.

1990a. *History from Below: The "Vocabulary of Elisabethville" by André Yav: Texts, Translation, and Interpretive Essay.* Amsterdam: John Benjamins.

1990b. *Power and Performance: Ethnographic Explorations through Popular Wisdom and Theater in Shaba (Zaire).* Madison: University of Wisconsin Press.

1990c. "Presence and Representation: The Other in Anthropological Writing." *Critical Inquiry* 16:753–72.

1991a. *Time and the Work of Anthropology: Critical Essays 1971–1991.* Chur, Switzerland: Harwood Academic Publishers.

1991b. "Anthropology and the Suppression of Time: Review Article." *Transition,* no. 53:55–61.

1991c. *Language and Colonial Power* (paperback edition of Fabian 1986). Berkeley: University of California Press.

1991d. "Of Dogs Alive, Birds Dead, and Time to Tell a Story." In *Chronotypes: The Construction of Time,* ed. John Bender and David E. Wellbery, 185–204. Stanford, Calif.: Stanford University Press.

1992. "White Humor." *Transition,* no. 55:56–61.

1995. "On Ethnographic Misunderstanding and the Perils of Context." *American Anthropologist* 97:1–10.

1996. *Remembering the Present: Painting and Popular History in Zaire.* Berkeley: University of California Press.

1998a. *Moments of Freedom: Anthropology and Popular Culture.* Charlottesville: University Press of Virginia.

1998b. "Etnické artefakty a etnografické objekty: O spoznávaní vecí" [Ethnic artifacts and ethnographic objects: On recognizing things]. *Slovenský národopis* [Slovak ethnology] 46:302–13.

1999a. "Remembering the Other: Knowledge and Recognition in the Exploration of Central Africa." *Critical Inquiry* 26:49–69.

1999b. "Culture and Critique." In *The Practice of Cultural Analysis: Expos-*

ing Interdisciplinary Interpretation, ed. Mieke Bal, 235–54. Stanford, Calif.: Stanford University Press.

———. 2000. *Out of Our Minds: Reason and Madness in the Exploration of Central Africa*. Berkeley: University of California Press.

———. 2001. "Time, Narration, and the Exploration of Central Africa." *Narrative* 9, no. 1:3–20.

Fay, Brian. 1987. *Critical Social Science: Liberation and Its Limits*. Ithaca, N.Y.: Cornell University Press.

Feld, Steven. 1982. *Sound and Sentiment: Birds, Weeping, Poetics, and Song in Kaluli Expression*. Philadelphia: University of Pennsylvania Press.

Feleppa, Robert. 1986. "Emics, Etics, and Social Objectivity." *Current Anthropology* 27:243–55.

Fillmore, Charles J. 1982. "Ideal Readers and Real Readers." In *Analyzing Discourse: Text and Talk*, ed. Deborah Tannen, 248–70. Georgetown University Round Table on Languages and Linguistics 1981. Washington, D.C.: Georgetown University Press.

Friedman, Jonathan. 1987. Review essay on M. Sahlins, *Islands of History*. *History and Theory* 27:72–98.

Friedrich, Paul. 1986. *The Princes of Naranja: An Essay in Anthrohistorical Method*. Austin: University of Texas Press.

Frobenius, Leo. 1907. *Im Schatten des Kongostaates: Bericht über den Verlauf der ersten Reisen der D.I.A.F.E. von 1904–1906, über deren Forschungen und Beobachtungen auf geographischem und kolonialwirtschaftlichem Gebiet*. Berlin: Georg Reimer.

———. 1985–1990. *Ethnographische Notizen aus den Jahren 1905 und 1906*. Edited by Hildegard Klein. 4 vols. Wiesbaden: Franz Steiner.

Galton, Francis. 1891. *The Narrative of an Explorer in Tropical South Africa: Being an Account of a Visit to Damaraland in 1851*. 4th ed. London: Ward, Lock and Co. (Originally published in 1853 and reprinted in 1971 by Johnson Reprint Co., New York.)

———. 1972. *The Art of Travel; Or Shifts and Contrivances Available in Wild Countries*. New Abbot, Devon: David and Charles Reprints. (Reprint of the 1872 edition by J. Murray, London, first published in 1855.)

———. 1974. *Memories of My Life*. New York: AMS Press. (Reprint of the 1908 edition published by Methuen, London.)

Geertz, Clifford. 1988. *Works and Lives: The Anthropologist as Author*. Stanford, Calif.: Stanford University Press.

Gell, Alfred. 1992. *The Anthropology of Time: Cultural Constructions of Temporal Maps and Images.* Oxford: Berg.

George, Kenneth M. 1990. "Felling a Song with a New Ax: Writing and the Reshaping of Ritual Song Performance in Upland Sulawesi." *Journal of American Folklore* 103/407:3–23.

Gibson, Gordon D. "Samuel P. Verner in the Kasai, Amateur Anthropologist." Manuscript. Washington, D.C., Smithsonian Institution.

Ginsburg, Carlo. 1976. *The Cheese and the Worms.* Baltimore: Johns Hopkins University Press.

Goody, Jack. 1986. *The Logic of Writing and the Organization of Society.* Cambridge: Cambridge University Press.

———. 1987. *The Interface Between the Oral and the Written.* Cambridge: Cambridge University Press.

———. 1991. The "Time of Telling and the Telling of Time in Written and Oral Cultures." In *Chronotypes: The Construction of Time,* ed. John Bender and David E. Wellbery, 77–96. Stanford, Calif.: Stanford University Press.

Graebner, Fritz. 1911. *Methode der Ethnologie.* Heidelberg: Carl Winter.

Gusdorf, Georges. 1973. *L'avènement des sciences humaines au siècle des lumières.* Paris: Payot.

Güssfeldt, Paul, Julius Falkenstein, and Eduard Pechuël-Loesche. 1879–1907. *Die Loango-Expedition: Ausgesandt von der Deutschen Gesellschaft zur Erforschung Aequatorial-Afrikas 1873–1876: Ein Reisewerk in drei Abtheilungen.* Leipzig: Paul Frohberg. (Part 1 by Güssfeldt and part 2 by Falkenstein, 1879; part 3/1 by Pechuël-Loesche, 1882: part 3/2 by Pechuël-Loesche, 1907].

Gysels, Marjolein. 1996. "Genre, Intertextualiteit en Performance: Een etnografische studie van de hadisi: een orale traditie in Lubumbashi, Zaïre." Ph.D. diss., Department of Anthropology, University of Amsterdam.

Habermas, Jürgen. 1967. *Zur Logik der Sozialwissenschaften.* Special issue of *Philosophische Rundschau.* Tübingen: J. C. B. Mohr.

———. 1988. *On the Logic of the Social Sciences.* Cambridge, Mass.: MIT Press.

Hacking, Ian. 1982. "Language, Truth, and Reason." In *Rationality and Relativism,* ed. R. Hollis and S. Lukes, 185–203. Cambridge, Mass.: MIT Press.

Hamacher, Werner. 1996. "Premises." In *Premises: Essays on Philosophy and Literature from Kant to Celan,* 1–43. Translated by Peter Fenves. Stanford, Calif.: Stanford University Press.

———. 1997. "One 2 Many Multiculturalisms." In *Violence, Identity, and Self-Determination,* ed. Hent deVries and Samuel Weber, 284–325. Stanford, Calif.: Stanford University Press.

Hammersley, Martyn, and Paul Atkinson. 1983. *Ethnography: Principles in Practice*. London: Tavistock.

Handler, Richard. 1998. "Raymond Williams, George Stocking, and Fin-de-Siècle Anthropology." *Cultural Anthropology* 13:447–63.

Harbsmeier, Michael, 1989. "Writing and the Other: Travellers' Literacy, or Towards an Archeology of Orality." In *Literacy and Society*, ed. Karen Schousboe and Mogens Trolle Larsen, 197–228. Copenhagen: Akademisk Forlag.

———. 1994. *Wilde Völkerkunde: Andere Welten in den deutschen Reiseberichten der Frühen Neuzeit*. Frankfurt: Campus.

Heelas, Paul. 1984. "Emotions across Cultures: Objectivity and Cultural Divergence." In *Objectivity and Cultural Divergence*, ed. Stuart C. Brown, 21–42. Supplement to *Philosophy* 1984. Cambridge: Cambridge University Press.

Hilton-Simpson, M. W. 1911. *Land and Peoples of the Kasai: Being a Narrative of a Two Years' Journey among the Cannibals of the Equatorial Forest and Other Savage Tribes of the South-Western Congo*. London: Constable and Co.

Hobart, Mark. 1985. "Texte est un con." In *Contexts and Levels. Anthropological Essays on Hierarchy*, ed. R. H. Barnes, Daniel de Coppet, and R. J. Parkin, 33–53. Oxford: Oxford University Press.

Hodder, Ian, ed. 1978. *The Spatial Organization of Culture*. London: Duckworth.

Hodgkin, Thomas. 1956. *Nationalism in Colonial Africa*. London: Muller.

Honneth, Axel. 1994. *Kampf um Anerkennung: Zur moralischen Grammatik sozialer Konflikte*. Frankfurt: Suhrkamp.

———. 1996. *The Struggle for Recognition: The Moral Grammar of Social Conflicts*. London: Polity Press.

Hughes, Diane Owen, and Thomas R. Trautmann, eds. 1995. *Time: Histories and Ethnologies*. Ann Arbor: University of Michigan Press.

Humboldt, Wilhelm von. 1963 [1830–35]. *Schriften zur Sprachphilosophie*. Edited by Andreas Flitner and Klaus Giel. Stuttgart: Cotta.

———. 1988. *On Language: The Diversity of Language-Structure and Its Influence on the Mental Development of Mankind*. Translated by Peter Heath. Cambridge: Cambridge University Press.

Huntington, Patricia J. 1998. *Ecstatic Subjects, Utopia, and Recognition: Kristeva, Heidegger, Irigaray*. Albany, N.Y.: SUNY Press.

Hymes, Dell. 1964. "Introduction: Towards Ethnographies of Communication." In *The Ethnography of Communication*, ed. John J. Gumperz and Dell Hymes, 1–34. Menasha, Wis.: American Anthropological Association.

————. 1974a. *Foundations in Sociolinguistics: An Ethnographic Approach.* Philadelphia: University of Pennsylvania Press.

————. 1974b. *Reinventing Anthropology.* New York: Vintage Books. (Originally published by Random House in 1969.)

Jackson, Michael. 1989. *Paths toward a Clearing: Radical Empiricism and Ethnographic Inquiry.* Bloomington: Indiana University Press.

Jarvie, Ian C. 1969. "The Problem of Ethical Integrity in Participant Observation." *Current Anthropology* 5:505–8.

————. 1975. "Epistle to the Anthropologists." *American Anthropologist* 77:253–65.

Jay, Martin. 1986. "In the Empire of the Gaze: Foucault and the Denigration of Vision in Twentieth-Century French Thought." In *Foucault: A Critical Reader,* ed. David Couzens Hoy, 175–204. Cambridge, Mass.: Basil Blackwell.

Jenkins, Ron. 1994. *Subversive Laughter: The Liberating Power of Comedy.* New York: Free Press.

Jewsiewicki, Bogumil, ed. 1992. *Art pictural zaïrois.* Sillery, Québec: Septentrion.

————. 1999. *A Congo Chronicle: Patrice Lumumba in Urban Art.* New York: Museum of African Art.

Jewsiewicki, Bogumil, and David Newbury, eds. 1986. *African Historiographies: What History for Which Africa?* Beverly Hills: Sage.

Joyce, T. A. 1932. "Emil Torday: Obituary." *Man,* n.s., nos. 53–55:48–49.

Jules-Rosette, Bennetta. 1975. *African Apostles: Ritual and Conversion in the Church of John Maranke.* Ithaca, N.Y.: Cornell University Press.

Keesing, Roger M. 1989. "Exotic Readings of Cultural Texts." *Current Anthropology* 30:459–79.

Kirshenblatt-Gimblett, Barbara. 1998. "Folklore's Crisis." *Journal of American Folklore* 111/441:281–327.

Kojève, Alexandre. 1969. *Introduction to the Reading of Hegel.* Edited by Allan Bloom, translated by James H. Nichols, Jr. New York: Basic Books.

Komesaroff, Paul A. 1986. *Objectivity, Science and Society: Interpreting Nature and Society in the Age of the Crisis of Science.* London: Routledge & Kegan Paul.

Kramer, Fritz. 1987. *Der Rote Fes: Über Besessenheit und Kunst in Afrika.* Frankfurt: Athenäum.

————. 1993. *The Red Fez: Art and Spirit Possession in Africa.* London: Verso.

Kuhn, Thomas S. 1962. *The Structure of Scientific Revolutions.* Chicago: University of Chicago Press.

Larsen, Mogens Trolle. 1987. "The Mesopotamian Lukewarm Mind: Reflections on Science, Divination and Literacy." In *Language, Literature and History: Philological and Historical Studies Presented to Erica Reiner*, ed. F. Rochberg-Halton, 203–25. American Oriental Series, vol. 67. New Haven, Conn.: American Oriental Society.

Lebzelter, V. 1934. *Eingeborenenkulturen in Südwest- und Südafrika.* Leipzig: Karl W. Hierseman.

Lips, Julius. 1966 [1937]. *The Savage Hits Back.* Hyde Park, N.Y.: University Books.

Lourau, René. 1988. *Le journal de recherche: Matériaux d'une théorie d'implication.* Paris: Klincksieck.

Lynch, Michael, and Steve Woolgar, eds. 1988. *Representation in Scientific Practice.* Special issue of *Human Studies* 2, nos. 2–3. Dordrecht: Kluwer Academic Publishers.

Mack, John. n.d.[1990]. *Emil Torday and the Art of the Congo. 1900–1909.* Seattle: University of Washington Press.

MAGD = Mittheilungen der Afrikanischen Gesellschaft in Deutschland. Berlin, 1878–89.

Maquet, Jacques J. 1964. "Objectivity in Anthropology." *Current Anthropology* 5:47–55.

Masquelier, Bertrand, and Jean-Louis Siran, eds. 2000. *Pour une anthropologie de l'interlocution: Rhétoriques du quotidien.* Paris: L'Harmattan.

Middleton, Dorothy. 1972. Introduction to Francis Galton, *The Art of Travel,* 1–17. New Abbot, Devon: David and Charles Reprints.

Miller, Daniel. 1987. *Material Culture and Mass Consumption.* Oxford: Basil Blackwell.

Mishler, Elliott G. 1991. "Representing Discourse: The Rhetoric of Transcription." *Journal of Narrative and Life History* 1:255–80.

Mitchell, J. C. 1956. *The Kalela Dance: Aspects of Social Relationships among Urban Africans in Northern Rhodesia.* Rhodes-Livingstone Paper No. 27. Manchester: Manchester University Press.

Mitchell, W. J. T. 1994. *Picture Theory.* Chicago: University of Chicago Press.

Mondada, Lorenza. 1994. "Verbalisation de l'espace et fabrication du savoir: Approche linguistique de la construction des objets de discours." Doctoral dissertation in Linguistics, University of Lausanne.

Mudimbe, V. Y. 1988. *The Invention of Africa: Gnosis, Philosophy, and the Order of Knowledge.* Bloomington: Indiana University Press.

Mühlmann, W. E. 1968. *Geschichte der Anthropologie.* 2d ed. Frankfurt: Athenäum.

Munn, Nancy D. 1992. "The Cultural Anthropology of Time: A Critical Essay." *Annual Review of Anthropology* 21:93–123.

Nash, C., ed. 1990. *Narrative in Culture: The Uses of Storytelling in the Sciences, Philosophy, and Literature.* London: Routledge.

Northrop, F. S. C., and Helen H. Livingston, eds. 1964. *Cross-Cultural Understanding: Epistemology and Anthropology.* New York: Harper & Row.

Novick, Peter. 1988. *That Noble Dream: The "Objectivity" Question and the American Historical Profession.* Cambridge: Cambridge University Press.

Olivier de Sardan, Jean-Pierre. 1996. "La violence faite aux données." *Enquête,* no. 3:31–59.

Olson, David, Nancy Torrance, and Angela Hildyard, eds. 1985. *Literacy, Language, and Learning: The Nature and Consequences of Reading and Writing.* Cambridge: Cambridge University Press.

Ong, Walter J. 1958. *Ramus: Method and the Decay of Dialogue.* Cambridge, Mass.: Harvard University Press.

Onwumelo, John A. 1966. "Congo Paternalism: An Isolationist Colonial Policy." Ph.D. diss., University of Chicago.

Ortner, Sherry B., ed. 1999. *The Fate of Culture: Geertz and Beyond.* Berkeley: University of California Press.

Owusu, Maxwell. 1978. "Ethnography of Africa: The Usefulness of the Useless." *American Anthropologist* 80:310–34.

Pearson, K. 1914, 1924. *The Life, Letters and Labours of Francis Galton.* 2 vols. Cambridge: Cambridge University Press.

Pels, Peter, and Oscar Salemink, eds. 1994. *Colonial Ethnographies.* Special issue of *History and Anthropology* 8, nos. 1–4.

——, eds. 1999. *Colonial Subjects: Essays on the Practical History of Anthropology.* Ann Arbor: University of Michigan Press.

Pluciennik, Mark. 1999. "Archeological Narratives and Other Ways of Telling." *Current Anthropology* 40:653–78.

Pogge, Paul. 1880. *Im Reiche des Muata Jamwo: Tagebuch meiner im Auftrage der Deutschen Gesellschaft zur Erforschung Aequatorial-Afrika's in den Lunda-Staaten unternommenen Reise.* Beiträge zur Forschungsgeschichte Afrika's, no. 3. Berlin: Dietrich Reimer.

Pomian, Krzysztof. 1990. *Collectors and Curiosities: Paris and Venice 1500–1800.* Translated by Elizabeth Wiles-Portier. Oxford: Polity Press.

Pool, Robert. 1989. "There Must Have Been Something . . . Interpretation of Illness and Misfortune in a Cameroon Village." Ph.D. diss., Department of Cultural Anthropology, University of Amsterdam.

Pratt, Mary Louise. 1977. *Toward a Speech Act Theory of Literary Discourse.* Bloomington: Indiana University Press.

——. 1992. *Imperial Eyes: Travel Writing and Transculturation.* London: Routledge.

Probst, Peter. 1989. "The Letter and the Spirit: Literacy and Religious Authority in the History of the Aladura Movement in Western Nigeria." *Africa* 59: 478–95.

Richter, Dolores. 1980. *Art, Economics and Change.* La Jolla, Calif.: Psych/Graphic Publishers.

Rooij, Vincent A. de. 1996. *Cohesion through Contrast: Discourse Structure in Shaba Swahili/French Conversations.* Amsterdam: Ifott.

Rorty, Richard. 1980. *Philosophy and the Mirror of Nature.* Princeton, N.J.: Princeton University Press.

Sahlins, Marshall. 1985. *Islands of History.* Chicago: University of Chicago Press.

Said, Edward. 1979. *Orientalism.* New York: Vintage Books.

Sanjek, Roger, ed. 1990. *Fieldnotes: The Makings of Anthropology.* Ithaca, N.Y.: Cornell University Press.

Schildkrout, Enid, and Curtis A. Keim, eds. 1990. *African Reflections: Art from Northeastern Zaire.* New York: American Museum of Natural History.

——, eds. 1998. *The Scramble for Art in Central Africa.* Cambridge: Cambridge University Press.

Schipper–De Leeuw, Mineke. 1973. *Le Blanc et l'occident au miroir du roman négro-africain de langue française.* Assen: Van Gorcum.

Scholte, Bob. 1966. "Epistemic Paradigms: Some Problems in Cross-Cultural Research on Social Anthropological History and Theory." *American Anthropologist* 68:1192–1201.

Schön, Erich. 1987. *Der Verlust der Sinnlichkeit oder Die Verwandlungen des Lesers: Mentalitätswandel um 1800.* Stuttgart: Klett-Cotta.

Schousboe, Karen, and Mogens Trolle Larsen, eds. 1989. *Literacy and Society.* Copenhagen: Akademisk Forlag.

Schrire, Carmel. 1995. *Digging through Darkness: Chronicles of an Archeologist.* Charlottesville: University Press of Virginia.

Schütt, Otto H. 1881. *Reisen im südwestlichen Becken des Congo: Nach den Tagebüchern und Aufzeichnungen des Reisenden bearbeitet und herausgegeben von*

Paul Lindenberg. Mit 3 Karten von Dr. Richard Kiepert. Berlin: Dietrich Reimer.

Schütz, Alfred. 1967. *Collected Papers,* vol. 1. Edited by M. Natanson. The Hague: Mouton.

Scott, James C. 1990. *Domination and the Arts of Resistance: Hidden Transcripts.* New Haven, Conn.: Yale University Press.

Siran, Jean-Louis. 1998. *L'illusion mythique.* Paris: Institut Synthélabo, Les empêcheurs de penser en rond.

Stagl, Justin. 1980. "Der Wohl Unterwiesene Passagier: Reisekunst und Gesellschaftsbeschreibung vom 16. bis zum 18. Jahrhundert." In *Reisen und Reisebeschreibungen im 18. und 19. Jahrhundert als Quellen der Kulturbeziehungsforschung,* ed. B. I. Krasnobaev, Gert Robel, and Herbert Zeman, 338–53. Berlin: Camen.

———. 1995. *A History of Curiosity: The Theory of Travel 1550–1800.* Chur, Switzerland: Harwood Academic Publishers.

Stocking, George W., Jr. 1983. "The Ethnographer's Magic: Fieldwork in British Anthropology from Tylor to Malinowski." In *Observers Observed,* ed. G. W. Stocking, 70–120. History of Anthropology, vol. 1. Madison: University of Wisconsin Press.

———, ed. 1991. *Colonial Situations: Essays on the Contextualization of Ethnographic Knowledge.* History of Anthropology, vol. 7. Madison: University of Wisconsin Press.

———, ed. 1992. *The Ethnographer's Magic and Other Essays in the History of Anthropology.* History of Anthropology, vol. 8. Madison: University of Wisconsin Press.

———, ed. 1996. *Volksgeist as Method and Ethic: Essays on Boasian Ethnography and the German Anthropological Tradition.* History of Anthropology, vol. 8. Madison: University of Wisconsin Press.

Stoller, Paul. 1989. *The Taste of Ethnographic Things: The Senses in Anthropology.* Philadelphia: University of Pennsylvania Press.

———. 1995. *Embodying Colonial Memories: Spirit Possession, Power, and the Hauka in West Africa.* London: Routledge.

Street, Brian V. 1984. *Literacy and Theory and Practice.* Cambridge: Cambridge University Press.

Svenbro, Jesper. 1987. "The 'Voice' of Letters in Ancient Greece: On Silent Reading and the Representation of Speech." *Culture and History,* no. 2:31–47.

———. 1988. *Phrasikleia: Anthropologie de la lecture en Grèce ancienne.* Paris: Editions La Découverte.

Szombati-Fabian, Ilona, and Johannes Fabian. 1976. "Art, History and Society: Popular Painting in Shaba, Zaire." *Studies in the Anthropology of Visual Communication* 3:1–21.

Tannen, Deborah. 1985. "Relative Focus on Involvement in Oral and Written Discourse." In *Literacy, Language, and Learning: The Nature and Consequences of Reading and Writing*, ed. David Olson, Nancy Torrance, and Angela Hildyard, 124–47. Cambridge: Cambridge University Press.

Tannen, Deborah, ed. 1982a. *Analyzing Discourse: Text and Talk.* Georgetown University Round Table on Languages and Linguistics 1981. Washington, D.C.: Georgetown University Press.

———. 1982b. *Spoken and Written Language.* Norwood, N.J.: Ablex.

———. 1984. *Coherence in Spoken and Written Discourse.* Norwood, N.J.: Ablex.

Taussig, Michael. 1987. *Shamanism, Colonialism, and the Wild Man.* Chicago: University of Chicago Press.

Taylor, Charles. 1992. *Multiculturalism and the "Politics of Recognition."* Princeton, N.J.: Princeton University Press.

———. 1993. *Multikulturalismus und die Politik der Anerkennung: Mit Kommentaren von Amy Gutman, Steven C. Rockefeller, Michael Walzer, Susan Wolf: Mit einem Beitrag von Jürgen Habermas.* Edited and introduced by Amy Gutman. Frankfurt: Fischer.

———. 1994. *Multiculturalism: With Essays by K. Anthony Appiah, Jürgen Habermas, Steven C. Rockefeller, Michael Walzer, and Susan Wolf.* Edited and introduced by Amy Gutmann. Princeton, N.J.: Princeton University Press.

——— 1995. "Overcoming Epistemology." In *Philosophical Arguments*, 1–19. Cambridge, Mass.: Harvard University Press.

Tedlock, Dennis. 1983. *The Spoken Word and the Work of Interpretation.* Philadelphia: University of Pennsylvania Press.

Thomas, Nicholas. 1989. *Out of Time: History and Evolution in Anthropological Discourse.* Cambridge: Cambridge University Press.

———. 1991. *Entangled Objects: Exchange, Material Culture, and Colonialism in the Pacific.* Cambridge, Mass.: Harvard University Press.

———. 1994. *Colonialism's Culture: Anthropology, Travel and Government.* Cambridge: Polity Press.

Thompson, David W., et al., eds. 1983. *Performance of Literature in Historical Perspectives.* Lanham, Md.: University Press of America.

Thompson, Robert F. 1974. *African Art in Motion.* Berkeley: University of California Press.

Thomson, Joseph. 1881. *To the Central African Lakes and Back: The Narrative of the Royal Geographical Society's East Central African Expedition, 1878–80.* 2 vols. London: Sampson Low, Marston, Searle and Rivington.

Torday, Emil. 1913. *Camp and Tramp in African Wilds: A Record of Adventures, Impressions, and Experiences during Many Years Spent among the Savage Tribes round Lake Tanganyika and Central Africa, with a Description of Native Life, Character, and Customs.* London: Seeley, Service & Co.

———. 1925. *On the Trail of the Bushongo: An Account of a Remarkable & Hitherto Unknown African People, Their Origin, Art, High Social & Political Organization & Culture, Derived from the Author's Personal Experience amongst Them.* London: Seely, Service & Co.

Torday, Emil, and T. A. Joyce. 1911. *Notes ethnographiques sur les peuples communément appelés Bakuba, ainsi que sur les peuplades apparantés: Les Bushongo.* Brussels: Musée Royal de l'Afrique Centrale.

Tshonda Omasombo, Jean, ed. 1993. *Le Zaïre à l'épreuve de l'histoire immédiate: Hommage à Benoît Verhaegen.* Paris: Karthala.

Turner, Victor. 1986. *The Anthropology of Performance.* New York: PAJ Publications.

Tyler, Stephen A. 1984. "The Vision Quest in the West, or What the Mind's Eye Sees." *Journal of Anthropological Research* 40:23–40.

Van Maanen, John. 1988. *Tales of the Field: On Writing Ethnography.* Chicago: University of Chicago Press.

Vansina, Jan. 1961. *De la tradition orale: Essai de méthode historique.* Tervuren: Musée Royal de l'Afrique Centrale.

———. 1965. *Oral Tradition: A Study in Historical Methodology.* Translated by H. M. Wright. London: Routledge and Kegan Paul.

———. 1973. *Oral Tradition: A Study in Historical Methodology.* Paperback edition. London: Penguin.

———. 1985. *Oral Tradition as History.* Madison: University of Wisconsin Press.

———. 1986. "Afterthoughts on the Historiography of Oral Tradition." In *African Historiographies: What History for Which Africa?* ed. Bogumil Jewsiewicki and David Newbury, 105–10. Beverly Hills, Calif.: Sage.

———. 1994. *Living with Africa.* Madison: University of Wisconsin Press.

Vedder, Hans. 1934. *Das alte Südwestafrika: Südwestafrikas Geschichte bis zum Tode Mahereros 1890.* Berlin: M. Warneck.

Walu Engundu, V. 1999. "Images des femmes et rapports entre les sexes dans la musique populaire du Zaire." Ph.D. diss., Department of Anthropology, University of Amsterdam.

Weinrich, Harald. 1973. *Le temps.* Paris: Seuil.

Werbner, Richard, ed. 1998. *Memory and the Postcolony: African Anthropology and the Critique of Power.* London: Zed Books.

White, Bob. 1998. "Modernity's Spiral: Popular Culture, Mastery, and the Politics of Dance Music in Congo-Kinshasa." Ph.D. diss., Department of Anthropology, McGill University, Montreal.

White, Hayden. 1980. "The Value of Narrativity in the Representation of Reality." *Critical Inquiry* 7:5–27.

Williams, Robert R. 1992. *Recognition: Fichte and Hegel on the Other.* Albany, N.Y.: SUNY Press.

———. 1998. *Hegel's Ethics of Recognition.* Berkeley: University of California Press.

Wissmann, Hermann. 1889. *Unter deutscher Flagge quer durch Afrika von West nach Ost: Von 1880 bis 1883 ausgeführt von Paul Pogge und Hermann Wissmann.* Berlin: Walther and Apolant.

Wissmann, Hermann von, Ludwig Wolf, Curt von François, and Hans Müller. 1891. 3d ed. *Im Innern Afrikas: Die Erforschung des Kassai während der Jahre 1883, 1884, und 1885.* Leipzig: Brockhaus. (First published in 1887.)

Wolff, Willy. 1889. *Von Banana zum Kiamvo: Eine Forschungsreise in Westafrika, im Auftrage der Afrikanischen Gesellschaft in Deutschland.* Oldenburg and Leipzig: Schulze.

Woolgar, Steve, ed. 1988. *Knowledge and Reflexivity: New Frontiers in the Sociology of Knowledge.* London: Sage.

Wylie, Alison. 1989. "Archeological Cables and Tacking: The Implications of Practice for Bernstein's 'Options Beyond Objectivism and Relativism.'" *Philosophy of the Social Sciences* 19:1–18.

Index